Social Innovation Scaling Process in East Asia:

Bridging the gaps between stakeholders

Ken Aoo

University Education Press

Contents

List of Tables iv
List of Figures v
Acknowledgements vi
About the Author xi

Chapter 1 : Introduction 1

1.1 What is / Why Social Innovation?   *1*
    1.1.1 What is Social Innovation?   *1*
    1.1.2 Why Social Innovation?   *5*
    1.1.3 Policy Development   *9*

1.2 Literature Review   *18*
    1.2.1 Innovation Theory and Social Innovation   *18*
    1.2.2 Development of Social Innovation Theories   *19*
    1.2.3 Other Relevant Theories   *30*
    1.2.4 The Gap in Current SI Literature   *35*

1.3 Research Design   *36*
    1.3.1 Research Questions   *36*
    1.3.2 Theoretical Framework   *37*
    1.3.3 Methodology: Case Studies and Process Tracing   *40*

1.4 Structure of the Book   *51*

Chapter 2 : Japan *59*

2.1 Country Context   *59*
    2.1.1 Political System   *59*
    2.1.2 Socio-Economic Conditions   *61*
    2.1.3 Civil Society and Social Movements   *64*

2.2 Case Analysis 1: Non-Profit Organization (NPO)   *65*
    2.2.1 Background   *65*
    2.2.2 Processes   *67*
    2.2.3 Analysis   *81*

2.3 Case Analysis 2: Environmental Pollution   *84*
    2.3.1 Background   *84*
    2.3.2 Processes   *84*
    2.3.3 Analysis   *87*

2.4 Case Analysis 3: Community-Based Integrated Care   *90*
    2.4.1 Background   *90*
    2.4.2 Processes   *91*
    2.4.3 Analysis   *94*

2.5 Summary   *95*

Chapter 3 : China   *104*

3.1 Country Context   *104*
    3.1.1 Political System   *104*
    3.1.2 Socio-Economic Conditions   *107*
    3.1.3 Civil Society and Social Movements   *109*

3.2 Case Analysis: Welfare Reform and the Development of Social Organizations   *110*
    3.2.1 Background   *110*
    3.2.2 Processes   *114*
    3.2.3 Analysis   *123*

3.4 Summary   *127*

Chapter 4 : South Korea   *132*

4.1 Country Context   *132*
    4.1.1 Political System   *132*
    4.1.2 Socio-Economic Conditions   *135*

4.1.3 Civil Society and Social Movements *140*

4.2 Case Analysis: The Development of Social Economy *141*

    4.2.1 Background *141*

    4.2.2 Processes *144*

    4.2.3 Analysis *153*

4.3 Summary *157*

Chapter 5 : Indonesia *162*

5.1 Country Context *162*

    5.1.1 Political System *163*

    5.1.2 Socio-Economic Conditions *166*

    5.1.3 Civil Society and Social Movements *167*

5.2 Case Analysis: Governmental Decentralization *169*

    5.2.1 Background *169*

    5.2.2 Processes *170*

    5.2.3 Analysis *178*

5.4 Summary *182*

Chapter 6 : Conclusion *185*

6.1 Findings *185*

6.2 Arguments *197*

6.3 Policy Implications and Way Forward *205*

References *211*

List of Tables

Table 1.1 The Different Levels of Social Innovation: From Micro to Macro ……… 3
Table 1.2 Examples of Social Innovation ……………………………………………… 4
Table 1.3 Analytical Framework Used for Case Analysis ……………………… 46
Table 1.4 List of Independent Variables and Hypotheses Used for Case Analysis … 47
Table 2.1 The Years of Establishment of Non-Profit Organizations in Japan ……… 73
Table 2.2 Primary Activity Areas of Non-Profit Organizations in Japan ………… 74
Table 2.3 Annual Income of Non-Profit Organizations in Japan (Fiscal Year 2013) 76
Table 2.4 Japanese Non-Profit Organization Headcounts by Type of Employment / Participation ……………………………………………………………… 77
Table 2.5 Scaling Patterns and Paths for Non-Profit Organizations, Japan ………… 83
Table 2.6 Scaling Patterns and Paths for Environmental Pollution, Japan ………… 87
Table 2.7 Scaling Patterns and Paths for Community-based Integrated Care, Japan 94
Table 3.1 Levels and Numbers of Administrative Units in China ………………… 106
Table 3.2 Summary of Social Security and Welfare Systems in Urban and Rural Areas in China …………………………………………………………… 113
Table 3.3 Scaling Patterns and Paths for the Development of Social Organizations, China ……………………………………………………………………… 125
Table 4.1 Types and Criteria of Social Enterprise in South Korea ……………… 145
Table 4.2 Scaling Patterns and Paths for Social Economy, South Korea ………… 154
Table 5.1 Scaling Patterns and Paths for Governmental Decentralization, Indonesia ……………………………………………………………………… 179
Table 6.1 Summary of the Findings of Causal Relationships and Patterns Found from Case Studies ……………………………………………………………… 194

List of Figures

Figure 1.1 Obama Administration Social Innovation Fund (Classic Program) *14*

Figure 1.2 Structure of the U.S. Social Impact Bond / Pay for Success Contract *16*

Figure 1.3 The Six Stages of Social Innovation *20*

Figure 1.4 Historical Analysis of National Parks as a Social Innovation *23*

Figure 1.5 Social Innovation Keyword Cloud *27*

Figure 1.6 The Welfare Triangle and the Third Sector *32*

Figure 1.7 "Care Diamond" Models: Welfare and Non-Welfare States *33*

Figure 1.8 Governance Network Diagram *35*

Figure 1.9 Four Stages in the Social Innovation Process *39*

Figure 1.10 Governance Spaces for Social Innovation Processes *40*

Figure 1.11 Excerpt from a Critical Turning Point Timeline *42*

Figure 1.12 Four Domains of Top-Down / Bottom Up and the Formation of "Alliances" *50*

Figure 2.1 Social Benefits in Japan by Category (Fiscal Year 1970-2015) *63*

Figure 2.2 Number of Registered Non-Profit Organizations in Japan *73*

Figure 2.3 Income Breakdown for Japanese Non-Profit Organizations *76*

Figure 2.4 Level of Public Interest in Nonprofit Organizations in Japan *81*

Figure 2.5 Model of the Community-based Integrated Care System *91*

Figure 4.1 Unemployment Rate and Poverty Rate in South Korea (1996-2007) *137*

Figure 4.2 Comparative Public Social Expenditure as a Percentage of GDP (1960, 1990 and 2016) *139*

Figure 4.3 Annual Growth of Social Economy Organizations in Seoul *152*

Figure 5.1 Map of Indonesia *162*

Figure 6.1 Resilience and Adaptability Cycle *186*

Figure 6.2 Four Types of Social Innovation Scaling *195*

Figure 6.3 Model of Inter-Sectoral Relations in a Social Innovation Initiative *199*

Acknowledgements

This research has its roots in my past work experience in the fields of international development and social innovation at an NGO, UNDP, and foundations. First and foremost, I would like to thank all the friends and people who I had the privilege of working with together with in different places and projects, including in Vietnam, Uganda, the U.S., and Japan. The inspiration for this book came from what I learned from all of you. Indeed, this work would not exist without you.

Second, I am profoundly grateful to my colleagues and students at Okayama University for their kindness, support, and patience in accepting an inexperienced researcher / teacher like me. I always enjoy conversastions with all of you.

Third, I would like to sincerely thank the members of my PhD Dissertation Review Committee, which became the basis of this book. I was extremely lucky to have such brilliant and kind supervisors, and to have the opportunity to benefit from them. Thank you to Professor Tsujinaka for accepting me as his PhD student, and encouraging (and forcing) me to pursue a challenging question. I would also like to thank Professor Kaigo for providing me with critical comments and suggestions (with a sense of humor) to polish my dissertation, and Professor Ohtomo for guiding me on the basics of social sciences in a seminar room with only my good friend Anisa and myself (which will become an unforgettable memory), and for providing me with some hints as to the final concept and model. And last but not least, to Professor Akashi, for always taking such good care of me as the head of committee. I truly enjoyed my student days in

Tsukuba. Discussion and help from colleagues such as Professor Leslie M. Tkach-Kawasaki, Dr. Huang Mei, Dr. Hiroyuki Tagawa, Dr. Tomoya Sagara, Dr. Takuya Hasegawa, Mr. Bakhrom Radjabov, and the staff at the Kokunichi Office made my life an easy and enjoyable one.

Next, I would like to thank the researchers and practitioners who are involved in social innovation and who have shared their rich knowledge and insights with me, including Professor Alex Nicholls at Said Business School of Oxford University, Professor Fergus Lyon, Middlesex University, Ms. Louise Pulford, Ms. Jordan Junge and Ms. Sojung Rim, Social Innovation Exchange (SIX), Dr. Christoph Kaletka and Mr. Dmitry Domanski, Dortmund Technical University, Professor Frances Westley, University of Waterloo, Professor Wang Ming, Tsinghua University, Professors Yuan Ruijung, Zhang Changdong, Ju Hua, and Li Yongjun, Peking University, Professor Park Taekyu, Koryo University, Professors Lee Byungtae and Lee Ji-Hwan, KAIST, Professor Jang Jongick, Hanshin University, Professor Cho Sangmi and Professor Choi Yoomi, Ewha Womans University, Ms. Choi Hojin, Ms. Park Sun Min (Camilla), Ms. Han Sunkyung and Ms. Park Ahyoung, C., Dr. Frank Hubers, Asia Centre for Social Entrepreneurship & Philanthropy, NUS Business School, Ms. Pauline Tan, Soristic / NUS, Professor Gillian Koh, Institute of Policy Studies, NUS, Professor Thang Leng Leng, NUS, Mr. Laurence Lien, the Asia Philanthropic Circle / Lien Foundation, Ms. Naina Batra and Mr. Kevin Teo, Asian Venture Philanthropy Network, Mr. Alfie Othman, Singapore Centre for Social Enterprise, Dr. Vannarith Chheang, Cambodian Institute for Strategic Studies, Professor Jeffrey Cheah, Universiti Sains Malaysia, Mr. Kal Joffres, Tandemic, Mr. David Hulse and Mr. Alex Irwan, The Ford Foundation, Mr. Muntajid Bilah, Knowledge Sector Initiative, Mr. Romy Cahyadi, UnLtd Indonesia, Ms. Dian Wulandari,

Instellar, Mr. Sunaji Zamroni, Institute for Research and Empowerment, Acharn Nuntavarn Vichit-Vadakan, Dr. Richard Carhart, and other colleagues at the School of Global Studies, Thammasat University, Acharn Juree Vichit-Vadakan, National Institute of Development Administration, Acharn Chalermpon Kongjit, Chiang Mai University, Dr. Rosalia Sciortino, Ms. Natalie Phaholyothin, The Rockefeller Foundation, Ms. Thanyaporn Jarukittikun and Ms. Linh Nguyen, Thailand Social Innovation Platform, UNDP, Professor Seiichiro Yonekura, Hitotsubashi University, Professor Hirotsugu Koike, Kwansei Gakuin University, Professor Yanyan Li, Komazawa University, Professor Tatsuaki Kobayashi, Gakushuin University, Mr. Akira Matsubara, C's, and Mr. Yoshinori Yamaoka, Mr. Hiroshi Tanaka and Mr. Gen Watanabe, the Japan Foundation Center. They are the real social innovators.

Special thanks must also be given to Professor Ken Ito, Keio University / AVPN and the participants in the research project "Social Innovation Ecosystems in East Asian Countries" funded by the Toyota Foundation for the exposure to the global social innovation literature and networks and different case studies in Asia. These members include Mr. Sunit Shresta and Ms. Haidy Leung, ChangeVenture, Dr. Lee Wonjae, Lab 2050, Ms. Shuang Lin, Ms. Sayaka Watanabe, re:terra, and Mr. Jonathan Chang, then Lien Centre for Social Innovation, Singapore Management University.

I would like to express my full gratitude to the Japan Foundation / Asia Center and its staff, especially to Mr. Koji Sato, Ms. Kazumi Yagi, Ms. Ai Goto, Ms. Mari Shogase, Ms. Natsuko Minemura, Mr. Hiroyuki Kojima, Dr. Tadashi Ogawa, Mr. Masaya Shimoyama, Ms. Yuko Noguchi, and Mr. Ben Suzuki, for giving me the chance to study from various social sector practitioners and academic researchers in Southeast and Northeast

Asia by generously providing me with the Asia Fellowship, and also for partnering with me (then Toyota Foundation) on the 2016 "International Conference on Asian Nonprofit Sectors," which became the starting point of this research.

I am grateful to my former colleagues at the Toyota Foundation, especially Mr. Kenta Kusuda, Mr. Hideo Tone, Ms. Michiru Sasagawa, Ms. Hiroko Isaka, Ms. Zi Xuan (Ivy) Gu, Ms. Mina Murai, Mr. Mitsuru Ohno, Ms. Atsuko Toyama, and many others. The five years I spent at the Toyota Foundation was a great learning experience for me. I especially do not know how to thank Mr. Hiroshi Ito, who patiently guided me and gave a great opportunity to interact with and learn from colleagues in Japan and other Asian countries. Again, I have learned a lot from working with great people such as Professor Akira Suehiro, Tokyo University / Gakushuin University, Professor Tsuyoshi Kato, Kyoto University, Professor Toichi Makita, Oberin University, Dr. Suzanne E. Siskel, Asia Foundation, Mr. Xu Yongguang and Ms. Peng Yanni, Narada Foundation, Mr. Cheng Gang and Mr. Tao Ze, China Foundation Center, Professor Chung Moosung and Professor Cho Moungi, Soongsil University, Professor Yang Keeho, SungKongHoe University, Ms. Lee Eunkyung, The Hope Institute, Mr. Hamid Abidin, Pirac / PFI, Acharn Surichai Wungaeo, Chulalornkorn University, Acharn Worawet Suwanrada, Chulalornkorn University, Ms. Ada Chirapaisarnkul, TYPN, Professor Shogo Takegawa and Professor Kim Sung-won, University of Tokyo, Professors Toru Morotomi, Emiko Ochiai, and Wako Asato, Kyoto University, Professor Fumikazu Yoshida and Professor Taisuke Miyauchi, Hokkaido University, Professor Masahiro Matsuura, Meiji University, Professor Tetsuya Murakami, Nihon Fukushi University, Dr. Keiichiro Oizumi, the Japan Research Institute, Mr. Koji

Akiyama, the late Mr. Masayuki Miyahara, and the staff of the Akiyama Life Science Foundation, Mr. Tatsuo Ohta, JACO, and Dr. Toru Honda, CARE, among many others. I would also like to express my apologies to my colleagues at the Nippon Foundation for leaving the place so early without being able to contribute them.

Ms. Eda Tseinyev gave me another helpful hand with correcting and editing my English writing. Without her I would never have had the courage to write this in English, and I really appreciate her kindness. Also thank you Ms. Gao Ting for checking my Chinese. Ms. Miho Fujii kindly helped me to design the cover of this book.

I am greatly indebted to my family, especially Tomoko, Ko, and Saki, and my parents for their kind understanding and full support for my PhD study, and the career change.

Finally, I want to thank my *senseis* – I was always lucky to have great teachers and mentors, such as Professor Robert Chambers and Professor Mick Moore, IDS, University of Sussex, Professors Tetsuya Sakai, Akio Yoshie, Yoichi Kibata, Masao Nishikawa, Haruki Wada, and Masahiro Shiba, University of Tokyo, Mr. Shiro Kato and Mr. Takeshi Murakami, Azabu Highschool, Mr. Kichito, Meisei Gakuin, and Mrs. Ziegler and Mr. Clark at Brightwood Elementary School, among many others. They all taught me what the respect, love, and joy of studying is. I cannot thank all of them in this limited space. But I would like to dedicate this book to the late Mr. Yasuhiko Torigoe, who opened the door to the rich world of scholarship for me, but who passed away without seeing that I am back following his path.

About the Author

Ken AOO has a mixed background in banking, international development, philanthropy, and research. He currently works at Okayama University as a Senior Assistant Professor in Social Innovation and International Development, and also serves as a Vice Executive Director in charge of the university's community support programs and SDG initiatives. He is also a Fellow at the Japan Foundation Center, an umbrella organization for grant-making foundations in Japan and in charge of the Center's international research programs, networking, and communication. Before joining the university, he worked 6 years as Program Officer / Director in Toyota Foundation and Nippon Foundation in charge of their international programs mainly focusing on Northeast and Southeast Asia. He also has working experience in Vietnam as an NGO staff member, and in Uganda and New York as a UNDP staff member. His current research interests include: the social innovation process and ecosystem, well-being, community development, and multi-stakeholder collaboration in Japan and elsewhere. He holds a PhD in Social Science (University of Tsukuba), MPhil in International Development (Institute of Development Studies, University of Sussex), and a BA in International Relations (University of Tokyo).

Chapter 1 : Introduction

This book aims to provide an empirical analysis of social innovation (hereunder abbreviated as "SI") processes in different Asian countries, with a special focus on both its causal mechanisms and how the interactions of stakeholders from different sectors affect the "scaling" processes of SI initiatives. As an introduction, this chapter first discusses the definition of SI, then examines why SI is becoming important in both policy and academic arenas, why there are high hopes for it in both post-welfare and pre-welfare state contexts, and next gives a brief overview of the development of SI-related policies and literature. Finally, it presents the research design, including research questions, theoretical frameworks, and methodology.

1.1 What is / Why Social Innovation?
1.1.1 What is Social Innovation?
A Working Definition of Social Innovation

Since the 1990s, "social innovation" has become a fashionable term for policy makers, businesses, civil society, media, and academics in various regions to use. In part because it is largely a practice-driven concept, different groups use the term in their own ways. For example, SI is often used in a sense equivalent to charismatic social entrepreneurs and/or social ventures that use cutting-edge technology to tackle various social issues.[1]

Although SI is still a developing concept, there is a growing common understanding among researchers working on SI theory, particularly in English-language literature. The details of the concept are dealt with in the literature review section (1.2.2) below, but for the purpose of practical use in the meantime, this study applies a two-fold definition as the working definition of SI, which is taken from recent scholarly works (Nicholls et al. 2015:2-5; Howaldt et al. 2016:27-28; Mulgan et al. 2007:8; TEPSIE 2014:14). First, SI is a new (by the very definition of the word "innovation") combination of products, services, or activities to meet a social need or to create social value.[2] Second, SI is also a process that changes existing cognition, values, behavior, capacity, relationships between stakeholders, and the distribution of resources and power within a society.[3] It is occasionally summarized as "innovations that are social both in their ends and in their means" (Franz et al.2012:3).

Different Levels of Social Innovation: From Individual Initiatives to Societal Change

There is also a shared view in recent literature of appreciating the multiple levels and scales of SI that take place, from the individual to the macro level. As summarized in Table 1.1, based on Cajaiba-Santana (2014:48) and Nicholls and Murdock (2012:4), there are at three[4] levels of SI, which are micro (individual), meso (organization), and macro (social system). A successful SI process does not entail the accomplishment of an individual or an organization alone. Rather, it diffuses and/or scales with the involvement of different societal actors, and ultimately leads to a systemic change (also called "institutionalization") in a society. Such a change reconfigures how people understand the world, what they hold as values and norms, and how they behave on a daily basis, as well as becoming the new rules and regulations in a society (Heiskala 2007:59; Pel and Bauler 2014:5; TEPSIE 2014:11; Westley and Antadze 2010:2).

Table 1.1 The Different Levels of Social Innovation: From Micro to Macro

Levels	Examples
Macro (Social system)	- Social recognition, values, norms, and behavior - Laws and regulations - Power / resource allocation and relationships among actors
Meso (Organization)	- Organizational practices and operations - Inter-stakeholder interactions and collaborations
Micro (Individual)	- New ideas and practices

Source: Developed by the author, revised from Nicholls and Murdock (2012:4)

Examples of Social Innovation Initiatives

If we use this definition of SI, it is evident that SI is not a recent phenomenon, but has indeed existed since the beginning of human history (Cajaiba-Santana, 2014:42; Mulgan et al. 2007:9; McGowan et al. 2017:1). As shown in Table 1.2, a wide range of historical initiatives are considered to be examples of SI, including some of the "newer" initiatives such as microfinance, sharing economy, fair trade, internet-based media, and socially responsible investment as well as initiatives of a more historical nature, such as public health and sanitation systems, modern university education, environmental movements, international labor standards, civil rights movements, feminism, and civic associations, to name just a few. The origins and processes of these SI initiatives are varied, from government-led policies, civil society or philanthropic initiatives, grass-roots and social movements, to societal changes caused by business and technology.

Table 1.2 Examples of Social Innovation

Author	Examples of Social Innovation
Mulgan et al. (2007)	- Free and universal national health service, welfare states, school system - Internet and new media - Microcredit, building societies, trade unions and cooperatives - New university models in industrial societies - New welfare models developed by modern philanthropy and civil society - Social movements (anti-slavery, ecology, feminism, civil rights, anti-apartheid, anti-poverty, etc.)
Haxeltine et al. (2017); Pel et al. (2017)	- Basic income - Digital fabrication workshops - Eco-villages and other intentional communities - Network of social entrepreneurs - Participatory budgeting - Slow food - Sharing economy, time bank, local currency, and transition movement
Phills et al. (2008)	- Charter schools - Community-centered planning - Emissions trading - Fair trade - Habitat conservation plans - Individual development accounts - International labor standards - Microfinance - Socially responsible investing - Supported employment
Westley et al. (eds.) (2017)	- National parks in the United States - The intelligence test - The legalization of birth control in North America - The internet - The global derivatives market - Indian residential schools - Dutch joint stock company

Tanimoto et al. (2013)	- Renewable energy funded by citizens - Reusable dishes - Mail delivery service provided by handicapped people
The Hope Institute (2017)	- Pulmu Farmers Cooperatives in South Korea - The Bann Mankong Community Upgrade Program in Thailand - Governmental "Social Management Innovation" in China - Indian social enterprises targeting the base of the pyramid (BOP) - Nonprofits and cooperatives entering the long-term care insurance scheme in Japan

Sources: Hazeltine et al. (2017); The Hope Institute (2017); Mulgan et al. (2007:9-11); Pel et al. (2017:7); Phills et al. (2008:40); Tanimoto et al. (2013); Westley et al. (eds.) (2017)

1.1.2 Why Social Innovation?
Different Expectations for Social Innovation

There seem to be some different expectations for what the outcome of SI will be. Based on Nicholls et al. (2015:2-3) which summarizes SI as a i) new social processes and ii) new social outputs and outcomes, we may re-categorize SI into three functions. First is *welfare*, to directly solve a social issue, or to provide necessary services, including education, health and care-giving, environmental issues, and employment among others, especially in situations where traditional service providers such as government or family systems are not able to provide such a function (Goldsmith 2010; OECD 2011). Second is *economic performance*, to transform a society in order to adapt to economic and technological changes such as globalization or a transformation in industrial structure, and to promote post-industrial, knowledge-based economic growth (Hamalainen and Heiskala eds. 2007; Sgaragli 2014). Third is the less-noticed aspect of *governance*, which is to improve societal relationships and integrity, often by empowering and enhancing the inclusion and participation of marginalized groups (BEPA 2011; Moulaert et al. 2013).

Welfare Regimes and Social Innovation

Such diverse expectations for SI come at least partly from the continuing debate on the future of the "welfare state" system in both developed and developing / emerging country contexts. The idea and prototypes of a welfare state system, in which the public sector takes on the primary responsibility of providing basic social services to its citizens as a universal right, emerged in the late 19th century.[5] And under the WWII wartime mobilization and the post-war social-democratic environment, it was established as a social welfare system in a few industrialized countries, mainly in Western and Northern Europe (Esping-Andersen 1990:18-19; Lowe 1993; Pierson 2002:64; Tada 2014:3-12).[6] Indeed, the welfare state system itself was (or still is) a major SI initiative.

However, since the 1970s, the idea of a welfare state has been challenged for its growing cost and put under reforms based on neo-liberal ideas to minimize government involvement and leave the operation of services to market mechanisms (Pierson 1996:145). New social risks and needs have also been growing which the classic welfare state models were not designed to take care of, such as domestic care responsibilities for older people and children (while a large proportion of women have already moved into paid work), lack of skills and sufficient knowledge to respond to changes in industry, and low-paid workers (such as lower skilled women) not being covered by adequate benefits when leaving the workforce (Hamada and Kim 2018; Taylor-Gooby 2004:2-5). Reflecting the shrinking resources available to meet different needs, a number of countries, including the U.K. under the Thatcher administration, switched to market-friendly reforms of the welfare state model. They outsourced social services to the private sector, non-departmental public bodies, and non-governmental sectors or created quasi-market systems such as public insurance systems to substitute for the direct provision of services by the public sector (Esping-Andersen 1996:6-10; Imai 2016:178; Morgan and Campbell 2011:28-32).

And after the 1990s, as demographic shifts including aging, low fertility, and women's participation in the labor market increased, there was another wave of efforts to restructure welfare state systems and to meet diverse needs in society based on available resources, rather than being based on any sort of ideological confrontation (Hamada and Kim 2018:15-15; Miyamoto 2006; Pierson 2002:65). The "Third Way" advocated by the Blair administration (1997-2007) in the U.K. was one of the attempts to "modernize" the welfare state system by connecting work and welfare, giving more power to local-level groups including civil society organizations, and utilizing market mechanisms under the monitoring and supervision of the government (Giddens 1998; Imai 2016:182-184; Ohmura 2013:256-260).

The situation is quite different in developing countries, including those in Asia.[7] In most Asian countries including Japan after World War II (WWII), priority was given to constructing a newly independent state, and/or to restore an economy damaged by the war. Thus, a universal welfare state system was considered an unaffordable luxury (Kim 2008; Masuda 2013:7).

However, decades of economic growth have elevated many countries from a poor to a middle-income country status, and governments now have greater financial resources compared to decades ago. They are also facing increasing pressure from society to support diverse needs and demands, and there is also a strong frustration in many countries from those needs not being fulfilled (Inoguchi 2014:115). The very legitimacy of the government itself is greatly affected by how well the regime can meet those requests. These needs and issues in societies include both traditional "developing country" types of challenges as well as newer ones, including health and medical care, social diversity and minority rights, education, an aging population, people with disabilities, environmental issues, the transformation of the socio-economic system to a more post-industrial one, inequality, and poverty. Facing the weakening of traditional social safety nets and service providers such as family or local community, Asian countries have gradually expanded the scope of social policy to meet these needs (Shen 2016; Sugaya 2013:5). But the level of benefits and services are still quite limited compared to those in developed countries. Also, these states seem to be reluctant to take on the full responsibility of a welfare state (Goodman and Peng 1996:207-209; Haggard and Kaufman 2008:256-261).

In either context, considering the proliferation of needs and issues in society, slowing economic growth, and limited or decreasing financial and human resources in public sectors, there is an even lesser chance that the state alone will be able to handle all the societal needs and risks in the future (Evers 1995:159; Ito and Kondo 2010:21-22; Miyamoto 2006:69). It also means that the need for social services accompanied by the "retreat" of the governmental sector from it creates more empty "public spaces" (Habermas 1994; Mukai 2015:208-211), or a "welfare vacuum" in society, especially at local or community levels, which need to be filled by different stakeholders in the society. Authors tend to agree that no one sector alone, including government, businesses, family, or civil society, can provide services to the full extent required, and that there is a need for stakeholders to collaborate and build a "welfare regime," "welfare society," or "welfare community" to deal with different social issues (Esping-Andersen 1999:36; Pestoff 2000; Pierre 2000:1; Salamon and Anheier 1998:225; Tsujinaka 2010:11-12).[8] SI also stems from the discourse on restructuring welfare regimes and is expected to be a tool to create such a "welfare community" by utilizing available resources.[9]

Social Innovation for Well-being

Moreover, some figures such as Mulgan point out that the purpose of SI goes beyond mere economic development, provision of services, and expansion of human rights movements. Instead, they propose more holistic, different social values to be fulfilled by SI. These values include the expansion of capabilities or the improvement of well-being or life satisfaction as the goal, although they admit that the methodology to measure this type of impact is yet to be developed.[10] By expanding its purpose in this way, SI becomes a framework to measure the "quality of growth as well as its quantity" (Mulgan 2012:57-60).

1.1.3 Policy Development
The United Kingdom: A "Prototype" of Social Innovation
The New Labour government in the United Kingdom (U.K.) from 1997 to 2010, led by Prime Ministers Tony Blair and Gordon Brown, enforced

extensive social policies under the flag of "The Third Way." One of its major goals was to reduce the inequality between different areas and groups by promoting work-welfare integration and regenerating local initiatives through supporting voluntary and community sectors, instead of going back to the "traditional" welfare state system existing prior to the Thatcherist reforms, which provided uniform welfare services. They introduced some new policy tools and mechanisms (Murray et al. 2010:90; Tsukamoto et al. 2007; Zimmeck 2010). First was partnerships with the voluntary and community sectors. The New Labour government changed the contract-based partnerships between the government and voluntary sectors during the Thatcher and Major administrations. The new administration concluded national and local "Compacts" as a framework document between voluntary and community sectors. Then local authorities, businesses, voluntary and community sectors, and others including academic institutions together developed a multi-sectoral Local Strategic Partnership (LSP) and other issue-based partnerships such as Local Area Agreement (LAA) or Local Public Sector Agreement (LPSA), with a specification of services necessary in the community. The result was evaluated by the regional Government Office, by the Comprehensive Area Assessment (CAA) framework. Second was new funding mechanisms. The central government provided funding for local regeneration through newly established Neighbourhood Renewal Funds (NRF) and Community Empowerment Funds (CEF) for some poor communities through LSPs. Third was voluntary sector reform and support for social enterprise. British charity and voluntary sector reform took place during this period and led to the amendment of the Charities Act (2006), and the creation of two new legal statuses: Charitable Incorporated Organisation (CIO, for nonprofits) and Community Interest Company (CIC, for community-based social enterprises).

As the result of the policy shift[11] made by the New Labour government, total public spending rose from GBP 449 billion in 1996-1997 to GBP 725 billion in 2009-2010, up to 47.4 per cent of the GDP. It did not shrink inequality as intended, but helped to empower the voluntary sector, to improve the circumstances of the poor, and to support building an inclusive society for the immigrant population (Giddens 2010; Lupton et al. 2013:38-41). Still, the new forms of partnerships between the government and other sectors faced a number of challenges, including issues with implementation, governance, and representation (Zimmeck 2010).

After the change of government to the Conservative-Liberal Democratic Party coalition in 2010, most of the partnership frameworks including LSP or LAA were either abolished or converted into voluntary arrangements, and public expenditure for the voluntary sector was cut drastically. However, the "Big Society" policy launched by the new administration continued to stress the role of civil society organizations, social enterprises, and communities, and provided funding through the Big Society Fund which utilized dormant bank accounts, and the Transition Fund (Economist 2010; Harada 2013).

The Compact and other related partnerships between governments, voluntary and community sectors, and other local stakeholders were an attempt to mobilize locally-led innovations based on principles shared among different sectors, and although the New Labour government rarely used the term SI during their time, this policy mix of i) devolution to local level partnerships, ii) independent funding to support local initiatives to provide social service and create employment, and iii) support for social businesses and nonprofits became a model for later SI policies.

The European Union

Following its emergence in the U.K., since the end of the 2000s,[12] with strong support from then-European Commission President Barroso, the term SI started to appear in some major European Union (EU) policy documents as a tool for the EU's poverty and social inclusion policy (BEPA 2011; European Commission 2010; 2013). After the European Financial Crisis, a number of EU member countries were forced to cut down on social spending, and SI was expected to substitute for social welfare services by creating employment, education, and training for vulnerable groups including immigrants and refugees, people with disabilities, the elderly, and unemployed women and youth.

In addition to the existing European Social Fund, a new EU Programme for Employment and Social Innovation (EaSI, 2014-2020) with a budget of EUR 919 million was created as an EU-level financing instrument to support member countries in the modernization of employment and social policies, improvement of job mobility, and promotion of microfinance and social entrepreneurship schemes (European Commission 2017).

The EU also supported numerous large-scale cross-country SI research projects (each with a budget of hundreds of millions of Euros) using the European Union's Seventh Framework Programme for Research, Technological Development and Demonstration (FP7, 2007-2013) and its successor Horizon 2020 (2014-2020).[13] The details of these research projects will be further described later in the literature review section (1.2.2).

The United States

In the United States (U.S.), the social policy of the Obama administration from 2009 to 2017 is well known for introducing the Affordable Health Care Act (so-called "Obamacare"), securing more equal rights for LGBT citizens, and implementing the Deferred Action for Childhood Arrivals (DACA) policy for young undocumented people.[14] It was also during the Obama administration when SI and related policy tools appeared in U.S. federal government policies. Soon after taking office in the aftermath of a major financial crisis, Obama created the White House Office of Social Innovation and Civic Participation and the Social Innovation Fund (SIF) by the Edward M. Kennedy Serve America Act in April 2009, for which he received bipartisan support[15] (Barnes 2010; The Economist 2010; Potts 2017).[16] The SIF was intended to bring evidence-based solutions to the most pressing social issues, such as health, education, housing, and employment. SIF funding goes to grantees who are existing grant-making organizations (including foundations, The United Way, nonprofit venture capitals, nonprofit alliances, and universities) through an open competition process, and then the grantees are asked to raise a one-to-one match for the government dollars from their own resources. Each grantee provides mixed funding to subgrantees, who are nonprofit organizations working in local communities. Each subgrantee is also asked to raise matching funds equivalent to what they received, and to implement programs to support the target population, typically in poor communities (Figure 1.1). As a result, Federal government funding from 2010 to 2016 totaled up to USD 352 million for fifty-seven awards, but the total funding matched to the federal money was USD 707 million.[17] According to a meta-analysis of thirty-eight final evaluation reports, forty-five percent of the programs went into youth issues, thirty-two percent to health, and twenty-four percent to economic opportunity (Zhang and Sun 2016:13).

Figure 1.1 Obama Administration Social Innovation Fund (Classic Program)

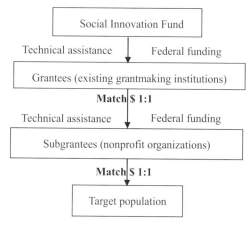

Source: Revised from Social Innovation Fund Fact Sheet, CNCS[18]

The goals of these policies, which came about in the aftermath of major economic and social crises, were to i) create funding mechanisms for nonprofit and social entrepreneurial projects both in the start-up and the growth stages, ii) create policy environments to enable innovative efforts, iii) utilize data and information tools to evaluate which interventions were truly effective, and iv) to do so without creating a new bureaucratic system or replacing existing funding frameworks. It came from a group of advisors like Michele Jolin,[19] who had experience both on the policy side and in supporting social enterprises at Ashoka, a global network of social entrepreneurs (Jolin 2008). Likely to be partly reflecting the ideas upheld by Jolin and other advisors with a social sector background, the SI policy frameworks during the Obama administration seemed to rely more strongly on the creativity and fundraising capacity of social sector organizations than European SI policies, while emphasizing the effective use of government funding by using financial terms like "returns on investment".[20]

Another feature during this period was the growing popularity of the Social Impact Bond (SIB), or the Pay for Success (PFS) contract, as it is usually called in the U.S., within national and local governments. The basic arrangement is to receive funding from a private investor prior to the implementation of a social intervention program by a service provider, with the government later repaying the investor upon the impact of the program being proven by an independent evaluator (Figure 1.2). These contracts became extremely popular after the first case in the U.S. in 2012 between New York City and the Urban Investment Group at Goldman Sachs to reduce the rate of reincarceration among adolescent inmates in New York City's Rikers Island prison, quickly expanding to over thirty states by early 2016 and soon included in SIF as a SIF Pay for Success Program awarded to nonprofit organizations and state and local governments. However, this kind of "financialization" was also criticized for focusing only on the particular issues that fit these financial tools, such as broad-scale preventive or early intervention programs, and not being able to recognize the real needs of the community, as well as the costs involved with setting up complicated mechanisms (Lake 2016:48-54).

Finally, during this period, around twenty states introduced at least one legal status for social enterprises such as Benefit Corporation (B-Corp) or Low-profit Limited Liability company (L3C). These new legal entities made it possible for a business pursuing socially-oriented goals to receive program-related investment from private foundations[21] and other investors, by accepting the obligation to consider social responsibility and to issue an annual benefit report compiled by an independent auditor (Murray 2012).

Figure 1.2 Structure of the U.S. Social Impact Bond / Pay for Success Contract

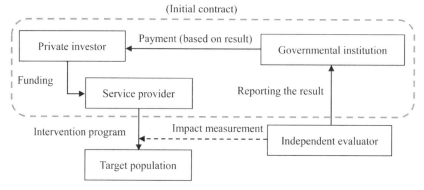

Source: Developed by the author

Asia

In Northeast and Southeast Asia, there is increasing pressure on governments to provide diverse social welfare services, especially in the aftermath of the major Asian economic crisis in the late 1990s and with changes in the socio-economic environment including rapidly aging societies, widening inequality, and slowing economic growth rates. Still, compared to Europe and the U.S., the policy application of SI in Asia has been mostly fragmental.

Arguably the champion of SI in Asia is the Seoul Metropolitan Government headed by Mayor Park Won-soon (2011-). Mayor Park set up the Seoul Innovation Bureau and mainstreamed SI as one of its major policy goals. Since then, the Seoul Metropolitan Government has introduced civic participation in policymaking processes, supported community-based organizations and social businesses, promoted sharing economy, and created supporting organizations including Seoul Innovation Park (C. 2018:7; Seoul Metropolitan Government 2015). Using Mayor Park's personal network with the international SI community including Geoff Mulgan and Social Innovation Exchange based in London, Seoul has been hosting a global annual "Future Innovation Forum" since 2015.[22]

Excluding the above-mentioned example, SI in Asian countries is mostly used as a vague slogan to support social entrepreneurs, or is mixed in with more general business / technological innovation. At the same time, there are both central and local governments in different countries putting in efforts to i) collaborate with civil society and other social sectors such as social enterprise, and to ii) create a favorable environment for the sectors, under different names such as "Social Management Innovation [*Shehui Guanli Chuangxin* 社会管理创新]" in China, or "Open Innovation" and "Public Service Innovation[23]" in Japan (Hope Institute 2017:268-270). A recent event in Japan is the use of SI in the draft of the "Basic Plan for the Use of Funding from Dormant Bank Account Grant[24]" in January 2018. In the document, it states that the organization who receives the grant should utilize the funding "to bring major social change (social innovation[25]) in the society". There is also strong interest from the business and financial sectors throughout Asia to utilize their resources for social investment (AVPN 2017; Mohan et al 2017a; 2017b).

1.2 Literature Review

SI is still an emerging concept and lacks a single, universally agreed upon definition. However, SI research has made significant progress and convergence in concept in recent years. There are also a variety of related concepts and theories. This section conducts a brief review of the theories and concepts that can support the development of a theory in this study. First, it shows how the theory of SI has developed, with some gaps between different regions especially in Europe, North America, and Japan and other Asian countries.[26] Second, it presents some other literature and conceptual frameworks to inform this research.

1.2.1 Innovation Theory and Social Innovation

As briefly mentioned above, SI as a process of change is nothing new to human history. However, SI as a term is fairly new, and prior to the current nomenclature, a similar idea had been described by different names including social invention, social diffusion, social change, social regulation, or transformation by different authors including Weber, Durkheim, and Tarde (Howaldt et al. 2014a:3; Moulaert et al. 2013:17-18). The word "innovation" (or "new combinations" / "creative disruption", which were the terms Schumpeter used originally), as widely known, comes from the classic works of Schumpeter, and it is worth noting that these early works mentioned not only business and technological phenomena, but also wider socio-cultural aspects (Jessop et al. 2013:113-114; Schumpeter 1937:166-168; Schumpeter 1994:83-84). One of the first authors who used the term "social innovation" explicitly was Peter Drucker in his book *Innovation and Entrepreneurship*. What he meant by the word was more in relation to society in general than business-specific, to address and adjust problems caused by the change of social structures. Among other social innovations such as the modern governmental administration system, banks, insurance, and newspapers, the two major issues he raised were first the replacement and training of blue-collar workers who will become redundant in the post-industrial society, and second the restructuring of outdated social policies and obsolete public-service institutions (Drucker 1986:257-260).

However, the later mainstream of literature relating to innovation, especially in the U.S. after the 1980s, when the government started cutting funding to nonprofits, became more focused on business and technological innovations at the micro level of individual social enterprises or social entrepreneurs. When they mentioned "social innovation," it usually meant an entrepreneurship dealing with "social" fields such as education and health (Christensen 1997; Defourny and Nyssens 2013:21-22; Goldsmith 2010; Rogers 1983). However, this approach was severely criticized by some authors such as Jessop et al. (2013:111) who called it "caring liberalism" that was trying to waive the responsibility of the public sector by letting it be handled by market mechanisms.

1.2.2 Development of Social Innovation Theories
Europe

The conceptualization and theorization of SI in the 2000s happened first in the United Kingdom and on the European continent, partly driven by the strong interest of policy makers. Two UK foundations, Young Foundation and Nesta, both led by Geoff Mulgan who worked for the Blair and Brown Administrations in 1997-2004, supported initial research works such as

Social Innovation: What it is, why it matters and how it can be accelerated (Mulgan et al. 2007) and *The Open Book of Social Innovation* (Murray et al. 2010).

In Murray et al. (2010) the well-known model of the stages of SI was introduced, where an SI initiative starts as a new idea, and being tested, disseminated or scaled up, finally reaches the stage of systemic change (Figure 1.3).

Figure 1.3 The Six Stages of Social Innovation

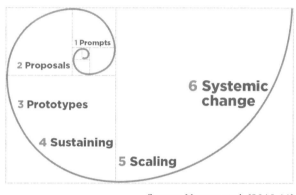

Source: Murray et al. (2010:11)

After the 2010s, as already mentioned, the EU began to support major SI research projects, including TEPSIE (Theoretical, Empirical and Policy Foundations for Social Innovation in Europe, 2012-2015),[27] SI-DRIVE (Social Innovation – Driving Force of Social Change, 2014-2017),[28] TRANSIT (Transformative Social Innovation Theory, 2014-2017),[29] CRESSI (Creating Economic Space for Social Innovation, 2014-2018),[30] and ITSSOIN (Impact of the Third Sector as Social Innovation, 2014-2017).[31] This body of literature including Cajaiba-Santana 2014; Domanski and Kaletka 2017; Haxeltine et al. 2015; Howaldt et al. 2014a; Moulaert et al.

2013; Nicholls and Murdock. 2012; Nicholls et al. 2015; Pel and Bauler 2014; TEPSIE 2014 and non-European authors who have close connection to their projects, such as the Hope Institute (2017) and Westley and Antadze (2010), though with differences in focus and emphasis, have still been able to develop considerable common conceptual frameworks and understandings. First, they established a clear conceptual distinction of SI from general (technology and business-oriented) innovation, social entrepreneurship, and social enterprise theories. This was accomplished by contributions from different academic disciplines such as the incorporation of structuration, institutionalism, agency, and social change theories. Second, they included non-business sectors and organizations such as governments, nonprofit organizations, cooperatives and other actors working on social economy and social issues as stakeholders in SI processes.[32] Third, a multi-dimensional understanding of SI was established, not only as an economic-technological phenomenon in one organization, but also as a change in understanding, cognition and framing in a society, societal and power relations, and systemic change in a society. Fourth, they paid attention to the process of individual SI initiatives leading to macro-level systemic change,[33] or the "institutionalization" of SI through scaling-up and diffusion. Finally, they showed a strong interest in connecting SI to the issue of social inclusion and empowerment of marginalized groups, inequality, and social justice.

Along with theoretical investigations, there were a large number of empirical analyses and case studies of individual SI projects, networks, sectors and global initiatives (Heals and Green 2016; Howaldt et al. 2014b; SI-DRIVE 2018). The theoretical nature of European SI literature seems to be in parallel with the expectations from the policy side (national governments and the EU) to utilize SI as a tool for social regeneration and inclusion, and to deal with severe social division and the exclusion of marginalized groups (including refugees and immigrants, youth, the poor, and unemployed citizens).

The United States

In the U.S., the Stanford Social Innovation Center was established in 2000 and in 2003, the first volume of the *Stanford Social Innovation Review* was published. During the 1990s and early 2000s, the focus of SI research in the United States was on social enterprises, coming from two different interests. First were those coming from the social entrepreneur and social venture backgrounds, applying business models and methodology to social issues, and second were nonprofit organizations shifting their operations to increase the amount of income-generating activities after the decrease in governmental funding. The meaning of SI at that time was more closely related to the financially sustainable application of a new product or methodology for a social cause (Dees 1998; Goldsmith 2010:13-14; SSIR Editor's Note 2003).

However, in the second half of the 2000s, SI literature in the U.S. began paying more attention to relationships between various actors. For instance, a well-known SSIR editorial, "Rediscovering Social Innovation" (Phills et al. 2008), re-defined SI and added being "just" and value creation for society as a whole, not only for a limited group. Interest has also been growing recently in a "systemic change approach" by connecting foundations or philanthropies, communities, and nonprofit sectors, something which cannot be accomplished by a social entrepreneur or social enterprise alone (Ganz et al. 2018; Kramer 2017).

Westley's Historical Analysis of Social Innovation Processes

Meanwhile in Canada, Frances Westley and her group based in Waterloo University developed an SI theory which shows similarity to the U.K. and European literature by distinguishing the difference between SI and social entrepreneurship and focusing on the impact of SI on change at the systemic level, including power and resource allocation, laws and common practices, and the basic beliefs that govern the society (Westley and Antadze 2010:3-4). Her group later conducted a historical analysis of SI initiatives[34] and discovered seven cross-cutting patterns (Westley 2017:240-254, Figure 1.4). First, they emphasized the importance of

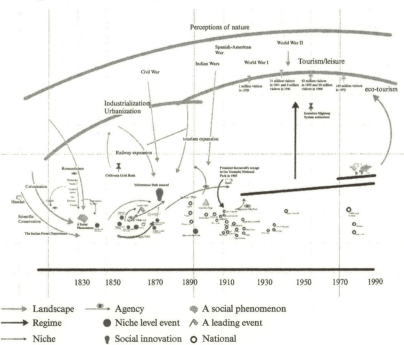

Figure 1.4 Historical Analysis of National Parks as a Social Innovation

Source: Antadze (2017:19)

meaning, that a new idea or social philosophy is behind a breakthrough, such as the creation of national parks driven by Romantic tradition, or the Internet based on the ideological foundations of counterculture. Second was the notion that SIs take time to unfold and therefore transcend the efforts of individuals. In some cases, the changes may take hundreds of years, and are not accomplished by one individual entrepreneur. For instance, different groups of agents like poets, explorers, academics, environmentalists, politicians, and managers all made a significant contribution at different times and in different ways to the establishment of national parks. A large-scale event like WWII may bring about drastic change, as it had on the use of intelligence testing and contraception methods. The third point is that the coherency of principles, not the consistency of practice, is important. Although different individuals and ideas participate in SI initiatives and the process transforms greatly over time, there is a surprising consistency with the initial conditions and ideas seen in the process. Fourth, combination with initiatives in the "adjacent possible" shapes the innovation itself. Each innovation, over time, combines and recombines with the adjacent possible, which is the alternative social phenomenon beyond existing reality. This may lead to the deterioration of the initiative, unless there is a person (like Margaret Sanger for the birth control movement) who can negotiate with different groups (the army, policy makers for poverty alleviation, and industries in Sanger's case). Fifth is the paradoxes and tensions which characterize SIs. Within an SI initiative, there may be ideas that are very different or in conflict with each other. For instance, national parks highlighted tensions between conservation and tourism, or between nature and culture. Still, such a paradox eventually works as a catalyst to evolution in the dynamics of SI processes. Sixth is that conflicts, oppositions, and opportunities stimulate combinations and re-combinations in SI. SIs develop new elements by having partners (for resource development) who may seem to be strange, and the combination defines future conflicts and debates within the initiatives. Seventh is the different effects positive and negative policy change have on SI development. Supporting policies create a stable environment for SI experimentation and development, while suppressive policies (such as the Comstock Act which illegalized birth control) stimulate a shadow network (which waits for the opening of a window of opportunity), conflict, and opportunistic behavior.

Japan and Other East Asia
In Japan, SI study has been conducted mostly by scholars with a business administration background (Kaneko et al. 2010; Nonaka et al. 2014; Takahashi et al. 2018; Tanimoto et al. 2013; Watanabe and Tsuyuki 2009), together with some others from social movement / nonprofit organization studies (Fujii et al. 2013; Hattori et al. 2010; Nishimura 2014). Thus, their conceptual frameworks mostly come from general innovation theories such as Schumpeter, Drucker, Christensen, and Rogers. With a few exceptions such as Fujisawa et al. (2017), Ohmuro (2009) or Tanimoto et al. (2013), most of them seem to have little connection with the recent SI literature (other than works on social enterprise and entrepreneurship) developed in Europe and North America. The strength of their research is in empirical analysis of individual cases or organizations, including for-profit companies and nonprofit organizations which create SI initiatives, and the relationships or ecosystems with other stakeholders surrounding them in a local community. Compared to European or American SI literature, they rarely

discuss the macro-level impact of SI or the processes of how individual SI cases can lead to systemic change, partly because of unavailable data and other technical limitations (Ohmuro, 2009; Tanimoto et al. 2013). Another characteristic, probably reflecting the interest of policy makers such as governments and foundations, is their strong focus on the individual "tools" of SI, including social enterprise, impact measurement (such as SROI, or social return on investment), or social investment bonds (SIB, Fujii et al. 2013; Laratta et al. 2011; Tsukamoto and Kaneko 2017).

SI literature in Japan and other Asian countries consists mainly of individual case studies (O'Byrne et al. 2014; Teets 2011; Zhao 2015), and not many theoretical works have been produced (Lin and Chen 2016; Shen and Li 2017). Among them, "The Social Innovation Landscape in Asia," a research project conducted by Korean think-tank NGO the Hope Institute, is arguably the most comprehensive attempt to investigate Asian SI initiatives. The Hope Institute team derived their conceptual understanding of SI from European SI literature, in particular TEPSIE (2014), and analyzed forty-six cases from five Asian countries, China, India, Japan, South Korea, and Thailand. As a result, they stressed the diverse political-economic-social contexts among Asian countries, as well as some characteristics observed in Asian countries which are different from European or North American countries, such as i) rapid and compressed socio-economic development led by the government, ii) a lack of consolidated frameworks to secure democratic and civic rights, and iii) weak governance in government sectors and the obstacles facing collaboration between the public and civil sectors often seen in developed countries (Hope Institute 2017:255-256). As a result, they argue that "SI in Asia has emerged as a response to growing challenges that often result from the "failure" of modern welfare states and free market capitalism," and presented seven characteristics of SI in Asia extracted from the most commonly observed terms in their case analyses (Figure 1.5), which are i) people-centered development, ii) community empowerment, iii) Information and communication technology (ICT) based civic engagement, iv) public sector leadership and local governance, v) social entrepreneurship, vi) intermediary organizations, and vii) cross-sectoral partnership.

Figure 1.5 Social Innovation Keyword Cloud

Source: Hope Institute (2017:255)

This research successfully illustrated the potential power of alternative developmental initiatives originating from grassroots movements, but it still omitted any capture of the process of scaling or the mechanisms for its causation. Other works include the "Research on the Social Innovation Eco-System in Asia" project supported by the Toyota Foundation which this author took part in, analyzing the scaling processes of SI initiatives from five countries (China, Japan, South Korea, Singapore, and Thailand, including Aoo 2019a and 2019b), and the special 2017 issue of *Stanford Social Innovation Review*, "Social Innovation and Social Transition in East

Asia," which highlighted examples from China, Hong Kong, Japan, and South Korea (SSIR 2017).

The Question of "Scaling"

While SI both as a policy term and a practice is becoming popular in different parts of the world, even giving rise to euphoria in the hopes that it can solve various social issues, there are also growing concerns that it is not being scaled as expected and delivering the expected outcome, or at least its results are not being felt by many, including many who need it most. Successful social entrepreneurs and social innovators have come to attract attention and funding from donors and the government with a slogan of "scaling what works," and their operations may grow at a remarkable speed. However, there are still many being left behind who could benefit from those services, and moreover the issues themselves or the root causes which lie beneath the problems are not being solved (Bradach and Grindle 2014; Ganz et al. 2018). This echoes the frustration seen in European SI documents which wonder why EU- or national-government funded SI initiatives do not "scale" and bring desired impact on a larger scale (Howaldt et al. 2014a:17).

Bradach and Grindle (2014) give practical advice on how to scale successful interventions to a level where they reach the "transformative scale": i) distributing through existing platforms, ii) recruiting and training others, iii) unbundling and scaling up parts with the greatest impact, iv) using technology to reach a larger audience, v) strengthening the field by either raising awareness of an issue or strengthening the players involved in that field, vi) changing public systems, vii) embracing the need for policy change, viii) considering using for-profit models for scaling, and

ix) altering people's beliefs, attitudes, and behaviors so that the change becomes the new social norm. Although most of these suggestions are concerned with disseminating individual programs to other areas and groups, others include some broader and crucial points, such as utilizing governmental or business sectors for scaling, and working on society at large to change their mindsets and attitudes.

Making It Big: Strategies for scaling social innovations[35] is a report prepared by Nesta. It is based on previous works done by Murray et al. (2010)[36] and interviews with different social innovators and presents four routes for SI scaling which do not rely on talented individuals: i) influencing and advising through advocacy, consultation or trainings, ii) building a delivery network by expanding the movement or replicating specific services, iii) forming strategic partnerships between governments, businesses, and social sectors,[37] and iv) growing the scale of a service-delivery organization. Here the ideas of size expansion (such as the case of BRAC in Bangladesh) and delivery networks are still there, but there is more emphasis on other multi-sectoral strategies such as campaigning and policy advocacy, building strategic alliances, creating common values and a mission by creating a brand and blueprint for social innovation (Gabriel 2014:22-27).

Social Innovation Ecosystems

Another emerging viewpoint in SI literature is a perspective that focuses on a national or local "SI ecosystem," which is a combination of social demands, actors, resources, processes dynamics and interactions between them (Aoo 2019a; Domanski 2018; Sgaragli and Giacomo Brodolini Foundation 2014). It seems to be a promising approach, especially to analyze the "missing link" of how individual SI initiatives connect to macro-scale impact. Still, so far it has gone little further than listing prominent institutions, projects and resources, and/or emphasizing the importance of having collective networks to generate SI (Guida and Maiolini 2014), and fails to provide an empirical analysis of the actual processes by which such ecosystems foster SI initiatives and develop them into scale, and how local contexts affect the processes.

1.2.3 Other Relevant Theories

Since SI literature is affected by various concepts and theories, there is a wide range of scholarship that is contributing to its development. Here are some of the most relevant theories and frameworks that serve to help develop this study.

Institutional Theories / Structuration Theories

Institutional / structuration theories have provided a strong basis for SI literature. Cajaiba-Santana (2014:43) points out the theoretical dichotomy of agency and structuralism in SI research. Authors such as Heiskala draw examples from institutionalism or structuration theories including Bourdieu, Giddens, and Max Weber to draw attention to the historical and organizational path-dependency and the way such dependencies reproduce and limit the possible development of historical processes (Heiskala 2007:53; Howaldt el al. 2014a:24-28).

Transitions Theories

Transitions theories, or social change theory, is the other side of the agency-structuration dichotomy. It emphasizes the role of agency, and "change agents" (Chiappero-Martinetti and Jacobi 2015: Goldsmith 2010). It helps the building of a social systems theory, but has also been criticized for being too abstract, and for its weakness in connecting empirical phenomena, especially the collaboration, negotiation and compromising mechanisms between different stakeholders, with a theoretical framework (Haxeltine et al. 2015:5).

Welfare Regime / Welfare Society Theories

Welfare nation / regime / society is another group of concepts which require attention to understand the current SI debate. Theories beginning with the classic Esping-Andersen work *The Three Worlds of Welfare Capitalism*, which presented three welfare state models (Esping-Andersen 1990), different welfare regimes or welfare society models have been proposed in order to investigate the arrangements between state, market, and other sectors including family, community, and the social sector. They are significantly helpful since they can be used as tools to measure how societal relationships, distribution of resources, and burden and risks change as an outcome of an SI initiative.

It should be noted that even in his 1990 book, Esping-Andersen set three models (Liberal, Corporatist, and Social Democratic) not only as variations of welfare states, but also as categories of welfare regimes based on a mix of contributions from the state, market, and family sectors. He also placed special emphasis on how the labor markets for different gender and age groups affect welfare coverage and the provision of care services (Esping-Andersen 1990:26-28, 222-226). In his later work (Esping-Andersen 1999:35-36) he further highlighted the role of non-state actors, especially family. However, these models still had limitations as frameworks targeting primarily industrialized societies, not resource-scarce contexts which lack significant input from the state.

Based on Esping-Andersen's categorization,[38] Salamon and Anheier (1998) added a nonprofit sector which functions either as a substitute for a welfare state (in a few countries which fall under the "liberal" category such as the U.S. and the U.K.), or as a complement, by receiving funding from the state and working as a service provider within a welfare state system in Western European and Nordic countries. Evers (1995) and Pestoff (2000), and Sakamoto and Tsujinaka (2012:24) proposed a model of a welfare mix concept made up of state, market, and private household and community, and the third sector, which includes both voluntary and nonprofit, cooperatives and other social economy organizations, as shown in Figure 1.6. They emphasized the intermediating role of the third sector

Figure 1.6 The Welfare Triangle and the Third Sector

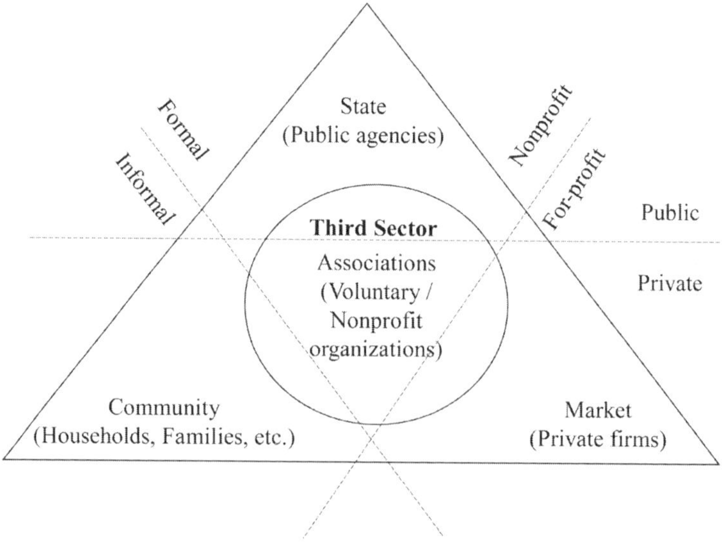

State
(Public agencies)

Formal
Informal
Nonprofit
For-profit

Third Sector
Associations
(Voluntary /
Nonprofit
organizations)

Public
Private

Community
(Households, Families, etc.)

Market
(Private firms)

Source: Pestoff (2000:42)

between different sectors, acting as "a part of the public space in civil societies" and bringing a synergetic mix of resources into welfare (Evers 1995:159-161, 173; Pestoff 2000:45-54).

Ochiai (2009); Ochiai et al. (2010), along with Ueno (2011) developed the "care diamond" (or "welfare quadrangle" as the latter proposes) model to illustrate how different sectors share welfare costs and risks. It consists of state, market, community (including nonprofit sectors), and family. Figure 1.7 shows examples of care diamonds representing two different welfare regimes, the first where the state provides services (Society A), and the second where the welfare state system is non-existent and family and community become the main care providers (Society B). Compared to the Evers-Pestoff model, which defined the third sector as an intermediary sector within a state-market-family/community triangle (thus demonstrating its role of covering the "welfare residual" of other sectors), this model has the advantage of showing the contribution of different sectors visually and is suitable for cross-country or cross-time comparisons.

Figure 1.7 "Care Diamond" Models: Welfare and Non-Welfare States

(Society A: Welfare state)   (Society B: Non-welfare state)

Source: Ochiai (2009); Ochiai et al. (2010); Ueno (2011:217)

Governance Network Theory

Although a state - market dichotomy model and government – market - community triangle are both useful as conceptual frameworks, they can describe very little about the complex and dynamic interactions between individual stakeholders within an actual policy process. To understand multi-stakeholder processes from micro (individual) to macro levels, it will be useful to apply other tools from different disciplines. The analytical frameworks and concepts derived from the study of "governance networks," led by Kooiman and Rhodes among others, allow us to investigate a detailed institutional mechanism and interactions.

As Figure 1.8 shows, the policy (defined as a desirable social output, such as a social service) is seen to come as a result of governance processes between various stakeholders including governments, businesses, service providers, and civil society. The actors can interact and negotiate in the processes, and there will be self-regulation to govern behavior within the network. The government is no longer the sole owner of the policy, but continues to intervene either as a stakeholder, or through providing a "meta-governance" to the network by setting guidelines, regulations, and standards for the policy (Abe 2016; Sorensen and Torfing 2006:4-5; Rhodes 1997:9-11, 36-45; Kooiman 2003:83, 104-106).

It is important to note that the governance network is not always supportive of SI and may in fact work conversely, but this framework enables us to analyze a wider range of stakeholders than traditional principal-agent or corporatist theories, as well as to illustrate the dynamic chain of processes that will formulate (or fail to formulate) a policy outcome, within a certain context and scope.

Figure 1.8 Governance Network Diagram

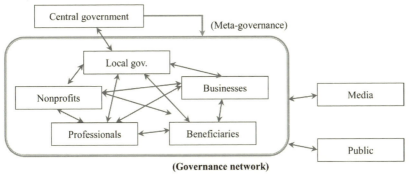

Source: Developed by the author

1.2.4 The Gap in Current SI Literature

As seen above, significant advances have been made in SI theoretical and empirical research. It has enabled SI theory to be a conceptual framework which is independent from more general innovation theory, and through connections with other related discourses, has created a sound theoretical basis to develop future practice and research. However, researchers have noted that there is still a significant gap both between i) practice and theory, and between ii) individual initiatives and macro-level impact / structural change (Cajaiba-Santana 2014:49; Haxeltine et al. 2017:15). They have stressed the need to develop a "middle-range theory" to bridge these gaps, especially the latter, but the challenge of how to trace and analyze the complexity of multi-sectoral SI processes has kept this an ongoing research challenge, apart from a few ambitious attempts such as Westley et al. (2017). Although Murray et al. (2010:87-100) have pointed out multiple paths that lead to scaling of SI initiatives from the growth of individual organizations, collaboration, licensing and franchising, replication, diffusion, dissemination, and the commissioning and adoption by authorities, the actual processes of scaling were largely still in the black box. This gap, which is closely linked to the policy maker and practitioner's challenge and desire to "scale up" SI initiatives and to bring about greater impact (Clarence 2014: 47; Goldsmith 2010:6; Howaldt et al. 2014a:61), remains one of the greatest questions still unanswered in the development of SI theory.[39]

Also, so far most of the major contributions to developing SI theories have come from Europe and North America. Other regions, including Asia, have mostly been merely providing empirical cases and evidence. In-depth analysis of SI processes in Asia to contribute to conceptual development is a relatively uncharted research area.[40]

The objective of this study is to fill in these major gaps, even partially, based on an empirical analysis of SI initiatives in selected Asian countries. It examines the processes of scaling, how different stakeholders and factors influence the processes, and how this leads to having (or not having, in some cases) macro-level impact on a society.

1.3 Research Design
1.3.1 Research Questions
This study intends to fill in the gaps in the existing SI literature, as stated above. The main question to be answered is:
"What are the factors and causal mechanisms that affect the scaling of (or the failure of) social innovation initiatives in selected Asian countries?" While answering this main question, the study also deals with a set of accompanying questions, such as: i) What are the roles of central and

local governments, businesses, and civil society[41] within these processes? ii) What are the governance mechanisms between multi-sectoral stakeholders that lead to successful (or not so successful) scaling? iii) Are "top-down" or "bottom-up" processes more successful in the scaling of initiatives? iv) Are "indigenous" or "foreign" ideas / initiatives more successful in scaling? v) How do other factors, including political and socio-economic systems, values and norms, legislation, crises, or the use of technology influence the processes? vi) What infrastructures and policies are helpful for enhancing the social innovation processes in different countries?

To answer these questions, this research conducts an empirical analysis of case studies and their comparison to investigate the SI processes and results (both successful and failed) in different countries, then investigates the causes of the differing results, the scaling patterns and the governance mechanisms. It also compares the differences and similarities between Asian countries, and between Asian and European countries. The details of the methodology are explained further in the following section 1.3.3.

1.3.2 Theoretical Framework
Processes of SI

This book attempts to fill the major gap of explaining the causal connection between individual SI initiatives and macro-level changes in a society. It pays particular attention to how SI initiatives scale up and diffuse through interaction with different stakeholders, and finally have (or fail to have) macro-level impact in a society. Figure 1.9 shows the four stages of SI scaling processes used for this study, a consolidation of the well-known six steps (i. Prompts – ii. Proposals – iii. Prototypes – iv. Sustaining – v. Scaling – vi. Systemic change) proposed by Murray et al. (2010). Each stage corresponds to the following step:

Stage 1: Ideation is the initial step when the new idea is brought in, either as a strange "invention" of a local practitioner or an entrepreneur or introduced as a foreign idea.

Stage 2: Incubation is when one or more individual organizations or projects, sometimes in collaboration with different stakeholders, attempt to materialize the new idea, often on the local community level. This is the area that most of the existing SI literature focuses on.

Stage 3: Acceleration is when the Incubation stage is successful, and the scale of the initiative expands. It should be noted that this may be accomplished through a) top-down implementation of the initiative as a policy or program of a national or local government (or another organization with sufficient resources, such as grant-making foundations), which is called "scale-up"; b) diffusion to or imitation of a successful initiative by other communities, often with certain adjustments or "localization", which is a bottom-up process and called "scale-out"; or c) a combination of both (Tamamura 2014:28).[42]

Stage 4: Institutionalization (also referred to as a "systemic change") is when the majority of the members in a society accept the idea as a "normal" or an unquestionably positive value, adopt the behavior, and new laws or regulations endorse the value. Here we should be cautious that the "goal" for an SI process is not to have it become a law or a policy, since there are numerous examples of new laws or governmental policies failing to become "embedded" within a society or meeting with opposition from stakeholders in the implementation stage and thus making hardly any impact.[43] Therefore, this study defines the SI initiative as having had macro-level impact only when there is some (even anecdotal) evidence that the idea is widely accepted in the society, and strongly embedded within the values, behaviors, and rules of the people and organizations.

Figure 1.9 Four Stages in the Social Innovation Process

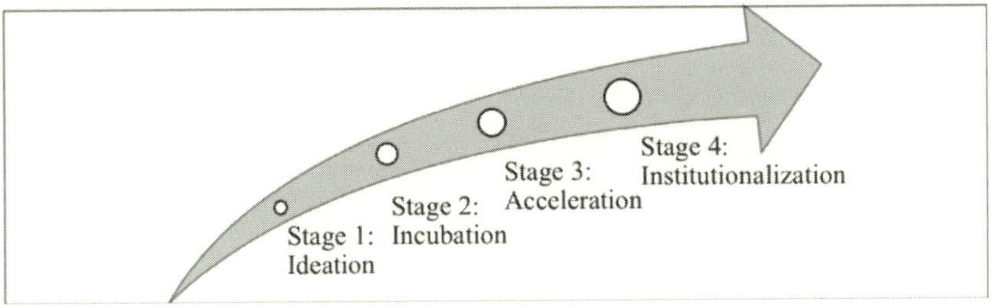

Stage 1: Ideation
Stage 2: Incubation
Stage 3: Acceleration
Stage 4: Institutionalization

Source: Developed by the author (revised from Murray et al. 2010:11)

This research pays particular attention to how SI processes may succeed or fail to scale or become institutionalized, corresponding to stages three and four in the categories described above. On the contrary, it does not investigate the details of individual projects or attempts (stages one and two) unless there is a strong connection to the scaling processes.

Multi-stakeholder Networks / Interactions

When analyzing the SI scaling processes, it seems natural to follow the path of one successful organization and all related actors surrounding that organization. However, it is obvious that no successful SI processes are achieved by one person or organization but are instead the outcome of multi-sectoral interactions and diffusions, similar to the way different microcredit organizations and projects flourished following the famous success story of Muhamad Yunus. Therefore, to conduct such analyses, this study attempts to investigate a sector-level interaction of different stakeholders, including governments, businesses, and civil society. As Figure 1.10 illustrates, this perspective owes a great deal to the findings of network governance theory but has been modified to fit the purposes of the study.

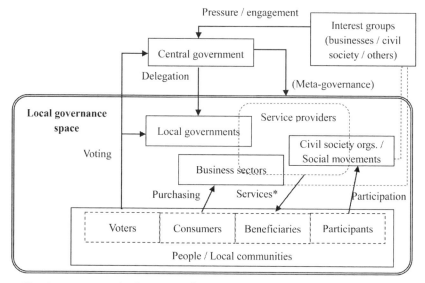

Figure 1.10 Governance Spaces for Social Innovation Processes

*Services may go under "purchasing" when beneficiaries can choose the provider.
Source: Developed by the author

1.3.3 Methodology: Case Studies and Process Tracing

To answer the research questions presented above, this study uses case studies as the main analytical tool, for two reasons. First, a large amount of quantitative data that we can use for statistical analysis is not available from the targeted Asian countries. If we try to collect a large number of samples, the homogeneity and comparability of the data may be questionable and run the risk of putting dissimilar samples together. Second, case study analysis is more suitable for the purpose of the study. To answer the questions stated above, this study attempts process tracing and causal process observation, to analyze possible mechanisms and causal contributions between various factors and outcomes (Brady et al. 2010:24; Collier et al. 2010:202-203; George and Bennett 2005:6, 27-31; Ragin 1993:36).

Case Studies and Process Tracing in SI Literature
As mentioned earlier, case studies in existing SI research tend to focus on individual SI projects or organizations, and to investigate how the initiative developed and the relationships with other stakeholders in terms of idea creation, financing, and operation or service provision.

A major attempt to apply process theory to SI initiatives and societal transformation can be seen in the TRANSIT project. Haxeltine et al. (2015) proposes:

> "Process theory is interested in discovering patterns in sequences of events, variance theory in explaining observed outcomes with the help of explanatory variables. ... process theories provide explanations in terms of the sequence of events leading to an outcome." (Haxeltine et al. 2015:6)

With their research focus on what they call the "relational perspective" and the change of social relations caused by SI initiatives, they do not set any specific data-analysis method in their methodological guidelines for case studies but ask each case to include actors and relations mapping and a timeline of processes and dynamics over time (Wittmayer et al. 2015:13-16). Still, there is a certain limitation to using TRANSIT case studies for analyzing multi-stakeholder processes of SI initiatives as to how they lead to macro-level societal change. First, the boundary of each case study is limited within an individual SI network (such as Ashoka network) and its national or local organizations. It is not very clear how such cases impacted transformative change in broader social contexts. Second, they pay more attention to "patterns, phases and turning points than to causes and factors" (Haxeltine et al. 2015:6), for the sake of using the results also for "quasi-quantitative comparative meta-analysis"[44] (Wittmayer et al. 2015:4) of "critical turning points"[45] (Pel et al. 2017:3-4, Figure 1.11). This seems to be sound reasoning for their research design, but as a result, they had to leave the causal linkage in a black box, and

Figure 1.11 Excerpt from a Critical Turning Point Timeline

The deceptive political breakthrough of basic income	December 17th 1994
On December 17th 1994, two Dutch ministers publicly spoke out in favour of the basic income. The endorsement by politicians in power suggested that basic income became a serious policy option. The apparent breakthrough soon proved deceptive, however. Read more	
5 related events	
	October 1985 publication influential basic income report WRR
1992 Report on basic income by Central Planning Bureau	
	September 1993 Newspaper interview series on basic income
September 1995 Political choice against basic income	
	2001 Tax reform: introduction 'by stealth' of little basic income

Source: Pel et al. (2017:5)

to state in their final Practice Brief that the "explanations for how processes of institutional change are unfolding in contemporary examples of transformative social innovation" are "an ongoing research challenge" (Haxeltine et al. 2017:15).

Also, as described above, Westley and her group have conducted case study analyses of SI initiatives. Their historical analysis presents examples of how SI initiatives can lead to macro level impact on societal rules, behaviors, and values. This is quite a unique and valuable contribution to empirically linking the micro level, when an SI initiative starts as a marginalized and peripheral movement, and the macro level or systemic change. However, they tend to focus on the description of the roles of individual persons, organizations and events, and omit any clarification or analysis of the structural relationships between different sectors / groups (such as industries, public authorities, or citizens) within these interactions and negotiations.

Target Countries and Cases: An Attempt at a Comparative Analysis
This study positions an individual nation as the basic unit of analysis, although it does not preclude the possibility of having sub-national regions with distinct cultural / historic distinctiveness such as the Basque region in Spain or Okinawa in Japan, or any rural community with a different local context compared to a megalopolis capital. The target countries for case study are China, Indonesia, Japan, and South Korea. These countries have been selected to compare the mechanisms caused by different contexts in governmental systems, socio-economic conditions, and cultural settings.[46] It may also help to investigate whether there is room for typological theorizing, or some common patterns for some sub-categories of SI

processes, such as in developed-country or developing country contexts, or with specific issues (George and Bennett 2005:235-236).

The main criteria for case selection are first, that the cases selected are cross-sectoral and do not consist of a single issue, to avoid being unduly constrained by the specific systems and contexts of certain sectors (for example, the medical care or education systems) – because of this criterion, we had to abandon many interesting initiatives, such as remote care services or online education. Second, cases which can be used by other countries as a reference, or in other words are not too context-driven, are selected – for example, Muslim philanthropy in Indonesia which is based on religious beliefs and traditions, or the Long-term Care Insurance system in Japan which is based on a considerable amount of financial outlay, had to be dropped. Even Singapore as a country had to be skipped due to its unique characteristics as a city-state and its governance and welfare schemes. Thirdly, cases that have already been in place for some time were chosen instead of on-going ones, so that we can evaluate the scaling processes as ones that are time-tested – again, we had to drop some of the interesting "latest" cases such as bicycle sharing or electronic payment platforms. Finally, since the study is based on a meta-analysis of primary and secondary literature, the availability of documents mainly in English or Japanese was a major concern. Thailand was another country passed over in this study due to this particular issue.[47]

It is obvious that increasing the number of countries will add a heavy burden on the study. And the diversity in political systems, economies, and cultural contexts in Asia makes the comparison even more challenging than the comparison of industrialized countries, as often done in the study of welfare regimes. However, it is also useful to compare SI processes in different countries to avoid getting too "embedded" in country- or issue-specific systems, historic paths, and discourses. Methodology-wise, it can be helpful in developing a theory to compare the "most different systems" and identify some elements of commonalities among variables and outcomes – to quote Przeworski and Teune: "If the relationship between an independent and the dependent variable is the same within the subgroups of the population, then again the systemic differences need not be taken into consideration" (Ito 2013:4; Meckstroth 1975:137; Przeworski and Teune 1970:35).

The cases that meet the criteria of considerable breadth beyond issues or sectors are the Non-profit Organizations (NPOs) in Japan, social organizations in China, social economy in South Korea, and governmental decentralization in Indonesia. For Japan, two additional sectoral cases (environmental pollution and community-based integrated care for the elderly) have been added to look further for the details of SI scaling mechanisms.

Methodology Design

The study was carried out in a three-step process. First, it conducts an analysis of the scaling processes of each individual SI case by using the following analytic framework (Table 1.3) to describe the four stages of SI and the roles of the different sectors (governments, businesses, and civil society)[48] in each stage.

The main source of information used for the case analyses is the meta-analysis of primary and secondary source documents. Primary sources include documents authored by the organizations and individuals involved, such as reports, websites, and other social media. It may also

Table 1.3 Analytical Framework Used for Case Analysis

Actor / Stage	Stage 1: Ideation	Stage 2: Incubation	Stage 3: Acceleration	Stage 4: Institutional-ization
Government	- -	- -	- -	- -
Business	- -	- -	- -	- -
Civil society	- -	- -	- -	- -

Developed by the author

○ minor / ◯ : major involvement from each sector
💥 : conflict with the initiative / ▭ : multi-sectoral alliance
💭 : new ideation / ▭ : legislation (central/ local levels)

include archival materials when accessible. Secondary sources include documents written by external authors, including monographs, academic papers, reports, and media articles on specific social issues, policies, or initiatives. Documents relevant to other issues, discourses, and academic discussions are included as well as literature specifically focusing on SI. Additionally, direct interviews with relevant academics and practitioners are used to supplement and triangulate the information. In other words, each case study in this study attempts to reconstruct the chronological and causal lineages of each initiative from the perspective of SI process development by using existing literature and other available materials.

Then as the second step, the study tests the following variables and hypotheses in each case as a causal process observation, asking whether we can say that the SI process succeeded or failed to scale because of these specific variables: i) whether the SI process was top-down or bottom-up; ii) whether there was a proliferation of multi-sectoral "alliances"; iii) whether the issue was recognized by a society as a major social priority or a crisis; iv) whether the SI initiative received support from existing business sectors, or whether a new sector was developed; v) whether a strong civil society and/or social movement was involved in the process; vi) other variables that had a causal relationship on the outcome of

Table 1.4 List of Independent Variables and Hypotheses Used for Case Analysis

Variables	Hypotheses
i) Scale-up (top-down) SI process or scale-out (diffusion) SI process or both	• Successful SI process happens when there is a scale-up (top-down) policy • Successful SI process happens when there is a bottom-up diffusion process • Successful SI process happens when there are both top-down policy and bottom-up diffusion processes
ii) Multi-sectoral "alliances" established and proliferated on different levels or the lack thereof	• Successful SI process happens when there is a multi-sectoral "alliance" formed at the central (national) level • Successful SI process happens when there is a multi-sectoral "alliance" formed at the local level • Successful SI process happens when there are multi-sectoral "alliances" formed both at the central and local levels
iii) Social consensus (or high priority) or remaining a marginal issue	• Successful SI process happens when social concern about the issue is high
iv) Support and cooperation from existing business sectors (or development of a new business sector) or the lack thereof	• Successful SI process happens when the mainstream business sectors (with pressure from a majority of consumers) start to cooperate, or when a new business sector emerges
v) Strong civil society and/or social movement or the lack thereof	• Successful SI process happens when there is a strong civil society sector and/or a social movement
vi) Other factors	• Political regimes (authoritarian / democratic) • Technologies or methodologies • The level of decentralization • Gender empowerment and equality

Developed by the author

whether the SI process ultimately had a macro-level impact in the society or not[49] (Table 1.4):

Two Axes: Top-Down or Bottom-Up, and Multi-Sectoral "Alliance"
Among other variables, this study pays particular attention to two factors. First is whether the initiative started as a "top-down" or a "bottom-up" process. There is a strong scholarly tradition which focuses on the authoritarian nature of Asian politics, by using different terms including "Asian values"[50] or "developmental state" (Chu et al. 2008:8-9; Inoguchi and Carlson 2006:4-8; Vatikiotis 1996:93; Williams 2016:29-30). On the other hand, there is another group of authors who emphasize the democratic and grass-root processes (such as "third-wave" democracies or participative development) since the democratization of Northeast and Southeast Asian countries in the 1980s and 1990s (Bell 2006:7-8; Huntington 1995:22; Kelly et al. 2012:33; Morris-Suzuki 2017:9-10). This study examines whether the "strongmen" types of politicians or "competent government officials" (World Bank 1993:94) could impose SI initiatives and deep-rooted societal changes, or more grassroot-oriented initiatives can do so.

Second is the existence and proliferation of multi-sectoral "alliances" at different levels. Here we need to clarify what multi-sectoral "alliance" means in this book. A vast amount of SI or social movement literature have spoken previously about multi-sector cooperation, partnership, or collaboration. Still, the difference of types or governance mechanisms within such cooperative efforts have been touched upon by only a few of them (Lyon 2012:139, 151; Van Dyke and McCammon 2010). While these types of partnerships establish the assumption (often unconsciously) that stakeholders from different sectors share a common goal and that they will cooperate to achieve that goal, and have been jokingly described as "hollow rhetoric" by Lyon (Park 2016:141-142), this paper refers to partnerships or relationships between stakeholders from different sectors that may or may not share values, interests, or goals but which still work to push an initiative forward, as an "alliance". The nature of such "alliance" is fairly open, less hierarchical and interdependent and often lacks formal negotiation between stakeholders, therefore each stakeholder acts based on their own values and interests.[51] Even when each shareholder is pursuing their own interest, this kind of "alliance" can help to push an SI initiative forward.

Although the idea of such an "alliance" originally comes from the scholars of local governance and network governance theory (Kooiman 2003; Rhodes 1997; Sorensen and Torfing 2006; Tsujinaka 2010), the term "alliance" is (strangely) taken from *Politics among Nations*, a classic of International Politics written by Hans J. Morgenthau. Morgenthau defined an alliance as a "function of the balance of power operating within a multiple-state system", and shows that an alliance can be formed not only when the parties share a common interest or ideology, but also simply to meet their own interests without any moral considerations, taking the example of changes in political alignments during the Thirty Years' War (Morgenthau 1968:175-183).[52] This study uses the word "alliance" to clarify that it appreciates different forms of partnerships or relationships, including cases of stakeholders competing for resources, or conflicts between different sectors that consequently push a process forward as "alliances," and analyzes how the formation of such "alliances" on the central or local level affects the processes.[53]

Combining two variants results in four domains divided by two axes (Figure 1.12) that will be used later to identify which process can cause an SI initiative to scale.

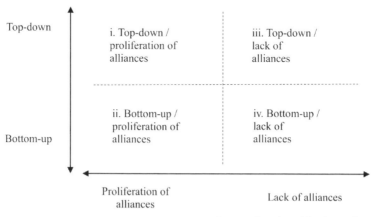

Figure 1.12 Four Domains of Top-Down / Bottom Up and the Formation of "Alliances"

Source: Developed by the author

After the case studies and hypothesis testing, as the third step, the study attempts to conduct a cross-case analysis to see patterns in causality. It merits early acknowledgement that the scope of this research is not limited to finding a general rule in which one of the variables will always lead to the institutionalization of SI initiatives. Literature on complexity theory warns us that the causal mechanisms of social phenomena cannot be described by such linear relationships and should be understood as interactions of intentions and actions (Byrne and Callaghan 2014:173; Jervis 1997:17, 35-39). And different culture and contexts, including historical "path-dependency" make such a "one-size-fits-all" understanding and prescription even less useful.[54] However, this study does not claim any sort of "representativeness" or to increase the inferential leverage by increasing the number of samples or issues, and prioritizes providing a limited number of in-depth analyses (Brady et al. 2010:23-24). Therefore, we should be aware that there may be different patterns of causal relationships beyond the ones identified by this study (George and Bennett 2005:157; Ragin 1993:44-46).

Finally, this study aims to clarify some of the causal mechanisms created by the interaction of different societal sectors in the SI processes, and how such initiatives do or do not have impact on the macro level. By doing so, it seeks to contribute to the middle-range theory which can explain the mechanisms under some certain circumstances, and possibly to provide some policy implications to scale the SI processes that are needed in society.

1.4 Structure of the Book

The structure of this book is as follows. Chapters two to five provide country case studies for Japan, China, South Korea, and Indonesia after providing a brief summary of country contexts that affect the case study processes. Chapter six presents some main findings and discussions from the case studies and cross-country analysis, policy implications, and conclusion.

---

1   For a few examples, the Asia Social Innovation Award invites social entrepreneurs who work on issues such as aging, environmental degradation, and poverty ("About the Award," Asia Social Innovation Award website: https://www.socialinnovation-award.asia/2017/about.html). The Horizon Prize for Social Innovation ("Horizon Prize Social Innovation in Europe," The European Commission website: http://

ec.europa.eu/research/horizonprize/index.cfm?prize=social-innovation) and the Aspirin Social Innovation Award ("The Award: Aspirin Social Innovation Award" page, Bayer Foundation website: https://aspirin-social-awards.org/the-award) both present awards to people who bring about pioneering technologies related to social issues such as mobility and health (All retrieved 2nd Nov. 2018).

2   How to identify the "social issues" and what the positive social changes are (and what they are not) is one of the major questions for SI, since agreement on these points will depend on the society in question (Domanski and Kaletka 2017).

3   Moore et al. (2012) describe the latter, borrowing the terminology from resilience theory, as the process of "release-reorganization-exploitation-conservation," by which existing resources in an ecosystem become available again and new lives begin to proliferate with new diversities.

4   In the case of Nicholls and Murdock (2012:4) they add "Network / movement" as another dimension, but here it is integrated with organization.

5   Some of the earliest prototypes are the Poor Relief System in Britain or Medical / Injury / Elderly Pensions in late 19th Bismarckian Century Prussia, but we need to note that these services were more of a charity or a favor, not a universal right (Tada 2014:6-9).

6   Most of these classical examples of welfare states are based on democracy, but Inoue (2014:28-29) notes that social security systems are often introduced by authoritarian / populist regimes such as in Argentina under J. D. Perón, or in Brazil under G. D. Vargas.

7   The authors pointed out that welfare state models from Europe / North America (represented by the earlier version of Esping-Andersen's model) could not be simply applied to Asian countries, due to different contexts such as the role of the state, business, organized labor, and other forms of social protections, and these different stakeholders acting as a "substitute" for or an "equivalent" of the welfare state (Estevez-Abe 2008; Zhang 2012).

8   Ueno (2011:217) even claims that the "welfare state" has already shifted to a "welfare society," following the upheaval and change of social welfare systems in actual policy.

9   We also need to note that there are criticisms of SI from authors who see it as another face of neo-liberalism which serves to release the state from its responsibility to

provide services based on universal rights (Jessop et al. 2013; Moulaert et al. 2013).
10 Inoguchi (2014:28-32), based on a series of cross-country AsiaBarometer surveys conducted from 2003 to 2007, categorizes three dimensions of well-being in East Asia, which are: i) material conditions (modern facilities and infrastructure), ii) non-material conditions (social relationships), and the iii) function of the public sector. He notes that there is a pattern of non-material conditions becoming more important as the economies develop, and non-material conditions tend to have a negative effect on subjective happiness in the societies.
11 Still there were some important similarities and continuities with the Conservative administrations, including the work and welfare connection, utilization of the charity sector as an executive arm of social service, and above all, the break with the traditional provision-based welfare systems.
12 European Commission website: President Barroso Discusses How to Boost "Social Innovation" (20th Jan. 2009) http://ec.europa.eu/social/main.jsp?catId=89&langId=en&newsId=445&furtherNews=yes (Retrieved 2nd Nov. 2018).
13 "FP7" page, Research Europa website: https://ec.europa.eu/research/fp7/index_en.cfm; "Horizon 2020" page, European Commission website: https://ec.europa.eu/programmes/horizon2020/en/ (Both retrieved 2nd Nov. 2018).
14 We should note that these policy and social changes (for example introducing affordable healthcare for all and accepting same-sex marriages in all states) are themselves a good sample of (controversial) SI initiatives, though I should not go into the details of each policy here.
15 "Social Innovation Fund" page, Corporation for National and Community Service website: https://www.nationalservice.gov/programs/social-innovation-fund (Retrieved 2nd Nov. 2018).
16 However, we should be aware that the Obama's Office of Social Innovation and Civic Participation was also a "variation" of former presidential initiatives to support community and voluntary activities, including Bill Clinton's AmeriCorps program and George W. Bush's Office of Faith-Based and Community Initiatives, each of them reflecting the respective president's personal preferences (Potts 2017:21).
17 "Funded Organizations" page, Corporation for National Community Service website: https://www.nationalservice.gov/programs/social-innovation-fund/funded-organizations (Retrieved 2nd Nov. 2018).

18 "Fact Sheet 2016 Social Innovation Fund", Corporation for National Community Service website: https://www.nationalservice.gov/sites/default/files/documents/CNCS-Fact-Sheet-2016-SocialInnovationFund_0.pdf (Retrieved 2nd Nov. 2018).
19 Jolin was appointed as a member of the White House Council for Community Solutions in 2010, after serving as a Senior Advisor for Social Innovation and a member of President Obama's Presidential Transition Team. She now runs a non-profit organization, Results for America, a nonprofit that informs policy makers by utilizing data and evidence. "Michele Jolin" page, Results for America website: http://results4america.org/people/michele-jolin/ (Retrieved 2nd Nov. 2018).
20 Still, the financial resources controlled by the White House Office of Social Innovation and Civic Participation were much smaller compared with the mainstream governmental funding controlled by Departments, and one of the major challenges for the Office was to get other departments to appreciate the collaborative working style with the social sector organizations (Potts 2017:26).
21 Foundations in the U. S. have an obligation to pay out more than five percent of their assets annually as grants or program-related investment, and by being registered as these legal entities (B-Corp or L3C), social enterprises became a qualified target for investment from foundations.
22 Future Innovation Forum 2018 website: http://www.seoulfif.co.kr/en/ (Retrieved 2nd Nov. 2018)
23 Cabinet Office, Government of Japan website: http://www5.cao.go.jp/keizai-shimon/kaigi/special/innovation/ (Public Service Innovation Platform [*Koukyou Saabisu Inobeeshon Pulattofuoomu* 公共サービスイノベーション・プラットフォーム] in Japanese, Retrieved 2nd Nov. 2018).
24 Cabinet Office website: http://www5.cao.go.jp/kyumin_yokin/shingi-kai/20180131/shiryou_1.pdf (Basic Plan for the Use of Funding from Dormant Bank Account Grant [*Kyuuminyokintou Koufukin ni Kakawaru Shikin no Katsuyou ni Kansuru Kihonhoushin* 休眠預金等交付金に係る資金の活用に関する基本方針] in Japanese, retrieved 2nd Nov. 2018).
25 Here the definition of SI is explained on page thirty-six as "a new solution to respond to social issues which is more effective, efficient, and sustainable than existing solutions" (translated by the author).
26 For details of SI theories in Europe, North America, and Japan, see Aoo (2018).

Domanski and Kaletka (2017) is an excellent summary of current SI literature written in English.
27 "TEPSIE: Growing Social Innovation" page, The Young Foundation website: https://youngfoundation.org/projects/tepsie/ (Retrieved 2nd Nov. 2018).
28 SI-DRIVE website: https://www.si-drive.eu/ (Retrieved 2nd Nov. 2018).
29 TRANSIT website: http://www.transitsocialinnovation.eu/ (Retrieved 2nd Nov. 2018).
30 CRESSI blog: http://cressi.sbsblogs.co.uk/2017/10/27/the-cressi-project/ (Retrieved 2nd Nov. 2018).
31 ITSSOIN website: http://itssoin.eu/ (Retrieved 2nd Nov. 2018).
32 Such emphasis on social sectors partly reflects the strong tradition of social economy literature in Europe, and the research works on social enterprise done by European scholars in EMES (*l'Emergence De Entreprises Sociales*) group and others, such as Borzaga and Defourny eds. (2001) and Defourny and Nyssens (2013).
33 It is called by different names, including societal transformation and macro-level change.
34 Westley et al. (2017) notes that although their samples were "successful" in terms of having impact on society, the impact was not necessarily a positive one, for instance the intelligence test.
35 Here "scaling" is used to show "when impact grows to match the level of need," rather than the growth of individual projects or social organizations.
36 For example, it sophisticates the six stages of SI (shown as Figure 1.3 above) proposed by Murray et al. (2010) to seven steps – i) exploring opportunities and challenges, ii) generating ideas, iii) developing and testing, iv) making the case, v) delivering and implementing, vi) growing, scaling and spreading, and vii) changing systems
37 Defourny and Nyssens (2013:48-49) warn of the risk of SI initiatives moving toward "isomorphism," a loss of dynamics coming from the pressure raised by legal frameworks or business-oriented practices.
38 They added another category (Statist) to Esping-Andersen's models (Salamon and Anheier 1998:228).
39 Yet Clarence (2014:51-53) notes that not all successful SI initiatives are suitable for scaling, or even necessary to scale, depending on their readiness, resources, receptivity, risks and returns for scaling (such as the possibility of quality of care

services being lost as a result of scaling).

40 A few exceptions are The Hope Institute (2017) and the country reports produced by the "Research on the Social Innovation Eco-system in Asia" project led by Ken Ito, funded by the Toyota Foundation (including Aoo 2019a and 2019b).

41 When this study mentions "civil society," it includes a wide variety of sectors and organizations which are not primarily governmental or for-profit, including non-profits, social enterprises, cooperatives, and other voluntary organizations and associations.

42 Still we need to be aware that literature use these terms in different way, like using "scaling out" for quantitative growth of a SI initiative (Haxeltine et al. 2015:27).

43 One (in)famous example was the 1920 prohibition law, or the Eighteenth Amendment to the U.S. Constitution, which attempted to ban the consumption of alcohol in the U.S.

44 As Pel et al. (2017:3-4) explains, this "quali-quantitative" approach has been intentionally taken to "move beyond anecdotal evidence" and to explain the processes through relational perspectives as a collective achievement, rather than "decomposing it into factors and causes."

45 The "crucial turning points" are what they define as "moments or events in processes at which initiatives undergo or decide a change of course" (Pel et al. 2017:4).

46 These four countries have different levels of economic development, political systems, and typologies of nation-society relationships. Inoguchi (2014:88-96) categorizes Japan and Indonesia as [weak state – strong society] while China and South Korea belong to the [strong state – strong society] category. They were also selected because of the Author's professional experience (as an NGO / UNDP / foundation staff member working mainly in Northeast and Southeast Asia) and familiarity with these countries.

47 I have to admit that one of the major limitations of this study is that documents in national languages (Chinese, Korean, and Bahasa Indonesia) could not be used to conduct the case analyses, and I look forward to receiving any feedback based on informational sources which I did not have access to. However, I am grateful for being able to use and benefit from the literature written by a number of scholars and practitioners, including ones written in Japanese.

48 The definitions and boundaries of these three sectors are indistinct, depend on

social and historical contexts, and are ever-changing – some of the various examples includes: grant-making foundations or financial institutions set up by governmental funding; community or religious organizations under strong control and support from the government; corporations claiming CSR (corporate social responsibility), CSV (creating shared value), or SRI (socially responsible investment) activities within or beyond their business boundaries; and "social economy" institutions which pursue both economic and social purposes (Prewitt 2006:356). In this study, social businesses / social enterprises / cooperatives / nonprofits which conduct business activities but hold social causes as their primary mission are included in civil society (or the "social sector," as it is increasingly being called).

49 Benett (2010:210-211) shows a way to test the strength of causation in process tracing by using the "hoop" test, "straw in the wind" test, "smoking gun" test, and "doubly decisive" test, by measuring whether a hypothesis is necessary / sufficient to establish causation.

50 "Asian values" refers to hierarchical and collective values in Asian societies often connected to Confucianism, and justifies governments' interventionist policies in economic and other areas. It became a strong discourse in the post-Cold War environment in the 1990s when East Asian countries developed as economic powers, and is often used to emphasize the heterogeneity between the Western and Asian societies, both from Asian speakers (like Lee Kuan-Yew) and external observers (Bell 2006; World Bank 1993:83-84, 158-159).

51 By its characteristics, the "alliance" is closer to what is called an "Issue Network," rather than the more official "Policy Network" or "Policy Community" defined by Rhodes (1997:38), but it should be differentiated since an "Issue Network" lacks the momentum to push specific initiatives to a certain outcome.

52 There is another group of management literature that mentions "alliance" as a voluntary relationship between autonomous and independent organizations / firms to achieve objectives, by mainly sharing or creating resources such as joint ventures, purchase partners, research and development partnerships, among others (Robinson and Stuart 2007; Tjemkes and Burgers 2012; Yasuda 2016), but this study does not apply this meaning to alliance.

53 This definition of "alliance" also corresponds to what Westley (2017:247) called "unusual partners," which are partnerships of stakeholders with different values,

ideals, or interests that still drive the initiative.

54 We should also be aware that the meaning for some concepts or variables, for example "democratic" or "bottom-up" processes, can be difficult to measure and even mean quite different things, depending on which context or country we are looking at (George and Bennett 2005:19).

Chapter 2 : Japan

2.1 Country Context

Japan was the first among Asian countries to achieve rapid economic development after WWII. While the post-war political, economic, and social systems were based until the 1980s on the close integration of the ruling Liberal Democratic Party (LDP), central ministries, and industries and businesses, social movements and volunteer activities were marginalized, if not regarded with suspicion by the mainstream. Despite this, problems that arose from Japan's rapid economic growth and societal changes such as environmental pollution, a rapidly aging society, and the changing employment and family structures grew and needed to be addressed, which led to some major SI attempts.

2.1.1 Political System

The modernization and nationalistic expansion of Japan which had been taking place since the late 19th century came to an end with its defeat in WWII in August 1945 (Masumi 2005:1-13).[1] Until 1952, Japan was under the occupation of the General Headquarters of the U.S.-led Allied Forces. Major political and economic reforms took place in this short period to transform the highly centralized political-industrial-military structure of pre-war Imperial Japan. Some of the major changes were i) disarmament, ii) enacting of a democratic and pacifist Constitution, iii) universal suffrage, iv) decentralization and introduction of elected local government heads and representatives, iv) agrarian reform, v) enactment of the Labor Union Act, and vi) dissolution of *zaibatsu* (conglomerates) (Fukunaga 2014:44-45, 65-74, 79-107; Noguchi 2015:71-72).[2]

However, the initial momentum behind democratization and reforms weakened, especially after the outbreak of the Korean War and the intensification of the Cold War. And from 1955, the pro-U.S. Liberal Democratic Party (LDP) held continuous power until 1993. Opposition parties including the Social Democratic Party of Japan (SDP) and the Japanese Communist Party (JCP) held roughly one third of parliamentary seats. Partly because the number of staff in central government ministries is small compared to other developed countries, the LDP politicians, ministerial bureaucrats, and businesses or interest groups formed alliances for individual policy areas, such as agriculture, medical care, construction, or education (Inoguchi and Fujii 2011:153; Muramatsu 1994; Shinoda 2011). As a result, LDP politicians, ministries in charge of specific issues, and interest groups (such as agricultural cooperatives, medical associations, industrial lobbying groups, or neighborhood associations) formed alliances to distribute subsidies and projects to the supporters of the LDP government in a system which lasted until the 1970s (Masumi 2005:25-26; Saito 2010:33-40; Tsujinaka 2012b:273).

Since the 1990s, ruling party coalitions have changed over time, but since 2012, the LDP has come back into power with its minority partner Komeito. Some authors point out that after the electoral reforms of 1994 and the Koizumi administration (2002-2006), the Prime Minister and the Prime Minister's Office (now the Cabinet Office) centralized power in terms of policy development (Estevez-Abe 2008; Rosenbluth and Thies 2010; Uchiyama 2010).

There are two levels of local government in Japan, which are the forty-seven prefectural level governments and the now 1,718 municipalities (cities, towns, villages, and wards).[3] Local governments have the power to set their own bylaws and account for around seventy-five percent of public spending. However, since more than two thirds of the total tax income belongs to the central government, projects are commissioned by the central ministries with subsidies to local governments (Muramatsu et al. 2001).[4] Mainly in urban areas in the 1960s and 1970s, the opposition won local government head elections, and some of the so-called "progressive municipalities" implemented their own welfarist policies such as free medical care in Tokyo in the early 1970s (Estevez-Abe 2008:139; Okada 2016; Tsujinaka 2003).

2.1.2 Socio-Economic Conditions

The post-war Japanese economy showed remarkable growth after the mid-1950s, and the annual rate of real economic growth stayed at around ten percent for nearly twenty years until the early 1970s.[5] This was the result of several factors, including i) a high personal savings rate, ii) the sufficient provision of labor force from rural areas, iii) a favorable international environment for trade and foreign exchange, iv) technological innovation, and v) export-oriented industrialization (Sawai and Tanimoto 2016:368-373; Yashiro 2017:21-32). It slowed after the oil shocks in the 1970s,[6] and after the burst of the so-called "bubble economy" in 1991, economic growth and other performance indicators stayed stagnant or fell (Noguchi 2015:289-295).

During this period of economic growth, the role of the government in social welfare services was rather limited, and public social expenditure as a percent of the GDP was only 3.5 percent in 1960, much lower than other OECD countries.[7] It was supplemented by family and corporations, such as children living together with (or sending money to) elderly parents, provision of care by female members of the family, corporate medical insurance and hospitals, retirement allowance and pensions, and housing (Ochiai 2013:87-90; Sawai and Tanimoto 2016:418-419; Ueno 2011:116-119). In 1961, the national pension and health insurance system was introduced (Kim 2014:245-259), but the benefit level was kept moderate. Even in 1990, public social expenditure amounted to only 11.1 percent of the GDP, which was much lower than other OECD countries including France (24.3 percent), Germany (21.4 percent), or Italy (20.7 percent).[8]

Along with economic growth, the aging of the population advanced rapidly. The proportion of the population over age sixty-five reached seven percent in 1971, but it took only twenty-four years to double to 14 percent, and now 33.9 million, or 26.6 percent of the population of 127 million is over age sixty-five, which makes Japan the most aged country in the world. Together with the movement of the younger generation to urban areas, a number of rural communities are facing the danger of not being able to sustain the community with an isolated and aged population (Masuda 2014).

This trend of rapid aging brought significant changes to public social welfare spending. As Figure 2.1 shows, in 1981 pensions became the top category in terms of social spending by category, and in 2015 it reached JPY 54.9 trillion (approx. USD 500 billion), or 10.3 percent of the GDP. Medical care is JPY 37.7 trillion (approx. USD 350 billion) or 7.1 percent of the GDP. Long-term care, included in welfare, is JPY 9.4 trillion (approx. USD 86 billion) or 1.8 percent of the GDP (National Institute of Population and Social Security Research 2017:10). Even compared to the OECD average, Japan spends 23.1 percent for social expenditure in 2016, which is higher than the OECD average of twenty-one percent, and close to other developed countries.[9] This shows that Japan's public social welfare has grown rapidly within these twenty-plus years, largely as a response to its aging population. However, Japan lacks a stable tax income to cover the expenditure, and it has resulted in serious governmental deficits. The accumulated gross governmental debt now reaches 230 percent of the GDP as of 2015 (Aoo 2017; Estevez-Abe 2008:291; Yashiro 2017:151). Another consequence of rapid aging and the burst of the "bubble economy" is relatively poor employment conditions such as an increase of part-time

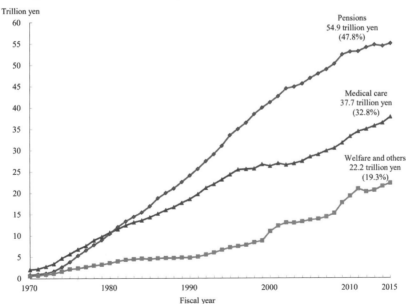

Figure 2.1 Social Benefits in Japan by Category (Fiscal Year 1970-2015)

Source: National Institute of Population and Social Security Research (2017:11)

employees and scarce social welfare services provided by employers for the younger generation compared to their parents and grandparents' generations (Inoguchi and Fujii 2011:153).

2.1.3 Civil Society and Social Movements

Local communities and mutual-help social groups have functioned as a traditional safety net since the pre-modern era (Najita 2009). In modern Japan, the state exerted strong control over social organizations, but an "associational revolution" took place after the 1940s and 1950s, due to the freedom of association set by the post-war Constitution and increasing waves of labor and social movements. In addition to pre-war associations like neighborhood associations and charitable foundations, new types of organizations such as membership associations, labor unions, cooperatives, corporate foundations, religious organizations, medical services corporations, and social welfare corporations developed under different laws (Tsujinaka 2003; Tsujinaka et al. 2010).

Social movements were also strong in the post-war period until the 1970s, but these were regarded with suspicion and marginalized from the government and mainstream businesses (Kawato et al. 2011). However, in the 1990s, volunteer activities received attention after the 1995 the Great Hanshin Earthquake, and it led to the enactment of the 1998 Specific Non-profit Activities Promotion Act (so-called "NPO Law") and creating a legal status for nonprofit organizations [*Tokutei Hieiri Katsudou Houjin* 特定非営利活動法人] , which are called "NPOs" in Japan (Estevez-Abe 2003; Yamaoka 1999).[10] During the time of the non-LDP coalition government led by the Democratic Party of Japan (DPJ) from 2009 to 2012, there was an attempt to utilize NPOs and other civil society organizations to take over more of governmental services under the name of "New Public" (Tanaka 2011:246-262) but was mostly abandoned after the restoration of the LDP government in 2012.

Following a major reform of Public Interest Corporations [*Koueki Houjin* 公益法人] systems in 2008, according to the Japan Association of Charitable Organizations (2013), there were 47,771 NPOs, 47,825 Medical Services Corporations [*Iryou Houjin* 医療法人], 19,498 Social Welfare Corporations [*Shakai Fukushi Houjin* 社会福祉法人], 5,543 Private School Corporations [*Gakkou Houjin* 学校法人], and 19,860 Public Interest Corporations (including Foundations and Associations with officially approved tax-exemption status), among others. However, Pekkanen points out the shortage of professional capacity in Japanese nonprofits, particularly that only a few professional nonprofit organizations are participating in advocacy or policymaking activities (Pekkanen 2006).

2.2 Case Analysis 1: Non-Profit Organization (NPO)[11]

2.2.1 Background

Issues in "Voluntary" Civic Activities

Here we review the history of voluntary non-governmental organizations in modern Japan. In pre-WWII Japan, based on the 1896 Civil Code, each private nonprofit organization (Associations [*Shadan Houjin* 社団法人] or Foundations [*Zaidan Houjin* 財団法人]) needed to have a supervisory government authority and to follow its instructions, including the details of its operational areas and activities. This did not change even after WWII, but with special laws, other legal entities were made possible such as Social Welfare Corporations [*Shakai Fukushi Houjin* 社会福祉法人], Private School Corporations [*Gakkou Houjin* 学校法人], Medical Corporations [*Iryou Houjin* 医療法人], and Religious Corporations [*Shuukyou Houjin* 宗教法人], among others. But after the 1960s, "voluntary activities" in various fields became popular (Nagashima 2016:76; Nihei 2011). This was made possible by the increasing numbers of middle-class citizens including educated women and students, and the leisure time created by economic growth and a modern lifestyle. Volunteers identified issues in local communities such as persons with disabilities, environmental issues, child and elderly care, and people with foreign backgrounds and started to provide social services themselves, going beyond protesting or filing petitions with the government. They pioneered the areas of support for refugees from the former Indochina region, international cooperation and development, environmental protection, and community-based social welfare activities, and in some areas including elderly care, started to become professionalized and receive fees for their service. The number of such groups was estimated to be around fifty to eighty thousand by the 1990s (Ushiro 2009:4; Yamaoka 1999:182).

However, these volunteers were unincorporated organizations without a judicial personality or tax exemption for donations. This caused a variety of problems including the group representative taking unlimited personal liability, no clear governance standards as a corporation, inability to register for international conferences, and a low level of recognition and trust from society. Against this backdrop, some groups from the community development or performing art sectors started researching and visiting the nonprofit sector in the United States and the voluntary sector in the United Kingdom. These members and others have formed networks and organizations including the Japan Networkers' Conference in 1989.[12] In 1994, the Nippon Institute for Research Advancement, a policy think-tank working with civil society leaders, issued a report on civic nonprofit activities (NIRA 1994). Other key organizations were established, including C's: An Association to Create Systems to Support Citizens' Activities in 1994, and the Japan NPO Center in 1996 (Hayase and Matsubara 2004; Tsujimoto et al. 2000:12-15, 34).

In 1993, the LDP lost control of the central government for the first time in almost forty years but soon returned in June 1994 by forming a triparty coalition with its long-time opponent the SDP and New Party Sakigake, a party formed by ex-LDP liberals and some from the SDP, which continued until June 1998. By 1994, all major political parties other than JCP had a research group on NPOs or the nonprofit sector.

On 17th January 1995, Western Japan was struck by the Great Hanshin Earthquake and while the government failed to respond immediately, around 1.4 million citizen volunteers joined the rescue and recovery activities and demonstrated their capability and expertise to the public. As a result, legislation to support volunteer activities suddenly became a major policy agenda (Kojima 2003:77-78).

2.2.2 Processes[13]
Legislation Process of the "NPO Law"
Soon after the Great Hanshin Earthquake, Chief Cabinet Secretary Igarashi made a statement indicating that the government was ready to create a framework to support volunteer activities. In February, the

Inter-ministerial Coordination Meeting on Volunteer Issues led by the Economic Planning Agency was formed.[14] The aim of the Coordination Meeting was to develop a bill as cabinet legislation, which is a normal process in Japan. However, the MPs of the triparty coalition and the opposition New Frontier Party both worked with civil society leaders such as Mr. Akira Matsubara of C's and proposed legislation by MPs. Following the negotiation, cabinet legislation was abandoned and the Triparty NPO Project Team agreed on the outline of the "Citizens' Activities Support Bill" in December (Harada 2017:82). During this period, stakeholders from civil society increased as a result of local forums organized in different parts of Japan. Moreover, the focus of agenda has shifted from supporting volunteer activities to creating legislation to set up a legal status for citizens' activity organizations, based on the discussions between the MPs and civil society leaders (Kojima 2003:89-92).[15]

Later, the LDP proposed an amendment to the outline which was less favorable in terms of the accreditation of "public benefit" status and its limitations on cost recovery, but following the reaction from other two coalition partner parties, pressure from the Keidanren, the most powerful networks in the business sector, and civil society networks including C's, Performing Arts Network, Shimin-Rengo Volunteer Network, as well as the necessity to show a strong result in the election campaign against the newly formed DPJ, the LDP finally made a compromise (Harada 2017:83). The name of the bill was later amended to "Promote Specified Non-profit Activities" due to the opposition of some LDP MPs in the Upper House, but was finally enacted in March 1998, coming into effect the following December.

Features of the NPO Law

The Law to Promote Specified Non-profit Activities,[16] or the so-called "NPO Law," had some distinctive characteristics reflecting the discussion and negotiation that took place during the legislative process.[17] First, the Law created a framework to provide a legal status ("Specified Non-profit Activities Organization" or so-called "NPO Corporation") for nonprofit organizations, but had no provision for tax exemption for NPOs. Second, the nature of "public interest" was defined not as an organization, but as its activities ("specified nonprofit activities") in then twelve different fields that can benefit an unspecified large number of people.[18] Third, it excluded organizations i) whose primary purposes were to disseminate religious teachings and/or promote political doctrine, or ii) who supported or opposed any candidate running for public office, any person holding public office, or any political party. Fourth, NPOs were mandated to apply for certification to prefectural or municipal level governments[19] (or then the Economic Planning Agency, if operating in more than one prefecture). Fifth, local governments were obligated to set their own bylaws for NPO certification, supervision, and information disclosure, instead of using a homogeneous standard created by the central government. Sixth, the processes of reviewing and taking necessary measures to make any adjustments was set in the Law to take place approximately three years after enforcement.

Some of these features, especially the limitation of activities, no setting of tax exemption, and the restrictions on political and religious activities were compromises for civil society.[20] Still, it was an epoch-making achievement that the Law clearly recognized the role of citizens contributing to the good of the public, by the wording of "specified nonprofit activities carried out by citizens as free social contribution activities… contributing to enhancing public interest" in Article One (Purpose) (Kashiwagi 2008:16-17; Kojima 2003:165-166, 179).

Amendment Process for Tax Exemption

As described above, the 1998 NPO Law prioritized creating a legal entity and did not put in place any tax exemption system for NPOs. But it established the reviewing and amendment process from the outset, which was done primarily to discuss tax exemption (Harada 2017:84). Both the Ministry of Finance, who was in charge of the taxation system, and the Economic Planning Agency were passive, but again a coalition of nonpartisan MPs and civil society leaders managed to pass the 2001 Revised Law. It set an "Approved Corporation" status which can enjoy tax benefits. Nevertheless, the benefits were limited in amount and the requirements, including testing for public support, were hard for most NPOs to fulfill (Kojima 2003:209-217). This was further eased by the 2011 Revised Law and the new Tax System for Donation under the DPJ-led coalition government.[21] Again, although the Tax Reform was presented by the Cabinet, the Revised NPO Law was presented by the nonpartisan NPO Parliamentary Group, maintaining the tradition of legislation process by nonpartisan MPs (Harada 2015:6; Kashiwagi 2008:144-152).

Developments after the Establishment of the NPO Law

The NPO Law was enacted concurrently with the 2000 Decentralization Law [*Chihou Bunken Ikkatsu Hou* 地方分権一括法] which greatly increased the scope of work conducted by municipal-level governments, and the Long-term Care Insurance System [*Kaigo Hoken Seido* 介護保

険制度] which began in 2000 (Ozaki 2001; Yamaoka 2001). Following these structural reforms, municipal governments outsourced their operations such as management and maintenance of public facilities and provision of social services to the private sector (Yamauchi 2002:42-44). NPOs provided a part of these outsourced services together with other for-profit businesses and nonprofit organizations (such as Social Welfare Organizations). Local governments also set bylaws and established NPO Support Centers to facilitate the cooperative structure and coordinate policies between the public sector and civic activities (Tsujimoto et al. 2000:18).[22]

The Long-term Elderly Care System in particular became a major income source for many NPOs. As the research conducted by the Economic Planning Agency which investigated 663 organizations registered as NPOs or applying for the status shows, forty-five percent worked primarily on health, medical or social welfare field (EPA 2000). In 2011, another study conducted by the Cabinet Office showed that the proportion of operational fees out of total income was 60.8 percent for all NPOs, but it occupied 74.6 percent for NPOs which had health, medical or social welfare field as their primarily operational field, highlighting these NPOs' dependence on public insurance systems especially of Long-term Care Insurance (Cabinet Office 2011:5).

In 2009, Prime Minister Hatoyama of the DPJ presented the "New Public Commons" as their policy, as "a new value to encourage people who join in the support of their neighbors in local communities and share the responsibility with the public sector, and to help those people as a whole society" (Harada 2015:4; Tanaka 2011:298-311). In January 2010, a New Public Roundtable was established, and in June the Proposals by the

Roundtable and the Government Actions toward Their Institutionalization were announced.[23] The recommendations included reforms for tax deductions for donations to NPOs and approval systems, along with support for social enterprises.[24] The subsequent Kan administration introduced subsidies to create employment in the NPO and social enterprise sectors. Authors such as Tanaka criticize this policy by stating that it could become pork-barrel politics without clear output goals, create an unsustainable income hike for those sectors, and harm its "civic" characteristics (Tanaka 2011:258-261). Still, it is true that recently there is a strong interest in social enterprise, especially among younger generations, which can utilize business approaches to solve social issues.

Moreover, the 2008 Public Benefit Corporation reform amended the 1896 Civil Code and allowed the general public to freely establish associations and foundations. This at least partly created an overlap with NPO status, and the new legal entities of association and foundation were widely used after the 2011 Great East Japan Earthquake and Tsunami for rescue and recovery activities (Japan NPO Research Association 2017:21-24).

Scale and Activities of NPOs

According to the statistics from the Cabinet Office, the number of registered NPOs was over 26,000 in 2008 (Ushiro 2009), and exceeded 51,000 by the end of April 2018 (Figure 2.2).[25]

NPOs have grown into a sector of considerable size. The Japan Institute for Labour Policy and Training (JILPT) estimated that the economic value created by the paid and unpaid staff working for NPOs is equivalent to JPY 892 billion (USD 8 billion). As a single industry, this is higher than the mobile phone industry or nonlife (property) insurance industry (JILPT 2016:30-31). Another study surveyed 2,720 NPOs in 2015 on the year the organization was established (not the year they registered but the year in which they began their activities as a group), as shown in Table 2.1. It shows that 16.7 percent were operating before the establishment of the 1998 NPO Law, but the majority were established in the 2000s, especially in the period between 2000 and 2004.[27]

Figure 2.2 Number of Registered Non-Profit Organizations in Japan

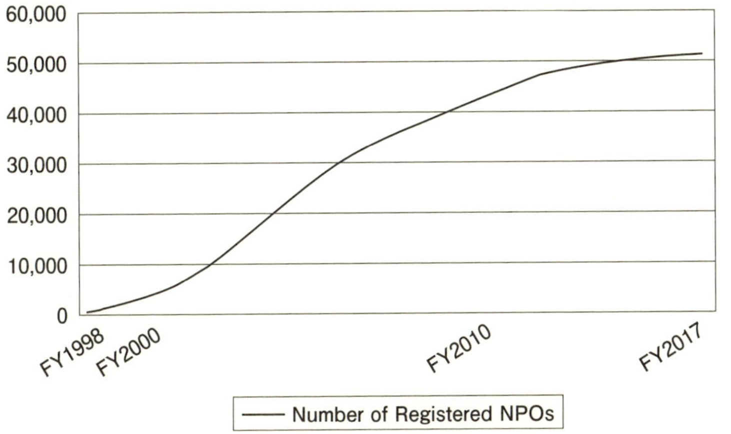

Source: Cabinet Office NPO website[26]

Table 2.1 The Years of Establishment of Non-Profit Organizations in Japan

Year the NPO was Established*	%
Before 1997	16.7%
1998-1999	6.5%
2000-2004	33.1%
2005-2009	20.3%
After 2010	17.2%

* The year NPOs started their activities, not registered year

Source: JILPT (2015:5)

In the same study, NPOs responded about their primary area of activities as shown in Table 2.2. Health, Medical and Social Welfare is the largest group, with 41.5 percent of NPOs responding with it as their primary area. Another question asked about the qualifications held by NPO staff, and the most common responses were (apart from driver's license) Certified Care Worker or Home Helper for the elderly care, which indicates that a number of NPOs are focusing on the provision of elderly care and other kinds of social welfare services (JILPT 2015:42). Still, according to a 2016 survey conducted by the Ministry of Health, Labour and Welfare, NPOs make up only five to six percent of home-based elderly care service providers or less than two percent of institutional care service providers, which is far less than other legal entities including Social Welfare Organizations, Medical Corporations, and for-profit companies (MoHLW 2016).

Table 2.2 Primary Activity Areas of Non-Profit Organizations in Japan

Primary Area of Activities	%
Health, Medical and Welfare	41.5%
Science, Culture, Arts and Sports	9.1%
Children	8.4%
Environmental Protection	7.5%
Community Development	6.9%

Source: JILPT (2015:6)

The annual income of NPOs in Fiscal Year 2013 is shown in Table 2.3. 35.5 percent (or 40.9 percent of respondents) reported that income was below JPY five million (USD 45,000), but the largest group had an income from JPY ten to thirty million (USD 90,000 to 270,000) with 17.6 percent (or 20.2 percent of respondents). 7.4 percent (or 8.4 percent of respondents) answered that they have an annual income of over JPY one hundred million (USD 900,000). Compared with the 2004 JILPT survey, NPOs reported larger incomes (JILPT 2015:5-11).[28]

Table 2.3 Annual Income of Non-Profit Organizations in Japan (Fiscal Year 2013)

Annual Income in FY2013	%
0	5.6%
0-1 million yen	14.0%
1-5 million yen	15.9%
5-10 million yen	9.4%
10-30 million yen	17.6%
30-50 million yen	8.6%
50-100 million yen	8.7%
Over 100 million yen	7.4%
No answer	12.9%

Source: JILPT (2015a:6)

According to the Cabinet Office study conducted in 2017, the average income of an NPO is JPY 32.3 million (USD 290,000) but the median is JPY 9.9 million (USD 90,000) which shows that a small number of the bigger organizations are pushing up the average while many stay small in terms of financial income (Cabinet Office 2018:24). The same survey showed that NPOs are relying on operational fees, by showing that 77.0 percent of total income comes from operational incomes, followed by 10.9 percent from grants and subsidies, 8.0 percent from donations, and 2.8 percent from membership fees (Figure 2.3). Many NPOs fail to obtain donations or membership fees from the public, and the median membership fee is JPY 63,000 (USD 570). Meanwhile, 37.1 percent of NPOs with Approved Corporation status (tax exemption benefit for donations) and 53.5 percent of non-approved NPOs have no income from donations (Cabinet Office 2018:21, 27-28). This corresponds with Tanaka (2008:28), who claims that the majority of NPOs do not raise money through donations.

Figure 2.3 Income Breakdown for Japanese Non-Profit Organizations

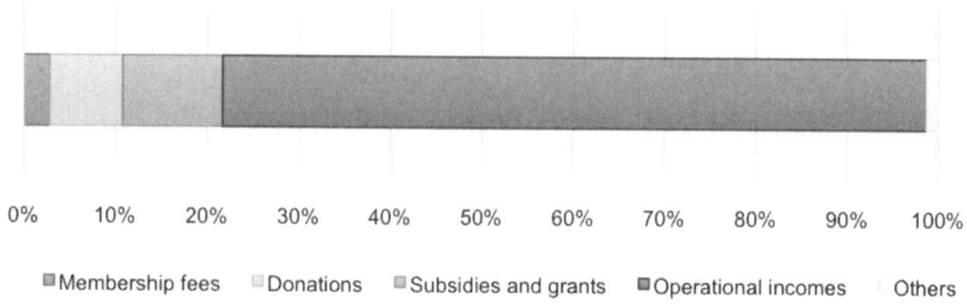

■Membership fees   ▫Donations   ■Subsidies and grants   ■Operational incomes   Others

Source: Cabinet Office (2018:27)

By comparing JILPT (2004) and JILPT (2015), we can see that the number of staff working for NPOs are increasing, both paid and unpaid. The percentage of paid staff in the organization (from 17.3 percent to 20.3 percent) and average number of paid staff (from 4.45 to 9.13) both increased during this period (JILPT 2015:10-11). However, the paid staff in NPOs usually receive a lower salary compared to other industries. JILPT (2015:8) indicates that the typical annual income of paid NPO staff is JPY two to three million (USD 18,000 to 27,000). The next group is from JPY one to two million (USD 9,000 to 18,000).[29] JILPT (2015:10) shows that the typical number of paid full-time staff for an NPO is between one and four (57.7 percent) and the average is 3.09, but the median is zero. Also, 48.1 percent of NPOs have between one and four part-time staff members, with an average of 6.04 and a median of one (Table 2.4). These figures show a picture that apart from a few large-scale organizations, NPOs operate by heavily relying on the work done by volunteers and unpaid board members.

Table 2.4 Japanese Non-Profit Organization Headcounts by Type of Employment / Participation

Types	Average (persons)	Median (persons)	Standard Deviation
Board Members	8.70	7	6.1
Paid Board Members	0.77	0	1.6
Full-time Staff	3.09	0	6.4
Part-time Staff	6.04	1	17.6
Paid Volunteers	4.42	0	29.8
Unpaid Volunteers (Secretariat)	0.85	0	2.1
Unpaid Volunteers (Others)	21.09	0	176.5
Interns	0.59	0	6.0

Source: JILPT (2015:10)

Change of Values through the Establishment of the NPO Law

One of the significant changes caused by the establishment of the NPO Law was the change in how Japanese society views the civic nonprofit activities. During the Cold War period, the word "citizens' movement" had an anti-governmental or anti-establishment image, partly because of their involvement in anti-war movements and protests against environmental pollution, and was generally avoided by the government and business sectors. It was first used with a positive meaning with slightly different wording in 1972, when the Tokyo Metropolitan government under Governor Ryokichi Minobe set up the "Citizen Activity Service Corner" [*Shimin Katsudou Saabisu Koonaa* 市民活動サービスコーナー] (Nagashima 2016:76; Nakamura 2000:32). Yamaoka, then a program officer at the Toyota Foundation, started a "Documentation of Citizen Activities" sub-program in 1984 as a part of the Foundation's Research

Grant Program, and it became an independent program called the "Grant Program for Citizen Activities" in 1986. Still, the word was not in common use (Toyota Foundation 2007:154-155).[30]

Also, the NPO Law was initially called the "Law to Promote Citizens' Activity" but after a debate with conservative LDP members in the Upper House, the name was changed to the "Law to Promote Specific Non-profit Activity." Those LDP members took issue both with the use of the term "citizen" and also with who would define "public benefit." The NPO Law finally accepting the citizen's initiative to define "public benefit" from their side was a major turning point, as this had traditionally been dominated by the government. Atsuko Doumoto, who was an MP in the Upper House from Sakigake during the legislation process, said that "The NPO Law had characteristics that changed the fundamental structure of Japanese society. The shift from a government-led system to an egalitarian democracy of citizens, or something of that kind. The conservative MPs at that time sensed this and were opposed to it."[31]

What civil society leaders like Yamaoka and Matsubara were feeling through the legislation process of the NPO Law was a "change of the times," and the "sense that the citizen and civil society are starting to come to the forefront in Japan." The processes of legislation, information disclosure and media coverage, and fora in different parts of Japan brought about a change of social cognition to see NPOs – who are not subject to any authority – as something positive, or "good" (Yamaoka 1999:82, 189-191). Furthermore, Yamaoka in his 2017 interview, states:

"The establishment of the NPO Law was a complete social innovation. People who felt the limitations of the one-hundred-year old

Public Benefit Corporation system started to simultaneously raise questions from different perspectives, conduct research, design and propose concrete policies, exchange views throughout Japan, and make numerous amendments to the Bill in the Diet through serious discussions, leading to a unique legislative process. Finally, it created a major hole in the Public Benefit Corporation system. It's not only about the process of the legislation. When we take the time to tackle an issue which lies at the foundation of society, even by going this way and that, it may create true social innovation."[32]

What Yamaoka had as his vision was replacing the uniform social services provided by the central government to allow more initiatives by local communities. Each community was supposed to think and create in their own way, through equal collaboration and shared responsibilities between citizens and local government (Yamaoka 1999:127-132; Yamaoka 2001:29).[33] He also found value in the NPO's nature as a "movement" and questions the argument which only focuses on the "business" or "management" of NPOs (Yamaoka 1999:149-151). Matsubara echoes Yamaoka by saying in his 2017 interview that society changed its perspective on NPOs from seeing them as "something done by left-leaning and heretical people" to a more positive view, and it led to local governments and businesses / foundations beginning to support NPOs, as well as bringing new people into the sector. He also emphasizes that the process brought "citizens" into public benefit activities for the first time, not allowing the governmental sector to dominate it.[34]

Conflict with the Needs of the Government Sector

At the same time, Matsubara points out that the two trends – first the citizens' activities to have the people's needs reflected in government policy and to become a route for civic participation, and second the governmental need to supplement its operations by utilizing NPOs - came into conflict.[35]

When we examine the literature on NPOs published in Japan during the 1990s, there are books showing the vision of nonprofit and voluntary sectors and organizations actively working in society, such as the translation of Peter Drucker's *Managing the Nonprofit Organization* (Drucker 1991; Hayashi and Imata 1999; Yamauchi 1997). However, in the 2000s after the enactment of the NPO Law there were more works focusing on more pragmatic NPO management and operations (Kashiwagi 2004; Sakamoto 2004; Tao 2004) or partnerships between NPOs and governments or businesses (Matsushita 2002; Ueyama 2002; Ushiro 2009; Yamaoka et al. 2001). This seems to show the role of NPOs being established in society, but also reflects a fading of the idealism which was prominent during the 1990s. Tanaka (2008) was one of the authors who warned of the risk of NPOs depending on governmental funding, but the economic stagnation after the collapse of the bubble economy in the 1990s brought about the shrinking of private nonprofit sectors between the end of the 1990s to the 2000s (Tsujinaka 2012a:13-14). Also the corporate foundations which eventually started to support NPO projects stagnated after the burst of the bubble economy in the 1990s.[36] This brought greater difficulty for NPOs in diversifying their sources of funding.

And in the 2010s after the Great East Japan Earthquake and Tsunami, the dependency of NPOs on the public sector become even stronger. Doumoto voiced her concerns that the citizens are losing their independent mindset and relying instead on the government.[37] The detachment between NPOs and the general public can be seen in a public opinion survey conducted by the Cabinet Office in 2016. As Figure 2.4 shows, while 37.6 percent say that they are either "very much interested (5.4 percent)" or "somewhat interested (32.2 percent)" in NPOs, the majority of 62.4 percent responded that they are either "not interested at all (15.4 percent)" or "not interested that much" in NPOs (Cabinet Office 2016:22).[38]

Figure 2.4 Level of Public Interest in Nonprofit Organizations in Japan

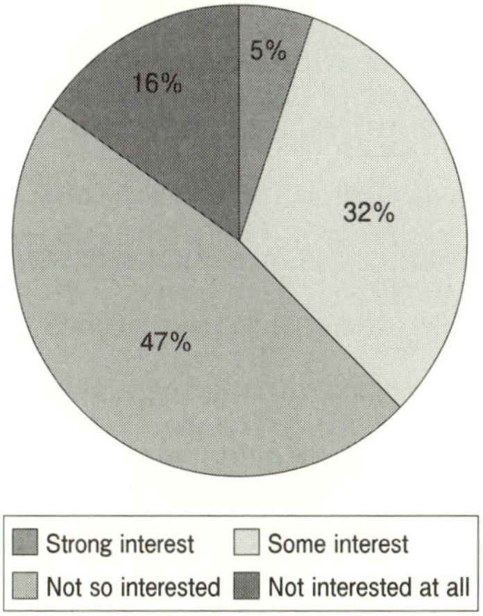

Source: Cabinet Office (2016a:22)

2.2.3 Analysis

The NPO scheme, which started as a central legislation, may seem to be a mere top-down process. It is also true that the "window of policy" opened by the 1995 Great Hanshin Earthquake had a significant impact on the process (Kojima 2003:231). However, we need to pay attention to the contributions of the civil society sector who made continuous efforts before the disaster and made the best of their opportunity after the Great

Hanshin Earthquake. Yamaoka recalls the process and says, "we were saying that the legislation would be enacted in the twenty-first century until we had the 1995 Great Hanshin Earthquake. But the disaster made the legislation possible without having discussion about civil society and the civic sector. We need to review that part from now on."[39] Because of their attempts to conduct research on overseas countries and to create networks that included different regions in Japan, they were able to prepare draft bills and provide input to the MPs in a short period of time, which led to the legislation by MPs instead of the Cabinet legislation as initially proposed. Also, these endeavors created a common understanding and vision (applied from overseas experience and knowledge, especially from the U.S. and the U.K.) among leaders in the civil society sector such as Matsubara or Yamaoka, and though they had differences in the details, the shared vision enabled the collaboration (Harada 2017:86).

The political environment during the legislation process – the LDP holding its claims first out of consideration to the other two coalition partners, and later out of necessity to compete with their main opponent, the newly established DPJ, and having supporting MPs in all major political parties including the LDP, SDP, Sakigake, DPJ, New Frontier Party, and the JCP, made it possible to unanimously pass the Bill in the Lower House.[40] Some conservative groups and business sectors also supported NPOs as a part of public administration reform / downsizing of governmental sectors. In such an environment, Matsubara, who played the role of the main lobbyist from civil society on the central level, switched his tactics from "making requests to politicians" to connecting various stakeholders through common interests. For example, he persuaded ministries that were in charge of international development, elderly care, and disaster

Chapter 2: Japan   83

prevention as well as MPs, political organizations, and religious organizations that NPOs may be useful in some way for their various agendas and operations.[41] This process and the "alliances" between different groups at the central level created a new model for MPs and civil society members to co-create a legislative process, which became a tradition in the NPO Law amendment process. The process also changed the mindset of society and enabled the change to the long-lasting Public Benefit Organization system which had continued since the nineteenth century.[42]

Next, the "alliances" were developed at local levels, mostly between local governments and NPOs. During the 1990s through the 2000s, both the decentralization process and the pressure to streamline the governmental system created more work for local governments, as well as outsourcing of operations to NPOs. As a consequence, NPOs have grown into a considerable sector in social service provision, especially in their partnerships with governmental sectors at local levels, as the processes in Table 2.5 show. But at the same time, NPOs became more dependent on

Table 2.5 Scaling Patterns and Paths for Non-Profit Organizations, Japan

	Stage 1: Ideation	Stage 2: Incubation	Stage 3: Acceleration	Stage 4: Institutionalization
			Central Alliance	
Government	※ (Suspicion from gov. and business)		○ (Bipartisan MPs)	▢ Local alliances (local govs. outsourced to NPOs)
Business	※	1995 Hanshin Earthquake moved the process	○ (Keidanren's support)	
Civil Society	○ ⌬ (Ideas brought from US/UK)		○ (Civil society as a key stakeholder in legislation process) → ▢ (NPO Law)	○ (local NPOs)

○ minor / ◯: major involvement from each sector
※: conflict with the initiative / ▢: multi-sectoral alliance
⌬: new ideation / ▢: legislation (central/ local levels)

governmental funding and operational income provided by the Long-term Elderly Care Insurance or other outsourcing of governmental services, such as the Designated Manager System for public facilities. On the other hand, most NPOs failed to raise funding from donations or membership fees, which indicates a weak linkage with the general public.

2.3 Case Analysis 2: Environmental Pollution
2.3.1 Background

In this section we examine the experience of environmental pollution, which is called *kogai* [公害], which literally means "public harm". Environmental pollution issues in Japan can be dated back to cases caused by the mining industry in the late 19th century, or even before modernization (Inoue 2006:9-11). By the 1950s, as post-war recovery and industrial development accelerated, there were already a number of health hazard phenomena reported in areas including Minamata, Yokkaichi, and the Jintsu river areas. Still they did not attract attention nationally, but were considered instead to be local problems for "farmers and fishers" who were in a marginal position in greater Japanese society (Fujikawa 2017:20; Tsuru 1999:59-60). Laws and regulations were either absent or lacked scientific standards and penalties by which to effectively stop the pollution, and local governments were largely supportive of industries (Iijima 2000:160).[43]

2.3.2 Processes

Initially, protests from local residents stayed small and local, and were not successful against powerful enterprises. Corporates, connected with governments and academics, denied that they were the ones causing the damage. For instance, in Minamata, the mechanisms behind how organic mercury was produced and how it caused damage to humans were not scientifically proven at that time, and although a group from the local Kumamoto University suggested that the "disease" was caused by organic mercury in 1959, authoritative scientists gave "scientific" evidence that what people in Minamata were suffering from was not caused by mercury (Miyogawa 2002:273-275).

The turning point was a public protest in three municipalities in Shizuoka prefecture in central Japan opposing the construction of a petrochemical complex by major companies. The movement had the cooperation of local school teachers and health professionals like pharmacists, and they conducted their own scientific investigations, study tours to other sites, and public education programs. It led to major public protests, and finally to statements of opposition being delivered by heads and representatives of three municipalities in 1964, and as a result, the businesses were forced to abandon the project. This became a role model for other areas suffering from pollution (Iijima 2000:152-154; Ui 2014:303).

Also, after the 1960s, some local governmental heads[44] such as Mayor Ichio Asukata of Yokohama city (1963-1978), Governor Ryokichi Minobe of the Tokyo metropolitan government (1967-1979), and Governor Ryoichi Kuroda of Osaka prefecture (1971-1979), were supportive of environmental protection and set stricter environmental regulations and policies such as the 1969 Tokyo Metropolitan Bylaw on Environmental Disruption Prevention, with detailed regulations and enforcement measures against violations (Miyamoto 2014a:198-201). Moreover, they concluded local-level agreements on pollution standards with corporates operating in their own areas. In 1964, after receiving complaints from local residents, Yokohama city, under the strong leadership of Mayor Asukata, made the first pollution prevention agreement with a local coal power plant, and this so-called "Yokohama model" spread to other areas. The number of industrial operators having an agreement with a local government grew from fourteen in 1965 to 854 in 1970, and 8,923 in 1975 (Ito 2016:22-23, 45-47; Okada 2016). These efforts provided a prototype for the central government to design regulations, and a government commission (the so-called *Kogai* Commission) gave a report in 1966 placing responsibility upon the parties causing environmental damage (Tsuru 1999:62).

And after the late 1960s, local residents and victims filed suits with the court to recover damages and were eventually compensated. Through these lawsuits and court decisions, the new idea of "environmental rights" was developed and became entrenched as a social value (Miyamoto 2014a:210-211). Environmental protection soon became a popular area for both civic volunteering and corporate CSR activities. As a result, there were over 15,000 environmental Japanese NGOs working on environmental protection in 2007 (OECD 2010:72).

Following these social pressures, legislation and institutional frameworks at the national level were finally developed. The Basic Law for Environmental Pollution Control was passed by parliament in 1967, and in the 1970 parliament 14 related laws were set or revised. In 1971, the Environment Agency was established as a central government agency. After the 1970s (especially after the post-1973 oil shocks), businesses followed the regulations and invested in pollution reduction (JICA 2004).[45] As an OECD report acknowledges, pollution in Japan is now among the lowest in OECD countries (OECD 2010:26).

2.3.3 Analysis

The case of environmental pollution was a major success as an SI initiative which managed to largely solve the major harms and problems caused by it.[46] It also managed to change people's mindsets and behaviors in a fairly short period of roughly twenty years and is now deeply embedded within the values of Japanese people (Miyamoto 2014a; Tomozawa 2014). Table 2.6 shows a summary of the process mainly in the 1960s and 1970s.

Table 2.6 Scaling Patterns and Paths for Environmental Pollution, Japan

	Stage 1: Ideation	Stage 2: Incubation	Stage 3: Acceleration	Stage 4: Institutionalization
Government	※		Local alliances (local gov. setting own regulations)	Central / local alliances (central gov.) (legislation)
Business	※ (Business not accepting responsibility)	※	/ ※ (Some businesses start cooperating)	(following regulations)
Civil Society	O (opposition by local residents staying marginal)	O (scaling after 1963-64 Shizuoka protests)	(academics and lawyers developing the idea of environmental rights)	(embedded as a social value in society)

O. minor / O : major involvement from each sector
※ : conflict with the initiative / ▢ : multi-sectoral alliance
☁ : new ideation / ▢ : legislation (central/ local levels)

Contribution from Different Sectors

We can see that this is a bottom-up process initiated by civil society / social movement which then expanded to local governments and finally to the central government and businesses. It first began as small, localized protests without much connection with other groups, but the 1963-64 Shizuoka movement became the watershed event for scaling, and grassroots movements formed by local residents and scientists, teachers, lawyers, and journalists in other areas created overwhelming pressure on governments and businesses to gradually change their behavior (Fujikawa 2017:22; Iijima 2000:161; JICA 2004; Ui 2014:213). Local governments also played an important role by setting additional regulations and pollution standards in their territories before national laws and regulations, and by enforcing them through compliance inspections. They also conducted negotiations with local businesses for stricter standards (Okada 2016), and led to the formation of local-level "alliances." Moreover, the lawsuits filed by local residents and supported by lawyers and academics led to court decisions in favor of local populations, such as the 1972 Yokkaichi Judgement. This pushed corporations to withdraw from appealing to higher courts and to instead accept their responsibilities (Ito 2016:20, 111-112; Miyamoto 2014b:13).

Corporations were reluctant at first to accept responsibility for the damages they had incurred or to reduce their pollution-creating activities. But when faced with strong social pressure, they began to assume responsibility for reducing environmental pollution.[47] Still, it was a time when Japanese companies were swiftly growing, so pollution/environment-related investment was a marginal cost and not a significant burden upon them. Corporates also enjoyed generous credit assurance schema to invest in pollution reduction measures. As they applied or developed state-of-the-art technologies, this actually supported the emergence of a new industry to produce anti-pollution equipment, such as stack gas desulfurization facilities or the utilization of liquefied natural gas (LNG).[48] The investment also worked as a cost-effective upgrade to overcome global competition (Ito 2016:9-10; JICA 2004).

Therefore, as a whole process we can say that having such bottom-up initiatives helped to develop local-level "alliances" between various stakeholders (local governments, businesses, and civil society including intellectuals) who had different values and interests but still were able to agree on change, and brought a width and depth of partnerships in the process.

The Development of Values

In terms of ideas and values, the role of lawyers and researchers who discovered and developed the positive values of "the environment" and "environmental rights" was crucial. Initially *kogai* was considered a local and "minor" event which only affected poor farmers or fishers, who were marginalized groups in a modern industrial society (Iijima 2000:147-149). Researchers like Dr. Shigeto Tsuru, who was an economist and worked as the chair of the Environmental Disruption Research Group, visited pollution sites including Yokkaichi, Chiba, Kurashiki, Shizuoka, and Yokohama and engaged with local residents, governments, and businesses. They also worked with the international academic community (International Social Science Council) to hold the 1970 International Symposium on Environmental Disruption in Tokyo, which made a declaration of "environmental rights" prior to the 1972 Stockholm Conference on Human Environment (Miyamoto 2014b:4-11; Tsuru 2001:334, 344). The concept of environmental rights was further developed by lawyers who supported lawsuits including the Osaka Airport Trial (Miyamoto 2014a:210-211, 342). Through these efforts, protecting the environment became a widely accepted positive value within the society (Tomozawa 2014:24).

2.4 Case Analysis 3: Community-Based Integrated Care
2.4.1 Background

This section provides another case analysis, examining community-based integrated care (CBIC), [*Chiiki Houkatsu Ke-a* 地域包括ケア] which is basically an elderly care provision system based on the collaboration of various professionals, service providers, and people in local communities. The CBIC was introduced to increase the efficiency and sustainability of the long-term care insurance (LTCI) scheme to provide long-term care[49] for older people. As mentioned above, Japan is the most aged country in the world, and in 2015 there were nearly thirty-four million people, or 26.7 percent of its population, aged over sixty-five (Cabinet Office 2016b:2). As the number of older people who need long-term care increases, it became more and more difficult for family members alone to provide such care, which requires hard work and attention around the clock. These types of "elderly-people problems" began receiving attention in the 1970s and 1980s, when the number of bedridden elderly reached 600,000 in 1984 and so-called "social hospitalization," which means older people occupying hospitals as a practical nursing home, became a social phenomenon (Campbell 2000:84; Yuuki 2011:55-57).

After local governments began directly providing elderly care services in the 1990s (Kawamura 2014:38), the LTCI[50] started in 2000 to provide in-kind care services for older people[51] by creating a public insurance scheme and quasi-market system by which the service users can select from different service providers (Sawada and Sumii 2014:11-13). In 2013, the number of older people who are qualified as eligible to receive services are 5.7 million, and approximately 4.9 million of them used the services[52] (Cabinet Office 2016b:24-25). However, the scheme soon faced the issues of a limited number of facilities and caregivers, especially for institutional care, and increasing financial resources spent on the system without having a taxation basis to cover the cost[53] (Estevez-Abe 2008:291; Takahashi 2012:9).

2.4.2 Processes

In 2003, the Elderly Care Study Group, an unofficial group held under the auspices of the Ministry of Health, Labour and Welfare (MoHLW), proposed the concept of CBIC, drawing ideas from the existing local practices of cross-sectoral care, including precedents in Onomichi City[54] and Wako City. According to the report published by the Study Group, they aimed to ensure the sustainability of the LTCI system by switching focus from

Figure 2.5 Model of the Community-based Integrated Care System

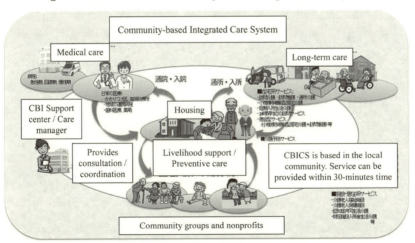

Source: Ministry of Health, Labour and Welfare website (translated by the author)

institutional care to "aging in place" supported by the CBIC. As in the model shown in Figure 2.5, the CBIC system was planned to be established in each local community, and to provide twenty-four-hour services through collaboration between different sectors and service providers such as housing, medical professionals, long-term care, rehabilitation, and local volunteers, among others (Elderly Care Study Group 2003).

Soon after the 2003 report, relevant laws (2005 Revised Elderly Care Insurance Act and 2006 Medical Care System Reform Act) were revised and CBIC was incorporated as a part of the LTCI system. Each local municipality was tasked with developing and managing their own CBIC system. And as of 2012, more than 7,000 Community-based Integrated Support Centers (including branches and sub-centers, financed by an LTCI scheme) are in operation,[55] responsible for coordinating with various stakeholders and resources such as medical and care professionals, social welfare offices, nonprofits, and volunteers in the community (Sawada 2014:198). There are also reported cases of "good practices" on local levels, typically mobilizing and collaborating different stakeholders for information-sharing and service provision.

For instance, there are cases of a local Social Welfare Council leading the facilitation of local residents in Takayama City and Tsuruta City (Ooi 2010) and a Medical Cooperative operating different types of care facilities in Nagoya (Hashimoto 2010). Another case which is often mentioned as a model for CBIC is Wako City, where an active government official (Mr. Tonai) worked to conduct a needs survey and organize service providers and experts within care plan meetings (Numao 2014:137-138).

Recently there was a case in which Fukuoka City subcontracted Hitachi Ltd. to develop a CBIC Information Platform to compile different medical and long-term care data and share it among beneficiaries and their families, medical and care professionals, as well as utilizing it for policy development (Fukuoka City 2017).[56] This seems to be a promising approach both to utilize the enormous amount of available data and to ease the difficulty for various stakeholders to share information and coordinate.[57]

Still, in most local municipalities and communities, the creation and management of the CBIC system is mostly done through face-to-face consultation between stakeholders, and there is a strong reluctance to actively take on such a responsibility, mainly due to the shortage of active coordinators who can organize collaboration between different sectors and institutions (Asakawa 2017; Miyamoto 2014c:36; Yuuki 2011). Local governments are suffering from a decreasing number of staff and lack of expertise, caused partly by continuing administrative reforms, and are not able to cover these complex tasks (Numao 2014:131-135). Community-based Integrated Support Centers, which frequently have to cover from five to ten thousand service users per Center (some over thirty thousand) frequently with fewer than ten staff per center, are not able to play this role either (Hirose 2014:227-228; Mitsubishi UFJ Research and Consulting 2010:24; Shirasawa 2011:241-242).[58] According to a 2013 survey conducted with 4,484 Centers, they responded that the creation of regional collaboration networks is the biggest challenge they face due to the limited capacity of staff, and nearly half of them (49.5 percent) did not conduct a community care meeting to build networks during the year (Hirose 2014:232-233). Also, in most areas, CBIC lacks the expected understanding, support and participation of stakeholders including politicians, medical experts, care service providers, and local volunteers (Maezawa 2011:72; Miyamoto 2014c; Takahashi 2012).[59]

The MoHLW recently has further expanded the concept of CBIC from elderly care to cross-sectoral care, by the new name of "Community Symbiotic Society" [*Chiiki Kyosei Shakai* 地域共生社会]. This concept is planned to mobilize local resources to meet the needs of not only older people but also other groups with needs, such as children and people with physical or mental disabilities, among others (MoHLW 2017). This is expected to solve the limitations of CBIC as operated within the framework of the LTCI scheme, which was by definition limited to supporting older people, but the results are still unclear.

2.4.3 Analysis

Considering these processes and issues, it is hard to say that CBIC is fully functioning as planned and helping to coordinate local practitioners as well as mobilizing local resources. Also, it has not yet been embedded within social value and norms within the society. Thus, at least for the present, it has to be described as "failed," or having only "partial" success

Table 2.7 Scaling Patterns and Paths for Community-based Integrated Care, Japan

	Stage 1: Ideation	Stage 2: Incubation	Stage 3: Acceleration	Stage 4: Institutionalization
Government		O (local gov.) →	O (MoHWL) → ☐ (Legislation)	O (local govs.) (Lack of local alliances)
Business				(The value of CBIC not embedded)
Civil Society	O ————→	O (local practices)		

O minor / ◯ : major involvement from each sector

※ : conflict with the initiative / ☐ : multi-sectoral alliance

💭 : new ideation / ☐ : legislation (central/ local levels)

as an SI initiative. Table 2.7 summarizes the above processes.

It is notable that CBIC was a heavily top-down process, initiated by a central government ministry (MoHLW). The change of the policy formation process in the 2000s and the concentration of power in the central ministries made this possible (Uchiyama 2010:8). Although the idea and model were taken from the best practices of local practitioners and local governments including Onomichi and Wako, it was not a well-developed or wide-spread social initiative before it became a central government policy.

The somewhat idealistic concept of CBIC lacks the broad support of the local governments who were entrusted to form and manage the system, or the existing businesses and service providers who benefitted from LTCI funding (including subcontracting for Community-based Integrated Support Centers) but did not find interest in "collaborating" with other stakeholders as expected in the CBIC. The systematic methods or technologies were underdeveloped. Also, most people who were quickly growing accustomed to the LTCI system and being "beneficiaries" of that system could not be motivated to participate and contribute to the system as volunteers or supporters of their neighbors. They felt CBIC was an excuse to reduce the service level of the LTCI systems (Numao 2014:122). In conclusion, it remained a government-led concept and policy, and could not find a wide range of support to develop and scale the initiative.

2.5 Summary

By comparing the three cases of NPOs, environmental pollution, and community-based integrated care, we can observe two factors that affect the successful scaling processes.

First, "alliances" of different sectors and stakeholders seem to be the crucial mechanism for both scaling and the initiative becoming embedded in the society. The environmental pollution process started as protests by local populations, but later different models of success were created at the local levels (such as Shizuoka or Yokohama) before coming to the central level, each with a strong "alliance" between a wide range of stakeholders, including local governments, businesses, and civil society. The proliferating "bottom-up" processes help to create such alliances in different places, thus contributing to the scaling of the SI initiative. NPOs, meanwhile, started as central legislation (and an "alliance" at that level) but later developed local partnerships mainly between local governments. On the contrary, in the case of CBIC, although there were different cases of best practice, it was not a wide-spread movement and the initiative came largely as a top-down concept and policy from a central ministry. It also lacked partners who found interest in and responded to the given opportunity. Such a "hollow" top-down policy is not working as expected or rooted in society.

Second, it seems to be that a strong social concern and/or a creation of new values and ideas which have positive meaning in the society propels the advancement of a process. In the case of environmental pollution, the social movement stayed relatively small and local until the 1970s, when urban residents began to feel that it was their own problem. Businesses reacted positively to the change, mostly because they felt pressure from society and the court decisions holding them responsible for the pollution. The new concepts and values created by academics and lawyers such as environmental rights or environmental protection changed people's mindsets and became a driver for continuing the activities in different sectors. Also the legal entity for NPOs was created utilizing the "policy window" opened by the Great Hanshin Earthquake, and later, with all their shortcomings, became a positive and a matter of course in society and hold a stable position mainly as a social service provider. In the case of CBIC, it is still not embedded as a strong social value which can motivate people to participate or contribute by taking action. Ideas can be imported from other countries, as in the case of nonprofit sectors in the U.S. and the U.K., or created / invented out of local knowledge and experience, as in the case of Dr. Tsuru and the other lawyers and journalists who developed the concept of environmental rights from interviewing local people.

1   As a result of the surrender, Japan lost its overseas territories and colonies, including Taiwan, the Korean Peninsula, Mainland China, and the South Pacific Mandate. The Okinawan islands were under U.S. occupation until 1972.

2   Still, due to the continuity of politicians and bureaucrats and the shift of U.S. policy to using Japan as part of the Western camp in the Cold War situation, there was continuity between pre- and post-war Japanese economic policies, industrial structure, and the members of the ruling groups (Noguchi 2015:7-14; Yui 2016:267-268).

3   "Cross-boundary Administration [*Kouiki Gyousei* 広域行政] page, Ministry of Internal Affairs and Communication website: http://www.soumu.go.jp/kouiki/kouiki.html (In Japanese, retrieved 2nd Nov. 2018).

4   According to the 2006 AsiaBarometer survey, Japanese people show relatively higher trust in local governments, with 53.7 percent saying they trust local governments "very much" or "to some extent," compared to 42.0 percent saying the same for the central government (Inoguchi and Fujii 2011:156).

5   8.8 percent (1955-60), 9.2 percent (1960-65), and 11.1 percent (1965-70) (Sawai and Tanimoto 2016:369).

6   The annual real GDP growth rate fell to 5.7 percent in 1976-78, and 4.0 percent in 1981-91 (Yashiro 2017:36).

7   For example, expenditure rates in other countries were 9.7% in the United Kingdom,

12.0% in France, 15.4% in Germany, and 10.7% in Italy. OECD Social Expenditure Update, OECD Social Expenditure Database website: http://www.oecd.org/els/soc/OECD2016-Social-Expenditure-Update-Figures-Data.xlsx (Retrieved 2nd Nov. 2018).

8 Source: same as above.

9 OECD Social Expenditure Database website. France 31.5 percent, Germany 25.3 percent, Italy 28.9 percent.

10 In 2008 the Civil Code was revised, and new laws were created to greatly ease the regulations on establishing associations and foundations.

11 In this section the abbreviation "NPO" is used to describe nonprofit organizations registered as a legal entity based on the 1998 Law to Promote Specified Nonprofit Activities Law, or so-called "NPO Law", which is also a term widely used in Japan for nonprofit organizations. Please note that when this article mentions "NPO", it does not include other nonprofit organization entities, such as foundations, associations, cooperatives, or social welfare organizations. But when it says "nonprofit organizations" it includes all of these private nonprofit organizations regardless of their registered legal entity.

12 Japan Networkers' Conference held a Networkers' Forum in October 1992, and discussed for the first time as a public meeting about the need to have a new legal entity for nonprofit organizations (e-mail from Yoshinori Yamaoka, dated 1st Oct. 2018).

13 For this section I greatly benefit from an extensive record of NPO Law establishment processes and the interviews of people involved which was archived and created by Machi-pot, a nonprofit organization: http://npolaw-archive.jp/ (In Japanese, retrieved 22nd Jun. 2018). The related documents are now in the National Archives of Japan.

14 It included eighteen central ministries and governmental agencies.

15 Interview with Noboru Hayase, Akira Matsubara, and Yoshinori Yamaoka, 15th Jul. 2011: http://npolaw-archive.jp/?page_id=35 (In Japanese, retrieved 22nd Jun. 2018).

16 [*Tokutei Hieiri Katsudou Sokushin Hou* 特定非営利活動促進法 *(1998年法律第7号)*] http://elaws.e-gov.go.jp/search/elawsSearch/elaws_search/lsg0500/detail?lawId=410AC1000000007 (In Japanese, Retrieved 23rd Jun. 2018).

17 "Act on Promotion of Specified Non-profit Activities", Japanese Law Translation website: http://www.japaneselawtranslation.go.jp/law/detail/?id=3028&vm=04&re=01 (Retrieved 2nd Nov. 2018).

18 Twelve areas were specified in the 1998 Law, which are health and welfare, social education, community development, culture / art / sports, environmental protection, disaster relief, local security, human rights protection and peacebuilding, international cooperation, gender equality, child support, and support for other organizations. They have since been expanded to twenty areas (June 2018).

19 Including Designated Cities.

20 Matsubara from C's later recalled that the civil society networks had to accelerate the legislative process by compromising, because the triparty coalition was expected to be terminated after the Upper House elections in July 1998. Interview with Noboru Hayase, Akira Matsubara, and Yoshinori Yamaoka, 15th Jul. 2011: http://npolaw-archive.jp/?page_id=35 (In Japanese, retrieved 22nd Jun. 2018).

21 As a result of these reforms, 1,078 of 51,809 registered NPOs enjoy the tax benefits awarded as an "Approved Corporation" [*Nintei Tokutei Hieiri Katsudou Houjin* 認定特定非営利活動法人]as of April 2018 (Cabinet Office NPO Website: https://www.npo-homepage.go.jp/ (In Japanese, retrieved 24th Jun. 2018)).

22 Ms. Akiko Doumoto, who became the Governor of Chiba Prefecture after serving as an Upper House MP, was one of the local government heads eager to support collaboration with NPOs. Interview with Atsuko Doumoto, Yoshinori Yamaoka, and Toshio Tsuji: http://npolaw-archive.jp/?page_id=53 (In Japanese, retrieved 23rd Jun. 2018).

23 Interestingly, one of the proposals made for governmental actions was to "propose social innovation models (for regulatory reform, public support, etc.) and consider building a scheme". "Proposals by the "New Public Commons" Roundtable and Government Actions toward Their Institutionalization", The New Public Roundtable page, The Cabinet Office website: http://www5.cao.go.jp/entaku/pdf/goverment-actions-english.pdf (page 7, retrieved 2nd Nov. 2018).

24 At the moment (Sep. 2018), there is no specific legal status for social enterprises in Japan. So, when this section says "social enterprise," it means an organization which pursues both social causes and business profit, often as a business corporation (or in some case as a NPO).

25 However, national newspaper The Mainichi Shimbun reported that around twelve percent of the NPOs they researched in Tokyo and another twenty cities are either not submitting reports to the local authorities or are inactive, and in some cases, a dormant NPO status was even sold to be used for illegal activities (*The Mainichi Shimbun* 4 Nov. 2018 "Some 12% of nonprofits in major Japan cities dormant, some used for crimes"). https://mainichi.jp/english/articles/20181104/p2a/00m/0na/015000c (Retrieved 6 Nov. 2018)

26 The Number of Certified NPOs [*Tokutei Hieiri Katsudou Houjin no Nintei Suu no Suii* 特定非営利活動法人の認定数の推移], The Cabinet Office NPO website: https://www.npo-homepage.go.jp/about/toukei-info/ninshou-seni (In Japanese, retrieved 1st Jul. 2018)

27 Weight is balanced between the three prefectures affected by the Great East Japan Earthquake and Tsunami and other areas (the same shall apply for the percentages hereinafter for the same study).

28 Still, the income of NPOs is relatively small. Ushiro (2009:5-10, 200) blames the NPO leaderships' mindsets which tend to consider "being a small organization as a value" and claims that NPOs should seek stronger partnerships with the public sector.

29 The majority of respondents for the individual questionnaires were the secretary generals of the NPOs, so the result may be showing a higher income than the salaries of general NPO paid staff (JILPT 2015:8).

30 Although Yujiro Hayashi, who was the Executive Director of the Toyota Foundation, had a strong interest in "citizens' participation," the foundation had to carefully explain the purpose to its donor, Toyota Motors Company, before setting up the Program (Toyota Foundation 2007:154).

31 Interview with Atsuko Doumoto, Yoshinori Yamaoka, and Toshio Tsuji: http://npolaw-archive.jp/?page_id=53 (In Japanese, retrieved 23rd Jun. 2018).

32 Interview with Atsuko Doumoto, Yoshinori Yamaoka, and Toshio Tsuji, same as above.

33 Koichi Kato, who continued to be the central figure supporting the 1998 NPO Law and its amendment processes from the LDP and corresponded with Professor L. Salamon from Johns Hopkins University before the Great Hanshin Earthquake, notes that "my major interest was how to place NPOs and volunteer works when thinking

about society after the impasse of the "Welfare State model," parallel to the interest of Yamaoka (Kojima 2003:74).

34 Interview with Akira Matsubara "What we aimed for with the NPO Law": http://npolaw-archive.jp/?page_id=492 (in Japanese, retrieved 21st Jun. 2018).

35 Interview with Matsubara, same as above.

36 Direct conversation with Mr. Hiroshi Tanaka, the Japan Foundation Center (5th Sep. 2018)

37 Interview with Doumoto, Yamaoka, and Tsuji, same as above.

38 In the same survey, only 26.9 percent of respondents answered that they are strongly or somewhat interested in Public Benefit Corporations, which means people still have more interest in NPOs compared to Public Benefit Corporations (Cabinet Office 2016a:24).

39 Interview with Doumoto, Yamaoka, and Tsuji, same as above.

40 Interview with Doumoto, Yamaoka, and Tsuji, same as above.

41 Interview with Akira Matsubara http://npolaw-archive.jp/?page_id=360 (In Japanese, retrieved 24th Jun. 2018).

42 However, when the Public Benefit Organization system was finally amended in 2008, it lacked a wide range of involvement from the civil society sector or MPs, and was developed mostly by the Cabinet Office, unlike the processes of NPO Law (Yamaoka 2007:598-601).

43 When the Ministry of Welfare tried to send the Environmental Pollution Prevention Bill to the parliaments in 1955/1957, strong opposition from business associations prevented it (Miyamoto 2014a:63-64).

44 They were often supported by opposition parties, and called as "Progressive Head " [*Kakushin Shucho* 革新首長].

45 Still, authors like Miyamoto (2014a:575-576) claim that businesses mostly transferred their operations to other countries and continued to pollute.

46 Still, in many areas pollution continued more or less, and continuing health hazards and conflicts had to be dealt with by local communities. One of these areas, the Mizushima area in Okayama had to go through lawsuits from 1983 until 1996, when they were settled. Mr. Terutomo Ota, who was involved in the case, recalls that a common understanding between governments, businesses, and society that environmental pollution has to be stopped was formed by the 1990s, and this

understanding urged the companies to take action (Iwabuchi 2018).

47 Some corporate leaders were eager to introduce new technologies and reduce environmental pollutions, such as Mr. Kikawada of Tokyo Electric Power who decided to introduce LNG instead of coal and oil for power generation as "a social mission" of the company (Ito 2016:49-50, 177).

48 For instance, the production of stack gas desulfurization facilities reached JPY ninety-five billion in 1975 (Ito 2016:84).

49 In this study we define long-term care as "care for people needing daily living support over a prolonged period of time," which may differ by contexts in terms of what to include, but typically includes help with activities of daily living (Colombo et al. 2011:38-39). In Japan, long-term care was separated from other medical care and consolidated as another "sector" in social services.

50 The LTCI system itself can be considered as a remarkable example of SI, providing care services for elderly citizens and shifting the burden of care from family (especially women) to society as a whole. However, this study does not discuss the LTCI system, partly because it depends heavily on funding both from the government and insurance premiums, and because it also has a risk of creating "silos" separated by beneficiaries and service providers. For a detailed analysis of LTCI as an SI and its limitations, see Aoo (2017).

51 Japan lacks a cash allowance as a part of long-term care system, which is different from other developed countries such as Australia, England, Germany, and Italy (Campbell et al. 2016:49-50).

52 The population over sixty-five years old in 2015 is approximately 33.9 million, so the majority of older people are not qualified as LTCI service users (Cabinet Office 2016b:2).

53 In 2012, the total amount spent for LTCI services reached JPY 7.7 trillion (USD seventy billion) (Hirose 2014:164).

54 Mitsugi Town (which became a part of Onomichi City in 2005) in Hiroshima Prefecture suffered from an increasing number of bedridden older people and started operating a regional health management center in 1985. The town also operated medical and home based long-term care services under Public Mitsugi Hospital (Sato 2003:76-93).

55 Around thirty percent of centers are directly run by municipal governments and

the rest are subcontracted to social welfare committees and other nonprofit organizations. MoHLW website "Operation of Community-based Integrated Support Center [*Chiiki houkatsu Shien Sentaa no Gyoumu* 地域包括支援センターの業務]": http://www.mhlw.go.jp/seisakunitsuite/bunya/hukushi_kaigo/kaigo_koureisha/chiiki-houkatsu/dl/link2.pdf (In Japanese, retrieved 17th Dec. 2017)

56 Fukuoka City Non-insured Services Information website [*Fukuoka Shi Hoken Gai Saabisu Jyouhou Teikyou Saito* 福岡市保険外サービス情報提供サイト] https://care-info.city.fukuoka.lg.jp/public/top (In Japanese, retrieved 20th Apr. 2018)

57 Hitachi and Fukuoka City Collaborating to Build Community-Based Integrated Care Information Platform by Analyzing Big Data [*Hitachi to Fukuoka Shi no Kyousou ni yori Biggu Deeta Bunseki de Chiiki Houkatsu Kea Jyouhou Puratto Fuoomu wo Kouchiku* 日立と福岡市の協創により、ビッグデータ分析で地域包括ケア情報プラットフォームを構築] Hitachi Ltd. website: http://www.foresight.ext.hitachi.co.jp/_ct/17116246?_CAMCID=lknjlhToJY-387&_CAMSID=COXTecBgsidA-55&_CAMVID=NOXTECBgsiDA&_c_d=1 (In Japanese, retrieved 20th Apr. 2018)

58 The Center has multiple responsibilities and tasks other than coordination, including applying for LTCI eligibility, developing care plans for preventive care services, providing information and consultation, educating and training older people and their caregivers, and protecting the rights of the elderly (Sawada 2014:198-199).

59 For example, Maezawa (2011:72) points out that most medical doctors only focus on the treatment of patients who visit hospitals, and are unaware of their roles in local communities, and patients are also used to being the "beneficiary" of medical care, and are not active in participating in the CBIC system. Asakura (2010), while showing some of good examples in which local stakeholders are building community-based care systems, still argues that more needs to be done to create such systems.

Chapter 3 : China

3.1 Country Context

Soon after the end of WWII, in 1949 China became the People's Republic of China (PRC), which led to some drastic transformation of its of political, economic and social systems based on the socialist ideology, including the Great Leap Forward and the Great Cultural Revolution. After the 1980s, the country changed its policy to Reform and Opening, but the Communist Party of China (CPC) still has a strong grip on the state and political systems. As market reform expands, socialist welfare systems ceased to be effective and had to be replaced by other means to support people with various needs.

3.1.1 Political System

Since the Qin dynasty which started in the 9th Century B.C., traditional Chinese dynasties essentially maintained a system of one Emperor and an empire divided into districts governed by bureaucrats, who were mostly civilians who passed a selection process based on their knowledge of Confucian classics and literature (Kishimoto 1998:18).[1] In 1911, the Qing dynasty, ruled by Manchurian emperors, were overthrown by the Xinhai Revolution and the Republic of China (RoC) led by President Sun Yat-sen was established. However, the RoC suffered from uprisings by warlords and later from a Japanese invasion. After the defeat of Japan in 1945, the RoC / Kuomintang and the CPC fought a civil war, until the former fled to

Taiwan at the end of 1949. On 1st October 1949, Mao Zedong announced the establishment of the PRC (Amako 2013:2-13).

A noticeable characteristic of the PRC's political system is the so-called "Party-state system", an influence of the CPC over other political and administrative institutions and other groups (Charlton 2010:224-226). The CPC has multiple means of exerting its authority including guidance of governmental bodies, party committees set up in various institutions, media control, and authority over personnel appointment (Tsujinaka et al. 2014:19-20), which in some literature called as "national corporatism" or "socialist corporatism" (Hishida 2010:7; Tang 2012:148-152). The CPC controls the legislation (National People's Congress), administration (State Council), justice (Supreme People's Court), military (People's Liberation Army), eight non-communist political parties, and eight people's organizations (including China Women's Federation, Communist Youth League, and All-China Federation of Trade Unions) (Amako 2015:22-30; Yu 2014:118).

Until the end of the 1970s, the PRC was involved in a number of international conflicts and domestic political turmoil including the Korean War, the Vietnam War, the Sino-Vietnam War, a confrontation and armed conflict with the Soviet Union, and the Great Leap Forward [*Da Yuejin* 大跃进] and the Great Cultural Revolution [*Wenhua Dageming* 文化大革命] (Amako 2013:12-90). It was only after the death of Chairman Mao and the end of the Great Cultural Revolution in 1976 that Deng Xiaoping and his group finally managed to turn the county's course to "Reform and Opening" [*Gaige Kaifang* 改革开放] and modernization in 1978. Along with economic reform, political reform, in particular a change in the relationship between the CPC and governmental bodies, was briefly brought onto the agenda in the 1980s, but it was crushed after the Tiananmen Incident in 1989 (Takahara and Maeda 2014:23-40, 80-85), and the Party-state system continues until today.

Another tradition of the PRC since Mao's time is the relatively strong autonomy of the local governments. According to Tsujinaka and Kojima (2014:22), the PRC has five administrative levels from central, provincial level, prefectural level, county level, and subdistrict level (Table 3.1).

Table 3.1 Levels and Numbers of Administrative Units in China

Level / Name of Major Units (with numbers for each of the major unit):[2]
i. Central [*Guo* 国]
ii. Province [*Sheng* 省] (23) / Autonomous Region [*Zizhiqu* 自治区] (5) / Municipality [*Zhixiashi* 直辖市] (4)[3] / Special Administrative Region [*Tebie Xingzhengqu* 特别行政区] (2: Hong Kong and Macau)
iii. Prefecture [*Diqu* 地区] / City [*Shi* 市] (332)[4]
iv. County [*Xian* 县] (1,456) / City [*Shi* 市] (369) / District [*Qu* 区] (857)
v. Subdistrict [*Jiedao* 街道] (7,194) / Town [*Zhen* 镇] (19,683) / Township [*Xiang* 乡] (13,587)

Source: Revised from Tsujinaka and Kojima (2014:22)

Especially since the Reform and Opening era, local governments have been given a higher level of autonomy in funding, personnel appointment, and administration (Tsujinaka and Kojima 2014:22-23). A number of new economic systems and other reforms were first tested in local special economic zones and cities, such as Guangdong, Fujian, Hainan, and Shanghai, before they were introduced at the national level (Takahara and Maeda 2014:64).[5]

3.1.2 Socio-Economic Conditions

Not long after the establishment of the PRC, in the early 1950s the CPC led by Chairman Mao started to "socialize" China's economic and social structures. Under state planning, enterprises became state-owned or collectivized, and rural villages were transformed into cooperatives and People's Communes [*Renmin Gongshe* 人民公社], units based on collective ownership and production (Tang 2017:30-41). The Great Leap Forward in the 1950s, which was an attempt to rapidly bring the Chinese economy into the heavy industrial stage, resulted in a failure and great famine causing the deaths of over twenty million people. The Great Cultural Revolution, driven by "Maoism," denounced anything considered "capitalistic" or part of "Western imperialism," and left the country's economy and industry greatly deteriorated in its aftermath (Marukawa 2013:33-37,48-49).

After the end of the 1970s, under Reform and Opening, collective farms were dissolved to incentivize individual farmers' production. New enterprises both in urban and rural areas flourished and resulted in creating new wealth. Privatization and restructuring of state-owned enterprises has been another issue but due to the bureaucracy's desire to control strategic industries and the vested interests of industrial groups, it is done only gradually and partially (Rana and Hamid 1996:198). It is also noticeable that the PRC has not renounced their socialist principles and planned economy, as apparent in the existence of the economic plans (Five Year Plans) and the central planning bureau (National Development and Reform Commission [*Guojia Fazhan he Gaige Weiyuanhui* 国家发展和改革委员会]) (Marukawa 2013:63-39; Tang 2017:27).

With a "socialist market economy" system, the economic growth rate after the Reform and Opening is remarkable, reaching around ten percent per annum from 1980 to 2010. This became the driver which made China the second largest economy in the world, and reduced severe poverty (people living on less than USD1.25 a day) from sixty-one percent of the population in 1990 to four percent in 2015 (United Nations 2015:14).[6]

The public welfare system in traditional China was limited, and measures were limited to communal grain storage to prepare for famines [*Yicang* 义仓 / *Shecang* 社仓] and provisional support for needy groups, which were often led by the local scholar-gentry in local communities (Li 2018a:288-296; Tao 2009:31). Under the Confucian tradition, direct and extended family was the main source of support and welfare, including the support of older parents by their children (Dixon 1981:7-9; Eastman 1994:28-31).

The change of welfare systems after the PRC is described further in the case study, but another issue worth mentioning is the birth control program known as the "one child policy." This began in 1979 and allowed only one child per couple (with exceptions for ethnic minorities and other groups). Although the policy has been relaxed recently, it dramatically accelerated the aging process and now China has more than 140 million people over the age of sixty-five, constituting 14.3 percent of the population (Zhu 2017:89). The "4-2-1" family structure caused by the policy, which means four grandparents, two parents, and only one grandchild, has made it difficult for younger families to provide care for the elderly (Nie 2016:351-352, 354; Xu and Zhang 2010:119).

Another unique social system in the PRC is the division between urban and rural populations. The average income of the urban population amounts to roughly double or triple that of the rural population. Although recently changing in some areas, people who are registered in rural areas were not allowed to move to urban areas, and even if they do, as many of them do to seek jobs (which are called *Mingong* [民工]), they do not have access to urban welfare systems and become a *de facto* "migrant" in their own country, which increases the risk of a lack of social welfare and stability (Ako 2012:55; Guo 2017:34).

3.1.3 Civil Society and Social Movements

From ancient times, Chinese society had a variety of guilds, associations and fraternities, for mutual help and in some occasions to survive under or revolt against autocratic rulers (Li 2018a:289-290, 296-297; Simon 2013: Chapters 3-4).[7] However, most of them were for serving extended family members, people from certain townships or regions, or for members only and not for general public benefit (Eastman 1994:292-302; Kishimoto 2012:115-116, 122). In the early 20th Century, during the end of the Qing dynasty and the RoC era, charitable associations and organizations emerged, mostly led by local elites (the scholar-gentry) working in poverty alleviation, education and training, and infrastructure development (Chen 2009; Fuma 2009). However, almost all of them were nationalized or disappeared soon after the PRC came into power (Okamura 2017:251; Yu 2014:116-117).

Under the PRC regime, only eight People's Organizations [*Renmin Tuanti* 人民团体][8] were officially allowed. These organizations were given the dual roles of communicating governmental decisions and policies to the society, and informing the government about the people's interests and demands, and they were given seats at the central

Chinese People's Political Consultative Conference [*Zhongguo Renmin Zhengzhi Xieshang Huiyi* 中国人民政治协商会议] and lower level government structures. Meanwhile, other independent organizations were not allowed to officially register or operate (Huang 2014a:89).[9]

Other types of nonprofit organizations, collectively called "social organizations" [*Shehui Tuanti* 社会团体 / *Shehui Zuzhi* 社会组织][10] prospered after the Reform and Opening era, as we see details in the case study below. The 2008 Sichuan Earthquake made private donations and volunteering popular with the public. According to Li (2018b:54), there were 662,000 officially registered social organizations (329,000 Associations [*Xiehui* 协会], 4,784 Foundations [*Jijinhui* 基金会], and 329,000 People-Run Non-Enterprise Units [*Minban Fei Qiye Danwei* 民办非企业单位] (PRNEUs)) by the end of 2015.[11]

3.2 Case Analysis: Welfare Reform and the Development of Social Organizations

3.2.1 Background

Welfare System under a Socialist Regime (1950s-1970s)

In socialist China after the collectivization movement in the 1950s, work integration became the main source of social security and welfare. Welfare benefits were provided through workplace units [*Danwei* 单位] such as state-owned enterprises and People's Communes (Dixon 1981:15; Zhu 2014:301-302). The level of welfare differed greatly depending on the units. If a person belonged to a state-owned enterprise in an urban area, he or she could enjoy generous benefits (sometimes called an "iron rice-bowl," meaning unbreakable benefits) including housing, retirement pensions, injury, disability, sickness, and maternity allowances, the use of facilities like canteens, nurseries, health clinics, sanatoriums, and other daily supplies and allowances provided by the workplace. These welfare systems were funded by different sources based on related laws and the unit's profits, and administered by unit members, with representatives from work unit managers, trade unions, and workers. Therefore, it could sometimes be difficult to control, and become quite costly for the unit[12] (Dixon 1981:40-43, 51-56; Guo 2017:35-36). Meanwhile, social welfare systems in the rural population were limited to only simple medical services. Other welfare – to provide the basic "five," which meant a minimum amount of food, clothing, housing, medical services, and a funeral (or education for children) were provided by the community only for people with "three nos," meaning no family, no working ability, and no income, such as the elderly, people who were widowed or orphaned, or handicapped people without any other assistance (Leung and Xu 2010:51).

The Transformation of Welfare Systems in the "Reform and Opening" Era

After the 1980s in Reform and Opening era, the restructuring of socio-economic systems continued, and millions of workers were laid off from the state-run enterprise, and the socialist welfare system itself was accused of hindering economic efficiency and was gradually rescinded (Shen 2014: Zhu 2014:303-304). But without having formal social safety nets, social issues and needs become more diverse and serious, including unemployment, an aging population, environmental issues, social protests and conflicts, and migrants from rural areas to big cities who were denied access to social services. According to Zhu, the Gini coefficient in China announced by the state statistics department in 2015 was 0.462, well over the 0.4 warning level of increased risk of social unrest (Zhu 2017:90). At first, local governments and the newly introduced "community" [Shequ 社区] were expected to provide this badly needed social assistance for vulnerable groups,[13] instead of the weakening work units. But soon it became obvious that most local governments and "operative units" (organizations to provide direct services such as medical and social care) under governmental bodies lacked the professional capacities and financial resources to meet all of the increasing and varying needs of society (Ma 2014:80; Xu and Zhang 2010:117; Yang et al. 2016:2299).[14]

As a result, the CPC and central government eventually had to directly engage with the increasing pressure from society.[15] The Party-government system took two different approaches to tackle this major challenge, especially after the mid-2000s when they proposed the "Harmonious Society" [Hexie Shehui 和谐社会] to adjust the increasing inequality and secure stable livelihoods for all as a major policy target (Tang 2012:121-122): first was to develop and provide more financial resources for social safety net schemes such as pension, medical insurance, unemployment insurance, minimum livelihood protection, and community service, as summarized in Table 3.2, and other poverty alleviation programs to support needy persons (Leung and Xu 2010:54; Okamura 2017:250; Zhu 2014). After the 2000s, these schemes began shifting from residual / selective benefits to universal coverage (Shen 2016:13-14). Second was to nurture a variety of non-state organizations which can support the vulnerable groups in society.[16]

Table 3.2 Summary of Social Security and Welfare
Systems in Urban and Rural Areas in China[17]

		Urban population	Rural population
Collective economy era	(Welfare provided mainly by work units)	Housing, medical services, pension, allowances, education, and recreation provided by unit	Co-working and co-production, simple medical services, and other minimum things provided only for "three nos"
Reform and Opening era	Pension	1991 for employees 2011 for all residents	2009 for all residents
	Medical insurance	1998 for employees 2007 for all residents	2003 for all residents
	Unemployment insurance	1999 for employees	None
	Minimum livelihood protection	1999 for all residents	2007 for all residents
	Community service	1987 community service	None in most areas

Source: Revised from Guo (2017:39)

Definitions

Here we should clarify what the term "social organization" or others mean in this chapter. Authors use different terms both in English and in Chinese to describe the ecosystem of social and nonprofit organizations in China, which may or may not correspond with the governmental terminology used to distinguish different types of organizations. Some of the popular terms are social organizations, civil organizations, NGOs, and civil society. In this case study, we use the term "social organizations" (SOs) [*Shehui Tuanti* 社会团体][18] to generally describe different organizations which i) principally pursue social purposes, ii) are non-governmental in a broad sense, and iii) are not primarily for-profit. It includes associations, foundations, People-Run Non-Enterprise Units (PRNEUs), and even other organizations which are legally registered as commercial enterprises, or which do not have any legal status at all.[19]

3.2.2 Processes

Ups and Down of Social Organizations after the Reform and Opening Era
The paths for social organizations in China were not straightforward ones, and they had to go through many ups and downs. SOs have flourished since the 1980s, when the Reform and Opening policy was promoted after the confusion of the Great Cultural Revolution. To allow the government to focus on modernization and economic growth, SOs were expected to provide the necessary resources for welfare and social services. Associations and organizations such as the Chinese Red Cross, YMCA, YWCA, academic associations, laborer associations, and professional associations among others were either revived or newly established. Foundations were established to collect funds from the public and international donors, starting from the China Children and Teenagers' Fund in 1981, followed by others including China Soong Ching Ling Foundation in 1982 and China Foundation of Disabled Persons in 1984. As a result, the number of registered associations and foundations at the Ministry of Civil Affairs exploded from around 5,000 in 1988 to over 150,000 in 1992. Still it was obvious that many of these were either semi-governmental or operating as a governmental arm (which were often called "GONGO", or government-organized NGO) or receiving strong support from the government, either to utilize their operational and fundraising capacities, or to shift governmental personnel as a result of public sector downsizing

(Wang 2011:14-17; Yu 2017:87-89; Zhao 2010:211).

After the 1990s, the government strengthened their control of SOs, especially for those operating in for-profit activities. After several waves of so-called "clean up and reorganization" of social organizations by the government in the 1990s, the number of registered SOs decreased until they hit a low point in 1998. Also, the government released formal regulations for different organizations (1988 Measures on Foundation Administration and 1989 Regulations on Social Group Registration and Administration). SOs now had to register both under the Ministry of Civil Affairs and under a governmental department supervising SO activities. This so-called "dual registration system" became a major obstacle for any SO to get registered, especially for those who did not have a connection with the Party-state system (Xu and Li 2008:14; Wang 2011:21-25).

Although imposing such a strong restriction on SOs, the Party-state system was aware of the increasing need to support the marginalized groups caused by the deepening reform and transformation of China's socio-economic structure. In 1998, new Provisional Regulations on People-Run Non-Enterprise Unit (PRNEU) Registration and Administration was released, and PRNEUs were introduced as a legal entity. These private-run institutions provided various services in the fields of education, health, and social services and the number of registered PRNEUs quickly grew to over 225,000 by 2012 (Huang 2014b:200).

The Beijing Women's NGO Conference held in 1995 also provided momentum for the emergence of so-called "grassroots NGOs." They operated in new areas such as environmental degradation, HIV/AIDS, gender, and other areas of social protection and community services. Many of them operated as an enterprise or without registration and received funding from foreign donors such as the Ford Foundation, World Vision, and Oxfam Hong Kong (Xu and Li 2008:3-8; Wang 2011:26-30). Some successful projects run by SOs represented by "Project Hope", a project to build schools in remote areas since 1989, also showed society the capacity of SOs (Liu 2008:29).

In 2004, State Council Regulations on Foundation Administration created a new type of foundation called a Non-public Funding Foundation [*Fei Gongmu Jijin Hui* 非公募基金会], which can receive funding only from specific individuals or organizations, different from Public Funding Foundation [*Gongmu Jijin Hui* 公募基金会] which can collect money from the general public. After this change, wealthy individuals and corporates established their own foundations (mostly Non-public Funding Foundations) and the number of foundations grew rapidly. According to the China Foundation Center website, the number of registered foundations is 5,775, holding total net assets of USD 15.6 billion, and with annual total of grant given from foundations of USD six billion by the end of year 2016.[20] Kojima and Kobashi (2014:22) report that the most popular areas of operation for these foundations are education and social services. Although the majority of foundations in China are "operating" foundations, which conduct programs by themselves rather than giving grants, there are some that appreciate the roles of SOs in identifying and tackling social issues, and are willing to support them. Some foundation such as Narada Foundation,[21] Dunhe Foundation,[22] and Youcheng Foundation[23] supported the SOs through grant-making, capacity building programs, and organizing networks and fora.

Also, in some areas like Shenzhen, Beijing, Nanjing, and Shanghai, governments have also initiated the development of "community foundations"[24] to collect funding locally and to provide services to local residents (Guo and Lai 2017).

The Charity Law: Targets and Logics

The Charity Law [*Cishan Fa* 慈善法] which is the umbrella law for SOs, finally passed by the NPC in March 2016 and took effect in September 2016 after a lengthy research and consultation processes, including visits to other countries including the U.S., the U.K., Canada, Singapore, Korea, and Japan (Li 2018b:161). It provides an overall definition of and regulations for charitable activities and organizations and their procedures, obligations, and relationships with the government. By defining the types of "charitable activities" in Article Three, it clarifies what kind of areas are prioritized by the government: support for the poor and the weak, disaster relief, education, science, culture, health and sanitation, sports, and environmental degradation and protection. These charitable activities became the *raison d'être* for Chinese SOs to win governmental approval and legitimacy – not as a right as in Western society, but as a player doing useful works in the society as approved by the Party-state system.[25] The dual registration system was abolished for the organizations meeting those requirements (Article Ten).[26] But SOs are newly requested to disclose detailed information about the organization as well as all donations and programs (Article Seventy-one to Seventy-five), in addition to submitting annual reports (Article Thirteen). Each local government at the district level and above is also tasked by the Charity Law with developing their own information platform and disclosing data and statistics related to charitable activities (Article Sixty-nine to Seventy) (Okamura 2017:256-257; Suzuki 2014:546-547).

A major shift observed in the Charity Law is the Party-state system relying more heavily on information disclosure to ensure sound governance and financial management of SOs instead of detailed and direct supervision from the government departments. Although the Charity Law still lacks some major provisions such as tax exemption for SOs, it provides a comprehensive framework for these organizations and opens up a new stage for their further development with a new and supportive approach.

The Ecosystem Surrounding Social Organizations

For SOs to develop and function to meet the immense demand for support and services, what need to be established beyond the legal and regulative frameworks are funding, human resources, partnerships with other stakeholders, and other forms of backing as an ecosystem. Here we examine some more of the crucial supporting (and not-so-supporting) environmental elements for the flourishing of SOs in China.

Local Governments: As an Experimental Site

In the Reform and Opening era, local governments were held responsible for providing different kinds of social services, but were also put under pressure to cut down on governmental structures and costs. As a result, looking at the provinces of Shanxi, Hebei, Jiangxi, and Fujian, the percentage of total expenditures on public goods fell from over seventy percent in 1970 to forty to fifty percent in 2000 (Tsai 2007:63). To solve this dilemma, they started to cultivate SOs[27] and contract services from them (Guo 2017:176; Yu 2016:65). In 2005, Beijing City officially introduced the public service procurement system to build a "Harmonious Society," and invited SOs to provide community services to support ex-offenders, youth, migrant workers from rural areas, and local volunteers (Koga 2010:139-145). Another case in Shanghai city reported by Suzuki (2014:549, 551-552) is the city government purchasing a variety of services including i) community services (social security, employment, health, elderly care, public sanitation, local environment, cultural activities, a charity supermarket, free meals, etc.), ii) support for local businesses, iii) social action support (petition support, legal aid, training), and iv) societal management (management of migrant workers from rural areas living in the city, conflict mediation, adoption support). The amount of services purchased totalled RMB 1.4 billion (USD 200 million) for the city, with another RMB six billion (USD one billion) for eighteen districts under the city in 2010. Li (2018b:187) estimates that services procured by local governments exceeded RMB fifteen billion (approx. USD two billion) in 2013.

To foster SOs with the capacity to meet these requests, some local governments have launched their own nonprofit incubation programs. For example, when the author visited Shanghai city in 2014, Rende Foundation had been contracted by the Pudong District government to manage the "Foundation Service Park" and was supporting twenty-seven new foundations working locally. The District also had the "Public Welfare Service Park" to support nonprofits and social enterprises.[28] Local governments including Beijing, Shanghai, and Shenzhen also conducted trials suspending the dual registration system in advance of the Charity Law and the decision made by the State Council at the national level in 2013 (Ma 2014:92; Hu and Guo 2016:231; Suzuki 2014:547, 552; Yang et al. 2016:2300). They functioned as an experimental ground for innovations, just as they worked for economic reforms during the Reform and Opening era.

The Role of Intellectuals

Another driving force in the flourishing of SOs was the researchers and academics who were involved in NGO and nonprofit studies, and the related legal and philosophical issues surrounding them. Beginning with the establishment of the NGO Research Center in Tsinghua University[29] in 1998 as the first research center on NGOs in China, others followed including Peking University (Center of Civil Society; Center for Nonprofit Organizations Law), Beijing Normal University (China Philanthropy Research Institute[30]), Shanghai Jiaotong University (Center for the Third Sector), Renmin University (China Institute for Philanthropy and Social Innovation[31]), and Sun Yat-Sen University (Center on Philanthropy[32]). These research centers played diverse roles, from proposing plans for possible legal and regulative frameworks throughout the discussion of the Charity Law and other laws and regulations, training human resources in the nonprofit and philanthropy sectors, and developing information platforms for SOs (Ma 2014:83-86).

They also played a crucial role in developing numerous concepts and terminologies that were acceptable in China's political environment. As the CPC and the government started to view the word "civil society[33]" with great suspicion, they translated it to the Chinese word "*gongming shehui*" [公民社会], which literally means "public people's society," and claimed that it includes the involvement of and interaction with the government and business, not only the social sector – thus it is interdependent and synergetic with the state and market systems and does not signal any confrontation between the state and society (Ma

2014:80, 86; Wang 2011:3, 10-12). When even *gongming shehui* became a "sensitive" word after 2011, authors like Wang Ming developed new concepts such as *"gongyi cishan"* [公益慈善] or *"gongyi quan"* [公益圈], which mean "Public Benefit Charity" or "Public Benefit Sphere" as a translation for the word "philanthropy" or "civil society," and expanded the meaning by including other social activities beyond the original words "charity" or "philanthropy."[34] These terms may seem like a bit like merely playing around with translation. But such manipulation of concepts and terms (mainly done in Chinese) had a crucial meaning in the development of policies which would be acceptable to the Party-government system, and in the creation of spaces for the legalization of SOs. Intellectuals also joined in to launch grassroots NGOs, think tanks, and other kinds of SOs (Li 2008; Li 2018b).

As a consequence, the CPC finally accepted the role of SOs in March 2014, with Premier Li Ke Qiang using a new slogan of "Social Governance" to achieve the fulfillment of social needs and participation of different stakeholders under the leadership of the government, and urging SOs to play a more active role in meeting those goals (Yu 2016:62, 66).

The Use of Information Technologies

As a relatively recent phenomenon, we can notice that Chinese SOs are using information technology quite effectively and on a large scale. Since the beginning of the internet, it helped to connect people with similar interests and form SOs with specific areas to work on (Wang 2011:33). In 2011, an IT company called Tencent started WeChat, a social messaging service, to which an online-payment service called WeChat Pay was added in 2013, soon becoming a necessity for daily life in China along with the preceding service Alipay. WeChat also became a platform for people who are interested in social sectors to discuss, inform, evaluate, or donate to SOs through online forums, increasingly from mobile phones. For example, during the "*Gongyi 99*" [公益99] campaign in 2017, RMB 830 million (USD 120 million) was collected from over twelve million people, together with RMB 300 million (USD forty-four million) from Tencent Foundation and RMB 180 million (USD twenty-six million) from partner corporations, for a total of RMB 1.3 billion (USD 200 million) in only three days. WeChat and other online platforms such as Alipay or Ant Forest are becoming a major tool for SO fundraising (Brennan 2017; Li 2018:63-65, 172-173).[35]

Information technology also works to share the information on SOs publicly. For example, the China Foundation Center website collects data on over 5,000 foundations and discloses it along with each foundation's "Transparency Index," which shows a score from zero to 100. Also, on each SO's website, it is becoming fairly common to show the names of online donors, even if it is for only one yuan on a real-time basis. Although such information disclosure can also be used by the government to monitor the SOs' activities, the accessibility to information is quite impressive. The active move of SOs towards increased transparency is accelerating fundraising and increasing trust from society as well as bringing in policy support. We can see that such innovative use of technology has made the information disclosure principle in the Charity Law possible.

The Control from the Party-State System
The CPC and government continued to hold ambivalent feelings about SOs, both expectations for them to contribute to solving social issues

and also suspicion about them being uncontrollable, and even becoming a potential threat to the regime (Kang and Han 2008; Tang 2012:198; Yu 2014:134). Therefore, the government policy has been a pendulum that swings from encouraging to controlling (Kang and Han 2007). The government and the CPC tried to control SOs through providing funding and in-kind support (like free office space), sending personnel,[36] setting up Party sections in the SOs, and in some cases chronically harrassing them (Suzuki 2014:541; Tsujinaka 2014:376). Even the enactment of the Charity Law does not signal their full support for civil society, as we can see through another Overseas NGO Management Law enacted in 2016 to ban the operation of all unauthorized foreign NGOs working in China (Jia 2017). On the other hand, Zhao, based on her observation of service-provision NGOs in Beijing, warned that SOs also tend to seek a connection with the government in order to receive protection and authority while outsourcing governmental functions (Zhao 2010:227-229).

The same holds true for virtual civil society. While "netizens" are claiming their rights and complaining about the corruption and wrongdoing of governmental officials, different governmental bureaus and departments are monitoring and controlling the information and individuals (Inoguchi 2014:60). Technological innovation does not automatically mean more freedom or more space for civil society (Ako 2012:56).

3.2.3 Analysis

As illustrated above, the development of SOs to fill the gaps created by the disintegration of socialist welfare systems first started at the central level in the 1980s, including the establishment of government-backed societies and foundations. But once the initial wave of momentum receded after the Tiananmen Square incident in 1989 and the following tightening control of SOs by the government, some local governments continued their experiments (often by offending the policies regulations set by the central government) together with local SOs and businesses.

And a noticeable feature of this case is the constant presence of groups from the civil society side who were willing to actively respond to the opportunities opened or suggested by the government side. Especially intellectuals, who were marginalized during the Great Cultural Revolution, became leading figures and worked together with other groups, both with insiders in the Party-state system and with other groups such as newly emerging entrepreneurs and people from rural areas (Tang 2012:200; Wang 2011:43-38). Later, the younger, well-educated demographic who were born in the 1980s - 1990s, including those who had studied abroad, joined the sector (Li 2018b:62-63; Tsujinaka 2014:375). Although they utilized information and knowledge from foreign countries such as the U.S., Europe, or other Asian countries, their initiatives also look like a revival of the social responsibilities that were once fulfilled by the traditional Chinese scholar-gentry, who "take the nation's great tasks as their own" [*Yi Tianxia Wei Jiren* 以天下为己任] (Liu 2008:27; Wang 2011:43; Yu 2017:170-176). Businesses joined at a later stage by providing funding to government-approved frameworks such as private foundations and online platforms, together with the general public supporting SOs through volunteering and donations (Table 3.3). Thus, we may say that this is an interesting combination of top-down and bottom-up approaches, and alliances between (mainly) intellectuals, civil society, and different levels of government.

Table 3.3 Scaling Patterns and Paths for the Development of Social Organizations, China

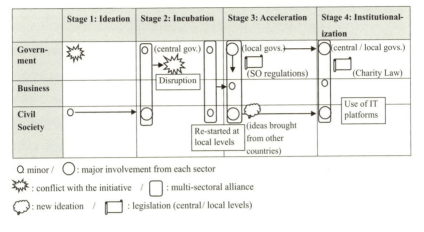

O minor / ◯ : major involvement from each sector
💥 : conflict with the initiative / ☐ : multi-sectoral alliance
☁ : new ideation / ☐ : legislation (central/ local levels)

However, we should not say this was a successful case without any concerns. One major risk factor is the gap between the resources and capacity SOs have (though already quite impressive) compared to the huge volume of social demands presented by Chinese society. If the government chooses to evade their responsibility of providing at least a minimum level of social safety net, SOs can now only cover limited areas (mainly major city areas such as Beijing, Shanghai, and Guangzhou) and issues (Yokohama 2012:82-83). Second, society's trust and support for SOs is still limited (Yu 2014:134), after major scandals involving financial mismanagement on the part of major SOs such as the Chinese Red Cross after the 2008 Sichuan Earthquake[37] (Ako 2014:199-200; Yang et al. 2016:2304). And finally, authors seem to concur (Suzuki 2014:537; Wang 2011:3; Yang et al. 2016:2298; Yu 2014:136) on the point that Chinese SOs exist in a different context from those in Western civil society, which are supposed to be autonomous from the government. Chinese SOs are under the strong guidance, supervision and control of the government, and we should not mistake the "grassroots" nature of some NGOs as a common trait of all SOs (Xu and Li 2008:12).

However, throughout the whole process of SO development, we can observe how SOs actively filled the major "vacuum" created by the work units and government's retreat from providing social services (Liu 2008:27; Yang et al. 2016:2294; Zhao 2010:229). Or in other words, it is also a process of different sectors coming to negotiate, cooperate, and co-govern the "public space" within the given context of the post-Reform era, to resolve the turmoil caused by the huge amount of inequality and frustration within Chinese society (Tsujinaka 2014:376-382). For instance, authors provide the different examples of public health system reform (Ma 2014), statements of protest from lawyers (Ako 2012), and incremental co-governance mechanisms developed in Hangzhou city (Wang and Liu 2017). This has the potential to affect the principle of the governance mechanisms in the Party-government system, as we can see in the new logic behind the Charity Law.

The emerging of SOs in China may be showing, as Li (2018b:28) claims, the importance of "bottom-up" elements in Chinese society. If that sounds too optimistic, it seems to be safe at least to say that SOs have successfully shown their presence in society as a crucial part of "socialist consultative democracy[38]" to deal with social tensions and problems, as President Xi reported in the Nineteenth National Congress of the CPC in October 2017. Again, it is still unknown whether the SOs have the capacity to solve the various needs within Chinese society, but as an SI process, we may conclude that i) it is a clear example of the process that is changing the relationships and resources distribution within the society, and ii) the effort is functioning to address and tackle diverse issues in the society.

3.4 Summary

The development of SOs in post-reform China shows us an example of how "alliance" of different sectors and groups including intellectuals, ex-party or government officials, business persons, and rural populations utilized the opportunities created by the post-reform crisis of welfare and social service provision, and how after many twists and turns, they expanded their space and resources within an authoritarian Party-state system. Even after the end of the initial "boom" in the 1980s, SOs continued to develop mainly on a local level and created a favorable environment including partnerships with local government, increasing online donation platforms, laws and regulations, and ideas, concepts, and values to facilitate the acceptance of the role of SOs by the Party-government system. In an environment cautious of any social sectors / organizations which may compete with the Party-state system, scholars and practitioners developed various concepts and values in order to be endorsed by the system. And with the help of the latest technologies to connect with public and government procurement systems, they were able to develop their own resource mobilization channels as well as a new governance structure between the government and society based on information disclosure as prescribed in the 2016 Charity Law.

---

1 It is a unique quality of the Chinese system that this scholar-gentry [*Shidafu* 士大夫 / *xiangshen* 乡绅] class was mostly formed through academic capability rather than noble lineage (Miyazaki 1963).

2   There are other categories especially for ethnic minority areas, but they are omitted in this list for simplicity.
3   Four Municipalities directly under the central government are large cities (Beijing, Tianjin, Shanghai, and Chongqing) which are divided into Districts and Counties.
4   Cities exist at two different levels (Prefecture-level Cities and County-level Cities).
5   However, Isobe (2008:45-47), based on detailed observation of the Guangdong province during the Reform and Opening era, argues that the independence of local leaderships should not be overestimated, and that basically they have been operating under a mandate from the central leadership.
6   Still, we need to note that there are huge regional differences and gaps in income and socio-economic conditions between different areas in China, especially between the so-called "East" (coastal regions with big cities, showing rapid economic development) and the "West" (inland regions, especially rural areas) (Guo and Min 2011:57).
7   Thus, such sects and associations were under oppression from the dynasties as a threat to the emperor's rule (Liu 2008:22)
8   The eight People's Organizations are: Communist Youth League of China, All-China Federation of Trade Unions, All-China Women's Federation, All-China Youth Federation, All-China Federation of Industry and Commerce, China Association for Science and Technology, All-China Federation of Returned Overseas Chinese, and All China Federation of Taiwan Compatriots. In 2000, the Ministry of Civil Affairs defined 25 organizations which do not require registration, including Chinese People's Association for Friendship with Foreign Countries, All-China Journalists Association, China Disabled Person's Federation, Chinese Red Cross and Soong Ching Ling Foundation, among others (Huang 2014a:102).
9   Other organizations include "Institutional Organizations," which were set up and funded by governmental bodies to provide services such as culture, education, health, and sports (Huang 2014b:202).
10 The definition of social organizations differs depending on which legal entities (and non-registered organizations / groups) the author includes. The definition in this study is given below in the case study.
11 The number of people's organizations and other semi-governmental social organizations operating in different administrative levels are far larger (6.9 million), but we shall not include them in the analysis (Tsujinaka et al. 2014:40).

12 As a result of generous benefits, the cost of welfare sometimes topped 50 per cent of the work place's wage bill. Later by the mid-1960s they were accused by the Maoist ideologues of being "welfarism" and "revisionist sins" that corrupted revolutionary virtues, but they were later reconstructed in the 1970s until they were finally dissolved in the Reform and Opening era after the 1980s to improve the competitiveness of state-owned enterprises (Dixon 1981:55;118;126).

13 Since the 1990s the government has been organizing Residential Committees [*Jumin Weiyuanhui* 居民委员会] and Community Organizations [*Shequ Zuzhi* 社区组织] to meet the need on grass-roots levels (Huang 2014a:90-91).

14 According to a 2006 AsiaBarometer survey, only 14.1 percent of respondents respond that they trust local governments "very much," which is significantly lower than 41.2 percent for the central government (Guo and Min 2011:52).

15 For example, the 2006 AsiaBarometer survey shows that 48.1 percent of respondents say that the social welfare system is unsatisfactory, which is the highest rate of discontent among other factors (personal life, governmental services, etc.) (Guo and Min 2011:46-47).

16 It is often called "socialization of welfare", but its meaning is to utilize the community and facilities for welfare and care, and is different from the old socialist model (Guo 2017:169-171).

17 Please note that the level of benefit differs depending on the schemes, regions, and other factors. For instance, Guo (2017) reported during her field research conducted in 2014 that an urban pensioner could receive RMB 2,000 to 4,000 per month, while a rural pensioner could only receive RMB sixty.

18 Please note that the Chinese government uses this word to describe either i) associations only, or ii) a wider category including associations, foundations, People-Run Non Enterprise Units, and People's Organizations. In the definition for this case study, it is closer to the latter (ii) but excludes People's Organizations and other semi-state organizations, and includes other organizations registered as commercial enterprises, or without registration but fitting the definition.

19 When social organizations in China do not have a connection with Party-government system, they may choose to be operate with a commercial enterprise [*Gongshang* 工商] registration, or without any registration (Zhao 2001:35).

20 China Foundation Center website: http://en.foundationcenter.org.cn/mission.html

(Retrieved 2nd Nov. 2018)
21 Narada Foundation website: http://www.naradafoundation.org/category/112 (Retrieved 2nd Nov. 2018)
22 Dunhe Foundation website: http://www.dunhefoundation.org/index_en.php (Retrieved 2nd Nov. 2018)
23 Youcheng Foundation website: http://old.youcheng.org/plus/list.php?tid=12/ (Retrieved 2nd Nov. 2018)
24 Please note that many of these "community foundations" are government-affiliated and their characteristics may be quite different from those of typical community foundations in the United States and other developed countries. Still, there are some strong community foundations developed by local intellectuals and businesses such as Guangdong Harmony Foundation in Guangzhou: http://www.gdharmonyfoundation.org/eindex.html (Retrieved 24th Mar. 2018).
25 This shows some similarity to how the NPO Law in Japan acknowledged the quality of "public benefit" as it applies to nonprofit organizations, not the organization itself but as demonstrated in their specific activities as stated in the Law.
26 Exceptions are for religious and foreign organizations.
27 According to Yu (2016:65), CPC Shenzhen City put up a large billboard with the slogan "Civil Society, Develop Together" in 2008 to propagate the role of civil society organizations in city development.
28 Site visit and interview with Ms. Ivy Gu, then Rende Foundation (22nd Dec. 2014). Other organizations such as NPI are organizing "Social Innovation Parks" in dozens of municipalities (Li 2018b:148).
29 NGO Research Center (NGORC), School of Public Policy and Management, Tsinghua University website: http://www.sppm.tsinghua.edu.cn/english/research/center/26efe4891f406f6b011f5ee4824e0041.html (Retrieved 21st Mar. 2018).
30 China Philanthropy Research Institute website: http://www.bnu1.org/ (in Chinese, retrieved 2nd Nov. 2018).
31 China Institute for Philanthropy and Social Innovation, Renmin University http://spap.ruc.edu.cn/displaynews.php?id=9526 (in Chinese, retrieved 2nd Nov. 2018).
32 Sun Yat-Sen University website: http://www.sysu.edu.cn/2012/en/research/research01/index.htm (Retrieved 2nd Nov. 2018).
33 The caution toward the word came both because of the Party-government system

becoming concerned about foreign influence over NGOs, and because of Marxist terminology depicting "civil society" primarily as a phenomenon of the bourgeoisie.

34 From Professor Wang Ming's Presentation at "2015 East Asia Civil Society Forum," Wuxi, Jiangsu Province, China (9th Oct. 2015).

35 According to a report published by the China Association of Fundraising Professionals, in 2014 over RMB 437 million (USD sixty-seven million) was donated through the top four online donation platforms, Sina Weibo, Tencent, Ant Financial and Alibaba. The total funds raised for Chinese charities was RMB 104 billion (USD sixteen billion) (CAFP 2015).

36 This also functioned as an absorption of governmental officers who retired or lost their jobs in repeated government restructuring after the 1980s (Tsujinaka and Kojima 2014:23).

37 The most infamous case is the "Guo Meimei case", a case which raised questions on the management of donations collected by the Chinese Red Cross – caused by an internet celebrity showing her luxurious life.

38 Xi Jinping's Report delivered at the 19th National Congress of the Communist Party of China (18th Oct. 2017). China Daily website: http://language.chinadaily.com.cn/19thcpcnationalcongress/2017-11/06/content_34188086.htm (Retrieved 4th May 2018).

Chapter 4 : South Korea

4.1 Country Context

The Republic of Korea (hereunder "South Korea") became an industrialized country during the 1970s and 1980s under military rule and later transformed itself into a democratic country after the democratization movement of the 1980s. The 1997 Financial Crisis and the following structural adjustment program led the country to further globalization and growth, but also brought a concentration of economic power in business conglomerates (*chaebols*) and big businesses, and an increasingly polarized society.

Facing severe inequality and poverty especially among the elderly and unemployed or irregularly employed youth in an economy with relatively weak social security nets compared to other developed countries, politicians, bureaucrats, businesses, and civil societies have been taking action and creating various policy frameworks to support marginalized groups by creating an environment more inclusive of those vulnerable populations, broadly labelled as "social economy".

4.1.1 Political System

Post-World War II South Korean Politics: From Military Rule to Democratization

Post-WWII South Korean politics has gone through major changes from colonial rule to military rule, and then to democratization. In 1910 the

Korean Empire was annexed to Japan and became its colony until the defeat of Japan in 1945. The occupation of the Korean peninsula was divided into the Soviet army in the Northern half and the U.S. army in the Southern half along the Thirty-eighth parallel north latitude. In 1948 the two parts separately declared independence as two republics, the Democratic People's Republic of Korea (North Korea) and the Republic of Korea (South Korea). The Korean War (1950-1953) caused millions of deaths, the division of families and immense damage to goods and infrastructure, and the ceasefire has left the two countries divided until now.

In post-war South Korea, anti-Communism became a national ideology under the first President Lee Seung-man (Mun 2015:75). President Lee was brought down by a student protest in 1960, but the short-lived democracy was overthrown by a coup-d'état in 1961 by an army group led by General Park Chung-hee. After a short period of military rule, Park became the civilian President of the Third Republic in 1963. In the 1970s, facing the challenge of a democratic movement led by Kim Dae-jung, Park put the country under martial law and introduced a new *Yushin* (meaning "renewal") Constitution in 1971.

A distinctive and enduring feature of South Korean politics is the strong confrontation between the so-called "progressive" and "conservative" camps. The former advocates for independence from U.S. influence, the unity of Korean people (unification with North Korea), and equitable economy. The latter defends the alliance with the U.S. and the free market economy. The two camps are strongly linked with regionalism within the South Korea, and the progressive was strong in the Southwest region (*Honam*), while the conservative had its stronghold in Southeast (*Yeongseo*),[1] with for example President Park originally coming from (and supported by) *Yeongseo* and his rival Kim Dae-jung from *Honam* (Onishi 2015:6-8).

After the assassination of President Park in 1979, the democratization movement became active during the 1980s, even with oppression from the military regime represented by the Gwangju Democratization Movement.[2] And following the 1987 Democratization Statement by President Roh Tae-woo, Kim Young-sam in 1993 became the first civilian and directly elected President after thirty years of military rule. The political landscape of South Korea changed further under two Presidents Kim Dae-jung (1998-2003) and Roh Moo-hyun (2003-2008) who took office after the 1997 Financial Crisis. As the first so-called "progressive" administrations, they increased the level of social welfare and also formally supported civil society organizations, including the enactment of the 2000 Nonprofit Private Organization Support Act (Akiba 2012:169; Isozaki 2004:67).

Later, pro-civil society policies were reversed by two Presidents from the conservative side, Lee Myung-bak (2008-2013) and Park Geun-hye. Park (2013-2017), the daughter of President Park Chung-hee, was impeached in 2017 after mass protests opposing a political scandal called "Choi Soon-sil gate," which referred to Park misusing her influence over business leaders to benefit a close friend. Moon Jae-in from the opposition party took office shortly after, becoming another President from the progressive side.

Local Governments and Decentralization

South Korean local governments have two levels. The first level is nine provinces and eight metropolitan / special cities. The second level is around 260 cities and districts dividing the first level. After the 1961 coup, local elections were suspended and the heads of local governments were appointed by the cabinet (for the first level) and provincial governors (for the second level) due to the concerns of the military government (Yeon 2012:50). After Democratization, Roh Moo-hyun introduced a decentralization policy to streamline the central ministries, and enacted the Special Law for Decentralization in 2004. The Law prescribed the principle of passing governmental functions to local governments, and expanding residents' participation in administrative processes including local referendums and volunteering (Cho 2007:27-30; Kang 2014:134). However, according to Yeon (2012:92-110, 173), the transfer of power and tax income to local government was delayed due to opposition from the members of the National Assembly who preferred to keep governmental funding as the source of their political power in their constituencies.

4.1.2 Socio-Economic Conditions
Economic Growth and the 1997 Financial Crisis
The severe destruction caused by the Korean War left South Korea as a largely agricultural country with widespread poverty, with a GDP per capita of only USD eighty-two in 1960 (Mun 2015:81-82). President Park Chung-hee turned the policy to a "developmental state" model, focusing on export-oriented industries under state-led economic planning, with support and loans from the U.S., Japan, and other Western countries (Seol and Haruki 2011:1). *Chaebols* (conglomerates) such as Samsung, Hyundai, and Daewoo were supported by the government as the drivers of the heavy and chemical industries (Hashiya 2000:366, 381-382). The annual growth rate reached an average of ten percent in the 1960s, which was called the "Hangang Miracle". The GDP continued to grow

steadily (other than a short period where it dropped after the 1978 oil shock) from six to eleven percent per annum, and the GDP per population increased from USD 592 in 1975 to USD 10,823 in 1995 (Hattori 2005:4, Mun 2015:95-98).

During this period of rapid industrialization, the population moved to urban areas, and the urban middle class formed a considerably large group in the society. Urban dwellers and rural poverty continued to be an issue, but at the same time macro income inequality was kept to a moderate level during the 1980s and 1990s, as the Gini coefficient was 0.31 in 1993 (Hashiya 2000:383, Hattori 2005:12).

The 1997 Economic Crisis caused a major change to the country. For the first time in eighteen years, the economic growth turned negative, -6.7 percent in 1998. After the crisis, financial and industrial system reforms were implemented as a condition of the IMF bailout program, including: i) re-organization of financial institutions and industries, ii) pro-market reforms and deregulations in industries, international trade, and labor liquidation, and iii) creation of social security nets to support the poor and unemployed groups (Hwang et al. 2016:6, Matsue 2014:280). As a result, South Korea's economy represented by *chaebols* recovered quickly after the crisis and became fit for global competition. However, because of changes in industrial structure and increasing globalization, although their asset size was growing,[3] they did not create jobs in South Korea as before and this led to increased unemployment and polarization (Kim 2013:18).

Through what was called "growth without employment," the unemployment rate jumped from 2.6 percent in 1997 to 8.6 percent in 1999, and the poverty rate from five percent in 1997 to twelve percent in 1999 (Kim 2008:104-105). Moreover, the quality of work was deteriorating.

Chapter 4: South Korea *137*

For instance, among the total number of workers (24.4 million) in 2010, only 10.5 million (forty-three percent) were regular employees, while the other 6.9 million (twenty-eight percent) were temporary or daily workers, 1.3 million (five percent) unpaid (referring to low-paid in-house workers in small family businesses), and 5.6 million (twenty-three percent) self-employed (Bidet and Eum 2011:72-73). Therefore, the poverty rate mostly continued to rise after the crisis, even with a low unemployment rate, as shown in Figure 4.1. In particular, severe poverty and social insecurity among groups including the elderly, women, and youth who are unemployed or have low-paid temporary jobs (called "working poor") became a serious issue in society after the 2000s (Defourny and Kim 2011:89; Kim 2016:156-158).[4]

Figure 4.1 Unemployment Rate and Poverty Rate in South Korea (1996-2007)

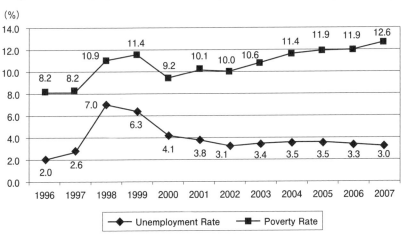

Source: Hwang et al. (2016:6)

Social Welfare Systems

Due to both a strong Confucian tradition and the policies implemented under the colonial rule of Japan, welfare in Korea was mostly covered by family systems (Hyun 2011:129; Kwon 1999:31-32; Matsue 2014:268). Social policies such as Livelihood Assistance Law (1961), National Health Insurance Act (1963), and National Welfare Pension Act (1973) were first introduced during the time of President Park Chung-hee. Nonetheless, the military government prioritized economic growth and showed reluctance to increase welfare spending as shown in their slogan "Growth First, Distribution Later," and the implementation of these programs was slow or suspended, with the coverage limited (Peng 2009).[5] For example, National Health Insurance was finally made a compulsory national scheme in 1977, but it covered only 26.7 percent of the population in 1981 and reached sixty-nine percent only in 1988. Other laws and schemes increased after the late 1980s, but the level of welfare expenditure remained at 5.7 percent of GDP in 1995, much lower than other OECD countries ranging between fourteen (Japan) to thirty-three (Sweden) percent. (Kim 2008:79-80, 87; Kwon 1999:93, 95, 143-144).

After the so-called "IMF Shock," with increasing business bankruptcies and layoffs, unemployed workers occupied streets and public spaces. Also, the rapidly aging society and low fertility rate, weakening family ties and increased participation of women in the job market all created an increasing demand for social services (Jang 2017:2598; Seol and Haruki 2011:4). The government implemented a variety of job creation programs and developed or expanded social support schemes under two "progressive" Presidents, Kim Dae-jung and Roh Moo-hyung (Kim 2008:104-116). Kim Dae-jung replaced the Livelihood Protection

Act with the National Basic Livelihood Security Act in 1999, overcoming opposition from bureaucrats by obtaining the strong support of civil society movements. The law introduced a welfare system which provides income and housing support for the poor based on universal coverage, and the proportion of beneficiaries (roughly 1.5 million persons) out of the total population reached 3.15 percent in 2007 (Jung 2009; Mendell et al. 2010:80-81). Still, following criticism from conservative politicians and bureaucrats that large-scale welfare spending will be a burden on the national economy, the welfare and pension payments remained low. As OECD statistics show, 2016 public social spending in South Korea is 10.4 percent of GDP, much lower than the OECD average of 21 percent (OECD 2016, Figure 4.2).

It also imposed a condition on the beneficiaries of the welfare payment who have the capability to work that they join a self-support program, to link welfare with work and to minimize spending (Matsue 2014:289). With the attempts of President Lee Myung-bak's administration to keep welfare expenditure to a low level, there continues to be a mix

Figure 4.2 Comparative Public Social Expenditure as a Percentage of GDP (1960, 1990 and 2016)

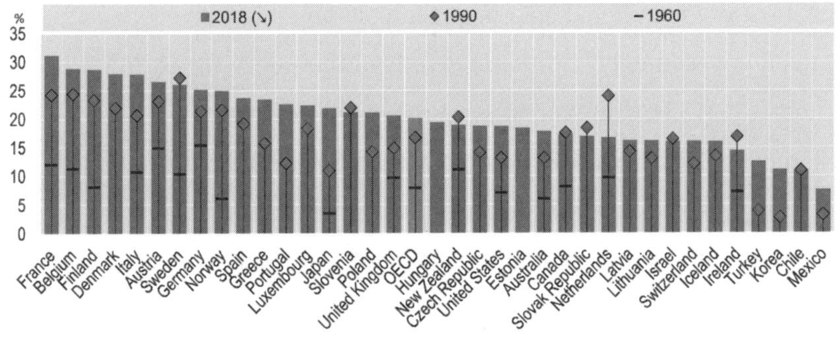

Source: OECD (2016)

of schemes that provide universal coverage (medical insurance, national pension scheme, long-term care insurance) but a low benefit level (Kim 2016:93-95; Takayasu 2014:12-13).[6]

4.1.3 Civil Society and Social Movements

During the period of military rule, the South Korean government took an oppressive attitude towards civil society organizations and allowed only government-led associations and cooperatives (Choi 2012:177-181).[7] However, anti-military social movements including labor unions, student movements, and Christian communities were strong during authoritarian rule (Kim 2000:60-61). They made a significant contribution to the democratization movement in the 1980s and later continued to exert political influence in the form of mass demonstrations, such as the 2008 demonstration against President Lee Myung-bak, or more recently the protests that led to the resignation of President Park Geun-hye in 2017.

It was after the 1990s when South Korean civil society changed its members from a state-led corporatism to a diversified range of associations (Tsujinaka and Choi 2004:136). During the presidency of Roh Moo-hyung (which was nicknamed "Participative Government"), civil society members had a major impact on policy advocacy, and also joined governmental committees to lead the policy formation process (Lee 2012:133). However, this group tends to work less on direct provision of social services. Park Won-soon, who was a lawyer and a social activist who led People's Solidarity for Participatory Democracy movements and later became the Mayor of Seoul Metropolitan Government, compares Korean and Japanese civil societies by saying "Korean society tends to think big and move dynamically, thus changes are fast. Japanese society's strength is that they are very detailed and can move on small experiments." (Park 2012:25)

There is another group in civil society in South Korea that has focused more on directly providing education, medical and other kinds of services since the time of the military regime. They are mostly connected to the business sector (such as Samsung Welfare Foundation or Asan Foundation established by the Chung family, the founders of Hyundai) or to religious groups, and basically respond to the government's requests to supplement social services (Kim and Hwang 2002:3). Onishi endorses this division by stating that South Korean civil society has two groups, i) the politically progressive group which work more on political advocacy and ii) the more conservative group which provides direct welfare services, based on the data collected by K-JIGS2 survey led by Tsujinaka (Onishi 2014:120-134).

4.2 Case Analysis: The Development of Social Economy

4.2.1 Background

Social Economy and Social Enterprise

In this chapter we deal with the development of social economy organizations including social enterprises, cooperatives, and other forms in South Korea as a social innovation initiative case study. According to scholarship led by Defourny and Develtere, who initiated EMES (*L'Emergence de l'Enterprise Sociale en Europe*), a key network for social economy / social enterprise research in Europe, the historic origin of social economy can be dated back to guilds, brotherhoods, and other forms of mutual-aid associations in medieval Europe and elsewhere in the world. Defourny and Develtere gave the definition of social economy as organizations that are based on the principles of: i) placing service to its members or the community ahead of making profit, ii) autonomy of management from governments, iii) a democratic decision-making process based on one vote per person, not based on ownerships, and iv) the primacy of people and work over capital in the distribution of revenue.[8] Since social economy, such as cooperatives, associations and other not-for profit organizations or shared economy, is based on collective values and norms, it is often placed in contrast with (or as an alternative to) capitalist economy (Defourny and Develtere 1999:4, 16, 19; Tomizawa 1999:27).

"Social enterprise (SE)", which describes an enterprise aiming for both social purpose and profit, is one of the legal entities used by social economy-related organizations among other schema such as cooperatives and nonprofit organizations. It is a legal status formally approved by legislation in a number of European countries such as Belgium (1996), Finland (2004), Italy (2005), the United Kingdom (2005), and Spain (2007). This legal status can be obtained by passing certain requirements to meet social purposes and the interests of different stakeholders, such as some restrictions on the uses of surplus (Mendell et al.2010:72; Yonezawa 2017:35-39).

Social Economy in South Korea

Apart from non-formal saving groups and the quasi-insurance system in traditional society, the consumer cooperatives which appeared in the 1920s during Japanese rule represented the first cooperatives in modern Korea. After independence, in the 1960s the South Korean military government set up agricultural, fishery, and forestry cooperatives and *Saemaul* organizations[9] in rural areas, and put them under state supervision.

Formal and informal credit unions and cooperatives emerged throughout the 1960s to 1980s as mutual support groups (Kim and Hwang 2002:3; Mendell et al. 2010:10-12). In the 1990s, a new wave of production community movements emerged to support the poor. Many of them failed (Akiba 2012:168), but others sustained and grew including Hansalim Consumer Cooperative, which was established in 1986 and grew to become a major distributer of organic products, having 540,000 households as its members and employing over 5,000 full-time staff in 2015 (Cheon 2018; Hansalim 2016:5). Other neighborhoods like Sungmisan *maul* (village) in Seoul started communal nurseries in the 1990s and this expanded to various cultural, housing upgrade, and other neighborhood activities (Kikkawa 2012:206-208).[10]

The Kim Dae-jung administration introduced the Self-support Program under the jurisdiction of the Ministry of Health and Welfare, based on the National Basic Livelihood Security Act in 1999 and operating under the slogan of "productive welfare." The program was an attempt toward work-welfare integration by engaging the poor in cooperative labor (as a condition for receiving welfare payments) with support from civil society organizations, some of them later becoming SEs (Akiba 2012:169; Shim 2011:159).[11] Another governmental initiative was the "Social Job" program introduced in 2003 by the Ministry of Employment and Labor (renamed the Social Service Work Program in 2007), which was a pilot program to create jobs and provide social services in ten specific fields including integrated education for disabled children, after-school classes, and forest conservation, with the support of civil society organizations (Hwang et al. 2016:8; Mendell et al. 2010:83-84).

Social activist Park Won-soon, while introducing the agenda of "social innovation"[12] through the Hope Institute, a nongovernmental organization which he led as the founder and an Executive Director (C. 2018), also became a social entrepreneur in the 2000s and launched the "Beautiful Store" to sell recycled goods and the "Beautiful Foundation" to collect donations from individuals and businesses and provide grants to civil society organizations and other social groups, by applying and modifying the models he saw in the U.K. (Oxfam), the U.S. (Goodwill and community foundations), and Japan (Seikatsu Club Co-op, WE21, and Workers' Collectives) (Park 2012:23; Ra 2015:iii).

4.2.2 Processes
The Creation of the 2006 Social Enterprise Promotion Act
The creation of the 2006 Social Enterprise Promotion Act was an epoch-making event as the first SE law in Asia. Since 2004, the Ministry of Employment and Labor (MoEL) has continued to propose making SEs a legal entity. The MoEL formed a taskforce in 2005 with academics (Dr. Hwang Deoksoon of Korea Labor Institute[13]) and civil society practitioners (Ms. Lee Eun-ae of Ewha Social Welfare Center / Work Together Foundation) to develop a draft of the SE Law (Lee 2012:134-135). Lee notes that the MoEL hastened to prepare the draft of the Law while Dr. Hwang and herself proposed conducting detailed research before drafting it (Lee 2012:134). This can be seen as a result of ministerial competition to have SEs fall under the jurisdiction of MoEL, not the Ministry of Health and Welfare who had been managing the Self-support Program since 2000. Hwang says the law was a "translated" version of the civil society agenda, which was aiming for a broader social economy concept with a European influence represented by Defourny and his group, such as democratic

governance or distribution principles (Hwang et al. 2016:5-6).

Social Enterprise Promotion Act and Its Scheme

The Social Enterprise Promotion Act (SEPA) passed the National Assembly in 2006 and came into effect in 2007. The aim of the law was to provide jobs to "vulnerable groups"[14] and integrate them into society, but it was missing the aspect of democratic governance emphasized by European literature. Thus, SEs were defined in the SEPA as "those companies that have been certified... that engage in business activities such as the production and sale of goods and services with the objective of achieving social goals, including providing vulnerable groups with social services or jobs, thus improving the local residents' quality of life" (Article Two, translated by Hwang et al. (2016:5)). Now the name "SE" can be used

Table 4.1 Types and Criteria of Social Enterprise in South Korea

Type of SE	Criteria
i. Work integration SE	SE that hires more than fifty percent[16] of employees from vulnerable groups
ii. Service provision SE	SE for which more than fifty percent[17] of service beneficiaries are from vulnerable groups
iii. Mixed-type SE	SE for which the percentage of beneficiaries and employees from vulnerable groups are both over thirty percent[18]
iv. Local community contribution SE (since 2011)	SE that focuses on contributing to one of the local communities decided by the Minister of Employment and Labor, and either more than twenty percent of employees or more than twenty percent of service beneficiaries are from that community
v. Others	Other types of SE which do not fall under one of the above categories and are approved by the MoEL's Expertise Committee

Source: Ra (2015:39-40)

only by organizations[15] certified by the MoEL, and is categorized into five different types with different criteria for each category (Table 4.1).

According to the Korea Social Enterprise Promotion Agency website (as of 2nd Nov. 2018), there are 2,030 SEs, 363 of them in Seoul.[19] Bidet and Eum analyzed the data of 251 SEs certified through 2009, and found that 43.8 percent were work integration type SEs, 29.2 percent were mixed, 14.7 percent were others, and 13.1 percent were service provision SEs. The areas of main activities for these SEs are social welfare (20.7 percent), environmental activities (16.3 percent), care services (13.1 percent), and others including childcare, education, health and culture (Bidet and Eum 2011:78; Kim 2015:189-196).

Certified SEs (and preparatory SEs) can enjoy generous support from the government, including i) tax benefits, ii) subsidies for personnel[20] and management costs, iii) loan provision, iv) expert consultation (management, finance, marketing, taxation, labor, and technology) and information provision, and v) priority purchasing of SE products by public organizations (Kim 2015:192-193; Ra 2015:40-46). Among these, the biggest benefit is the support of personnel costs. SEs can receive a maximum of five years of support (two years as a preparatory SE, three years as a certified SE) ranging from seventy to 100 percent of personnel costs. This accounted for ninety-seven percent of governmental expenditures on SE support in 2007, and seventy percent still in 2012. It created an incentive to be certified but also caused rent-seeking or cases of moral hazard such as SEs decreasing the numbers of employees after the initial five years period, or even going out of business once the period ended (Ra 2015:50-51).

According to Ra (2015:46, 49), 1,165 certified SEs are creating 22,533 jobs including 13,661 people (sixty percent) in vulnerable groups, including older people, unemployed youth, people with disabilities, North Korean defectors, and low-income people. However, sixty-five percent of SEs are work-integrated SEs, and only six percent are social service-providing SEs, far less in comparison to the sixty percent seen in Italy, and only one percent is local community service SEs. Hwang et al. (2016:5, 8) also note that the government's intention and support to use SE as its policy tool made SEs more dependent on the government. They also warn that when the majority of certified SEs are the work-integration type, it is not widely different from the Self-reliant Program focusing on job creation for the poor.

Proliferation of Schemes: Created Spaces

However, proliferation of legal entities and frameworks created by other governmental agencies created more spaces and options for people who are willing to participate in social economy organizations. After the enactment of the Social Enterprise Promotion Law, other ministries and local governments also established their own social economy organization schemes. Since 2010, Preparatory SE schemes were introduced to allow local governments and other ministries to approve organizations that do not yet meet the requirements for formal SE approval. In 2010, the Ministry of Interior and Safety created their own "*Maul* (community) Enterprise" scheme, and in 2011, the then-Ministry of Food, Agriculture, Forestry and Fisheries[21] developed another legal entity, the "Agriculture, Forestry and Fisheries Community Enterprise" (Kim 2016:195-196; Ra 2015:32).

One of the new articles of legislation that had the most significant impact is the Framework Act on Cooperatives (FAC) which was enacted in 2011 and went into effect in 2012. It was created as an umbrella law to allow setting up general cooperatives (aside from financial or insurance cooperatives) other than existing specific cooperatives (for example agricultural cooperatives) controlled by different government ministries.[22] The FAC created a specific category named a "social cooperative," which is a non-profit form of cooperative which does not distribute profit to its members. Cooperatives lacked the financial and other forms of support from the government that certified SE enjoyed, but the number skyrocketed, as 8,289 cooperatives were created in the first three years after the FAC was passed, including 362 social cooperatives. Their areas of operation differed from agriculture, manufacturing, environment and energy, education, culture, and social services. Around 100,000 people participated in cooperatives creation and invested KRW 130 billion (USD 118 million) (Jang 2017:2602-2605). Cheon (2018:76) and Hashimoto (2017:38-45) both describe the medical and elderly care services provided by cooperatives, which illustrates how these organizations are fulfilling the emerging needs of a rapidly aging society.

Hwang et al. (2016:13-16) also describe what they categorize as "alternative-economy SEs," which work on new issues (alternative energy, community-based finance, fair trade, community housing, local food, etc.) and have become drivers of social innovation. Most of them take the form of social cooperatives accepted by the FAC, which allows them to utilize democratic governance structures. This shows how civil society and communal actors in South Korea including those who are excluded from the old economic systems such as the self-employed, freelancers, early retirees, and unemployed youth are responding to the different opportunities opened to them and utilizing their entrepreneurial capacities (Jang 2017:2605).

Businesses[23]

Another group that strongly influenced social economy organizations was *chaebols* (conglomerates) and other big businesses. Hwang (2016) reports about several corporate social responsibility (CSR) initiatives that are funding or working with SEs to provide services to the disadvantaged population. Moreover, since 2014, LG and SK both established multimillion dollar funds to invest in SEs, especially in the "social venture" types of SEs rather than grassroots-oriented ones, partnering with Social Solidarity Bank and Korea Business School respectively.[24] Apart from business itself, there are several high-net worth individuals (the founders, or second- and third-generation family members) setting up investment funds, such as C Program established by five IT start-up billionaires,[25] or Root Impact from Chung Kyungsun of the Hyundai Group family.[26]

Also, apart from big companies sending their employees to SEs pro bono, SK, a major conglomerate group, has been supporting various postgraduate education and incubation programs for social entrepreneurs since 2013, including Social Entrepreneur MBA KAIST Business School (KAIST Social Entrepreneurship MBA Course / SK Social Entrepreneur Center),[27] Ewha Womans University (Social Economy Collaboration Courses for masters and doctorate degrees),[28] Hanyang University, Soonsil University, and Pusan National University (Happiness Foundation 2018:19). Some of them turn their own subsidiaries into social enterprises, such as Happynarae, which turned from a SK subsidiary working on maintenance, repair, and operation distribution, to a "social enterprise that helps social enterprises,"[29] or Beans and Berries coffee shop developed by Hanwha group, which changed into an SE.[30]

These contributions may be seen as support for social economy as part of large corporations' CSR activities, or their willingness to give back to society. Otherwise, this trend may also be viewed as a move to take advantage of the new business opportunities being created by social enterprises and other social economy organization schema.

Local Governments

As described above, local governments were given the power to approve preparatory SEs that contribute to their local communities in 2010. Some local government took further steps to promote the social economy environment in their district after the 2010 local elections, where the majority of governors and mayors came from opposition parties labelled the "progressive" side (Onishi 2014:241).

Chungcheongbuk-do province was the first to set their own ordinance to support social economy, and by 2012 had twenty-six certified SEs and thirty-four preparatory SEs. Nineteen are in service provision (domestic and care works), fifteen in production of goods, forty are private companies, and ten are nonprofits (Kim 2015:199).

The most likely candidate for champion of regional social economic policy in South Korea is Mayor Park Won-soon of the Seoul Metropolitan Government (SMG), who has already been mentioned above as a social activist / social entrepreneur. He became the Mayor in 2011 by special election and launched major reforms based on principles of participatory governance and social innovation (Lee 2017:18-19).

The SMG already had a SE promotion program since 2009, but a new "Comprehensive Social Economy Support Plan for the Creation of a Sustainable Economic Ecosystem" was launched in 2012 after holding discussions with stakeholders including local civil society members. This declared a clear shift "from supporting labor costs to forming an ecosystem,"[31] and since then related social economy policies have included: i) municipal ordinances to support fair trade (2012), cooperatives (2013), public purchases and marketing support for the products of social economy organizations (2014), social economy (2014), ii) the establishment of intermediary support organizations (Seoul Social Economy Center, Social Enterprise Development Center, Co-op Consultation Center,[32] Seoul Social Innovation Park), iii) the formation of peer networks for social economy organizations (Seoul Association of Social Enterprises, Seoul Social Economy Network, Seoul Community Enterprise Council, Seoul Regional Cooperative Association, and Seoul Community Business Association), iv) support for *maul* enterprise and communal activities, based on a model taken from the Sungmisan maul movement, v) the creation of a Social Investment Fund, vi) promotion of sharing economy, with a branding of "Sharing City," vii) the Local Social Economic Ecosystem Development Project, based on borough-level partnerships between local governments, social economy networks, and civil society, viii) the creation of Social Economy Zones, and ix) public purchases of social economy products (Seoul Innovation Center 2017; Seoul Metropolitan Government 2015).

Two major achievements were evident by 2015, according to SMG's report submitted to the Global Social Economy Forum (GSEF 2016). First was the growing number of social economy organizations - the SMG had 433 certified or preparatory SEs, 2,267 cooperatives, and 119 *maul* enterprises by the end of 2015. Figure 4.5 shows the annual increase since

2010, and we can see that the number of cooperatives is growing faster than SEs. Second was the increasing value generated by social economy organizations – an annual revenue of KRW 1.64 trillion (USD 1.5 billion) with 17,900 new jobs, both amounting to 0.4 percent of local GDP and employment.[33] Still, the support for SE labor cost subsidies decreased during this period, from KRW 22.7 billion for 400 SEs in 2011 to KRW 5.8 billion for 217 SEs in 2015 (GSEF 2016:24-27, 33, 36, 41, 49, 52, 81-83; Jung et al. 2015:8; Seoul Metropolitan Government 2015:13-14).[34]

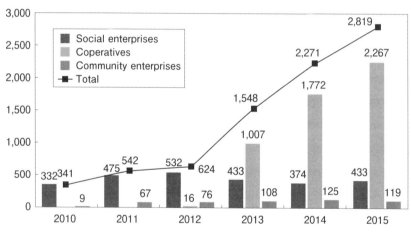

Figure 4.3 Annual Growth of Social Economy Organizations in Seoul

Source: Revised from GSEF 2015:34

Furthermore, Ra (2015:102-103) emphasizes that another aspect of the SMG policy of focusing on *maul* (community/village) is that it helps provide social capital in local communities, which is crucial for South Korean communities with weak capacity to conduct mutual-assistance activities.

Another change brought by Mayor Park is bringing his colleagues from civil society into the SMG systems and creating borough-level partnerships, which created closer coordination between the local government and civil society. However, there is also a concern that the capacity of civil society has been "drained" by the SMG.

It is significant that Mayor Park's ideas and the values behind these policies come from his background as a civil society activist. In an interview before he was elected as a mayor, he criticized the governmental approach of only focusing on the number of jobs or organizations created by SE support, and proposed building an ecosystem surrounding SEs and nonprofits. He also stressed that alternative values such as civic-centered, bottom-up, field-oriented, and local-oriented should be brought into policies. In the interview he also mentioned the influence of Geoff Mulgan of the Young Foundation in the U.K. and community development (*Machizukuri*) practices in Japan (Park 2012:14, 31).

4.2.3 Analysis
Process of Scaling

As a social innovation process, social economy in South Korea had appeared beginning in the 1970s, characterized as local efforts by social movements and communal activities. It held a marginal position in the economy until the 1997 Financial Crisis shocked the entire society and the need for social support and decent jobs became widely recognized. Together with concepts of social economy and social enterprise introduced from Europe, the idea gained wide support as a cure for the situation. Through two "progressive" Presidents with civil society backgrounds, Kim Dae-jung and Roh Moo-hyung, pilot programs managed by central ministries and implemented by civil society organizations were conducted in the early 2000s. Later, the MoEL established the SE certification scheme in

2006, but the top-down support system focusing on creating jobs resulted in inactive SEs doing little more than receiving government subsidies and employing people from disadvantaged groups. However, the emergence of different social economy organization schemes both on central and local levels, including cooperatives and *maul* enterprises, helped civil society actors to expand the ecosystem, together with the active involvement of some local governments such as the SMG led by Mayor Park Won-soon. As a whole, this is a process led mainly by a partnership of civil society and governments, with some key persons moving across sectoral boundaries, such as Mayor Park who turned from a civil society activist to the mayor of the biggest city in South Korea (Table 4.2).

Table 4.2 Scaling Patterns and Paths for Social Economy, South Korea

	Stage 1: Ideation	Stage 2: Incubation	Stage 3: Acceleration	Stage 4: Institutionalization
Government		(central ministries)	(MoEL) (SEPA)	(central / local govs.) (different legislations)
Business	Shared sense of crisis by "IMF Situation"		Inactive SE scheme under MoEL	Proliferation of schema (cooperatives, etc.) (private businesses and *chaebols*)
Civil Society	(communal / mutual support activities)	(pilot programs) (SE idea brought from Europe)		(different legal entities)

◯ minor / ◯ : major involvement from each sector
: conflict with the initiative / ☐ : multi-sectoral alliance
: new ideation / ☐ : legislation (central / local levels)

Different Origins of Social Economy Ideas and Its Manipulation

The idea of social economy in South Korea did not mean the same thing for different groups of people, and its origins were diverse. As we have seen, the tradition of anti-capitalist, anti-authoritarian social movements which existed since the military regime and engaged in cooperative labor as mutual support groups among the poor was one point of origin of the idea of social economy in South Korea (Jang 2017:2600-2601). However, it was not something acceptable to conservative groups in the society and was kept marginalized from the mainstream. One factor which helped to gain bipartisan support was blending the idea with concepts of social economy and SE introduced from European countries and the U.S. Since the early 2000s, a number of South Korean academics, policy-makers, and civil society activists visited Western European countries and picked up the concepts and practices of social economy, social enterprise, and cooperatives.

As a result, after the IMF crisis, both conservative and progressive groups began to expect SEs and social economy to solve the intensifying social issues in South Korea and agreed to support the initiative. Or in other words, because of the ideological confrontation between the two different camps while facing the need for increasing social services, agreeing was an easier option for both sides than taking other and more drastic measures, such as fully reforming the economic system or raising the level of social welfare provision by placing additional financial burden on the national economy. For instance, both the conservative and progressive party presented a draft for the Basic Law on Social Economy, but the values of social economy shown in the two drafts (increasing social services and welfare, creating employment, strengthening local communities, other contributions to societal public benefit, etc.) overlapped to a significant extent (Ra 2015:4-5).

This compromise led to the first legalization of SE in Asia (Defourny and Kim 2011:91; Hwang et al. 2016:4), and further development of social economy in South Korea. We can say that this was a creative manipulation of an idea, making it more acceptable for a wide range of social groups.[35] The idea was also fortunate to receive strong support from some key political figures including Kim Dae-jung, Roh Moo-hyung, and Park Won-soon, who had civil society backgrounds and strong affinity for the idea.

Government Control of Social Economy, or a Development of an Ecosystem?

Such bipartisan support created a favorable environment for social economy-related policies, but SEs also became a tool for governmental policy implementation and lost the independence from the state that was emphasized in the Western concept. Since the government-led SE scheme focused primarily on job creation for disadvantaged groups, together with generous subsidies from the government, it led to the inactiveness of certified SEs (Jang 2017:2602). It may be seen as a case of "state-led" top-down processes with a weak civil society, as some authors observe (Defourny and Kim 2011; Mendell et al. 2010).

Still, the proliferation of schemes for different social economy organizations, especially (social) cooperatives and the partnerships between some local governments and civil society provided broader spaces in society for different social groups, allowing for more innovative initiatives (Hwang et al. 2016:6). Therefore, if we look at the whole landscape of social economy in South Korea – not only the MoEL-certified social enterprises scheme – it appears more fruitful.

The Role of Local Ecosystems

It is still too early to decide whether local governments' social economy experiments will be able to take root and achieve the building of a more inclusive economy in regional areas. But at least compared to central government policies, it seems to be obvious that local governments are in a better position to reflect the reality of their communities and to develop local partnerships between different sectors. Perhaps the big question is whether there are grassroots initiatives to respond to the local governments' policies, as otherwise it may end up to be another government-driven and government-dependent program.

Although Jung et al. (2015:5) point out the "success" of "government-managed and government-directed" social enterprise promotion policies in the Seoul Metropolitan Government, we may need to see what will happen to the ecosystem that has been developed after Mayor Park leaves office.

4.3 Summary

Social economy development in South Korea was born out of the 1997 Financial Crisis and the following economic reforms (the so-called "IMF Situation") which created serious issues and concerns in a society with rather weak social safety nets, thus creating an opportunity for agreement on bipartisan social economy support policies to tackle the situation at hand. Ideas originating both in South Korean civil society and in European concepts framed the policies in central and local governments, with the support of political leaders who had civil society backgrounds. Although the social enterprise promotion policy led by the Ministry of

Employment and Labor seems to be ineffective, by focusing too much on creating employment and providing too many subsidies, the proliferation of schemes and legal entities for social economy organizations such as "social cooperatives", *maul* (community) enterprises, and others have created more options for people. Some local governments such as the Seoul Metropolitan Government are focusing more on creating a local environment that facilitates the activities of social economy organizations. These efforts seem to be more promising at the local level, with less governmental control but with supportive ecosystems and networks for social economy organizations.

---

1   For example, all the presidents during the military rule came from *Yeongseo*, which literally means "South of mountain" and includes areas such as Pusan and Ulsan. The region was also a strong supporter of President Park Geun-hye, the daughter of General / President Park.

2   The Gwangju Democratization Movement was a mass demonstration in Gwanju city suppressed by military corps in May 1980 which led to hundreds of deaths. Kim Dae-jung was sentenced to death by the military government (Hashiya 2000:399-400).

3   According to Kim (2013:2), the ratio of the five major *chaebols*' (Samsung, Hyundai Motor, SK, LG, Lotte) assets to GDP increased to 48.6 percent in 2010 from 32.8 percent in 2002.

4   According to Kim (2016:158), forty-seven percent of the elderly in South Korea fall under relative poverty, which is the highest in OECD countries.

5   For instance, President Park postponed the implementation of the National Pension Program after its introduction in 1973 due to a high inflation at the time. It was finally introduced in 1988 but still the coverage was limited, by only covering people who had made contributions for at least fifteen years (Kwon 1999:95, 98).

6   For example, the monthly payment from National Pension Scheme is KRW 96,400, less than USD100 (Takayasu 2014:61).

7   It was only in 2000 after democratization when the Act of Assistance of Non-Profit

Chapter 4: South Korea *159*

Civil Organizations was enacted and an entity for the general nonprofit organizations was legalized (Jang 2017:2595).

8   According to Defourny and Develtere, the latter two (democratic decision-making processes and possible distribution of profit to support the members) make the difference between social economy and nonprofit (based on Salamon and Anheier 1997) approaches (Defourny and Develtere 1999:19).

9   *Saemaul* means "new community / village." This was a government-led movement/organization in the 1970s to upgrade rural roads and infrastructure and to improve production through cooperative labor (Lim and Endo 2016:490; Hashiya 2000:383-384).

10 Cheon (2018:75-76, 79) describes the development of social economy organizations, the variety of services they provide (credit, consumer cooperative, production, community, logistics, education, medical and elderly care, cultural activities, and legal and professional services), and the network of such organizations as Wonju Cooperative Social Economy Network, which has 34 member organizations.

11 The self-support program created more than 58,000 jobs and training opportunities for vulnerable groups by the end of 2004, but only 5.4 percent of participants have managed to earn a minimum living wage and stopped receiving welfare spending (Kabumoto 2006:127-129)

12 The areas of SI the Hope Institute selected were: i) social invention, ii) community businesses, iii) community building, iv) social economy, and v) seniors' contribution to society (C. 2018;5).

13 Dr. Hwang is known as the person who introduced the concept (with reference to the U.K. and European experience) of SEs to South Korea through a presentation he made in a 2000 symposium (Lee 2012:133).

14 "Vulnerable groups" is a term used to describe people with low income, lack of education or work experience, the elderly, persons with disabilities, or those facing social discrimination.

15 Organizations that can apply for the certification are: i) associative corporations, ii) non-profit organizations, iii) consumer cooperatives, iv) welfare corporations (Bidet and Eum 2011:77).

16 Increased from thirty percent since 2017.

17 Increased from thirty percent since 2017.

18 Increased from twenty percent since 2017.
19 Korea Social Enterprise Promotion Agency website: http://socialenterprise.or.kr/kosea/company.do (In Korean, retrieved 2nd . 2018).
20 Three years for an SE (seventy to ninety percent of the personnel cost) and two more years for a preparatory SE (ninety to 100 percent), which means that a total of five years can be supported (Kim 2015:193).
21 Renamed the Ministry of Agriculture, Food, and Rural Affairs in 2013.
22 Since the military regime, different laws for specific cooperatives (Agricultural Cooperatives (1957), Fishery Cooperatives (1962), Forestry Cooperatives (1980), and Credit Cooperatives (1972)) existed (Ra 2015:30).
23 For this section I am extremely grateful to Ms. Park Sun Min, who kindly introduced various activities carried out by *chaebol*s and other business actors, as well as providing sources. However, the views and assessments of those activities are the author's own, including any misunderstandings.
24 *The Korean Herald*. 26 Oct. 2014 "LG Electronics, LG Chem to support social enterprises" http://www.koreaherald.com/view.php?ud=20141026000252 (Retrieved 24th Apr. 2018); The Happiness Foundation website: http://www.skhappiness.org/eng/innovation/training.do (Retrieved 24th Apr. 2018)
25 *Korea Joong-ang Daily*. 29 Nov. 2014 "Start-up Leaders Launch a Fund to Give Back" http://mengnews.joins.com/view.aspx?aId=2997911 (Retrieved 24th Apr. 2018)
26 Root Impact website: http://rootimpact.org/en/intro.php (Retrieved 24th Apr. 2018)
27 KAIST website: https://www.business.kaist.edu/programs/02040601 (Retrieved 24th Apr. 2018)
28 Ministry of Employment and Labor website: https://www.moel.go.kr/english/poli/poliNewsnews_view.jsp?idx=1424 (Retrieved 24th Apr. 2018)
29 Happynarae website: http://en.happynarae.co.kr/ (Retrieved 24th Apr. 2018).
30 *The Korean Herald*. 28th Mar. 2013, "Hanwa to Turns Cafes into Social Enterprise" http://www.koreaherald.com/view.php?ud=20130328000202 (Retrieved 24th Apr. 2018). The article says the Work Together Foundation is partnering with Hanwha to change the coffee shop chain into a social enterprise.
31 "From supporting labor costs to forming an ecosystem" page, SMG website: http://english.seoul.go.kr/policy-information/economy/social-economy/2-form-ecosystem/

(Retrieved 2nd Nov. 2018).
32 "What is co-op?" page, SMG website: http://english.seoul.go.kr/policy-information/economy/social-economy/3-co-op-city/ (Retrieved 2nd Nov. 2018).
33 This is still quite low compared to the targets that had been set (two percent of the GDP, eight percent of employment – benchmarked against the U.K. social enterprise sales (two percent) / employment (five percent) ratio). "What's a Seoul-type social enterprise?" page, SMG website: http://english.seoul.go.kr/policy-information/economy/social-economy/1-social-economy/ (Retrieved 2nd Nov. 2018).
34 GSEF (2016:34-35) explains the decrease as the period when SEs can receive support (up to three years for certified SEs, and up to two years for preparatory SEs).
35 Although as we saw in the case of SE certification, it may result in "losing" some of the core values of social enterprise / social economy as a result of negotiation between different groups.

Chapter 5 : Indonesia

5.1 Country Context

Indonesia, a country which boasts the fourth largest population in the world with over 250 million people and is the largest Muslim nation, has demonstrated a relatively stable democracy after the end of authoritarian rule under President Suharto at the end of the 1990s. It is also an example of a country whose unity has been successfully maintained despite its multiple ethnicities, languages, and cultures spreading over thirteen thousand islands (Figure 5.1), well-known as the Indonesian national slogan "unity in diversity (*Bhinneka Tunggal Ika*)".

Figure 5.1 Map of Indonesia

Source: Google Maps

After the end of Suharto's "New Regime" era, Indonesia went through a major governmental decentralization process – according to a report by the World Bank, a change from "one of the most centralized countries in the world into one of the more decentralized ones" (World Bank 2003). This chapter analyzes the process of government decentralization, including why it was needed, how it happened, and what emerged in its aftermath.

5.1.1 Political System

The territory of independent Indonesia came largely from the colonial Dutch East Indies, which were nationalized as colonies of the Netherlands in 1800 after being held by the Dutch East India Company. In the 1920s, nationalist movements in the colony represented by *Sarekat Islam* and its leader Oemar Said Tjokroaminoto started to aim for independence as Indonesia with "one nation, one people, one language," setting Malay (*Bahasa Indonesia*) which was used as a *lingua franca* in the region, as their national language, instead of Javanese, which was spoken by the biggest group in the population (Shiraishi 1997:7-12). *Pancasila*, which means "five principles" and consists of belief in God, Indonesian national unity, humanitarianism, Indonesian-style democracy through consultation and consensus, and social justice - were positioned by Sukarno and others including religious leaders as the philosophical foundation of the nation (Ramage 1997:11-13).

Following a brief occupation by the Japanese Army during WWII (1942-1945), Indonesian nationalists led by Sukarno declared independence in August 1945. After the four-year War of Independence, the Dutch finally recognized the sovereignty of Indonesia in December 1949 as a federation of independent states. But soon thereafter in August 1950, President Sukarno proclaimed the Republic of Indonesia to be a unitary state with a provincial system[1] to guard against the risk of disintegration and separatism (Beittinger-Lee 2009:39; Ricklefs 2008:269-270). After a short period of democratic experiment and freedom, Sukarno declared martial law under the rule of "Guided Democracy" in 1957, and drew closer to the Soviet and communist Chinese bloc, also leaning toward supporting the Indonesian Community Party (PKI). After 1965 September 30 Movement, military led by General Suharto crushed the PKI and eventually came into power.

The "New Order" regime under President Suharto (1966-1998) presented themselves as the champion of political stability and economic development, saving the country from the confusion of Sukarno's time. It lasted for thirty-two years and had a huge effect on Indonesia's political and socio-economic systems. Under Suharto as the highest patron, the New Order took a highly patrimonial and hierarchical, Java-centralized structure. The strong military involvement in politics (called "dual function" (*dwifungsi*) securing military seats in national and local parliaments) and the economy supported the system, and local governments were tasked only with implementing the projects coming from the central government. *Pancasila* was elevated to the national ideology, and by law all mass organizations were required to make it their sole principle, which meant denying any other cultural or regional identities as the basis for an organization. State dominance over society was accomplished by the restriction of political parties (PDI, PPP) and corporatism with Golkar (*Golongan Karya*), an association of groups, controlling social organizations and movements (Bunte and Ufen 2009:9-10; Shiraishi 2006;

Vatikiotis 1998:60-61, 92-95). Military centralization and the oppression of separatist movements and human rights violation continued in areas including Aceh, Iriyan Jaya, and East Timor, which was occupied in 1975 (Kimura 2013:49).

Local governments consist of provinces (*provinsi*), and districts (*kabupaten*) and cities (*kota*) under the province. There are also sub-districts (*kecamatan / distrik*) and villages (*desa / lelurahan / nagari / kampung*, etc.) under the districts and cities. During the Suharto era, local governments were, as prescribed by the Law No. 5/1974 on Standard Regional Governance, basically a subordinate of central governmental offices and lacked the funding or personnel to implement their own policies. Villages were also defined by Law No. 5/1979 on Standard Village Administration to be a uniform organ (based on the village (*desa*) model in Javanese society) to implement governmental projects and to mobilize local people (Shimagami 2012:72-76)

Suharto's long-lasting New Order regime came to an end in 1998 after the Asian Financial Crisis, upon which reform (*reformasi*) and democratization (*demokratisasi*) processes including revising constitutional and legal frameworks and governance structures, and installation of free elections, freedoms of speech, press, and associations took place (Bunte and Ufen 2009:23). After a few years of political confusion during three short-termed Presidents, Bacharuddin Jusuf Habibie (1998-1999), Abdurrahman Wahid (1999-2001), and Megawati Sukarnoputri (2001-2004), administrations led by President Susiko Bambang Yudhoyono (2004-2014) and Joko Widodo (well known as "Jokowi", 2014-) finally brought back a relatively stable political environment (Shiraishi 2010:9).

5.1.2 Socio-Economic Conditions

When Indonesia became an independent nation, its economy was still largely based on colonial plantations and the mining industry, and foreign enterprises controlled strategic parts of the country. In 1960, President Sukarno initiated the "*Benten*" Plan, which means "fortress," to build national industries within a foreign-dominated economy, but it was soon abandoned amongst political and diplomatic confusion (Hondai and Nakamura 2017:21-22).

Economic development advanced greatly during Suharto's time, with the help of Suharto's advisory team of Western-educated economists and technocrats,[2] high oil prices in the 1970s, and foreign investors and local (mostly Indonesian Chinese) entrepreneurs like Liem Sioe Liong (also known as Sudomo Salim, a close friend of the Suharto family), who worked as agents for both Indonesian political elites and foreign businesses. Under so-called "crony capitalism", the real GDP annual rate of growth from 1971 to 1981 averaged 7.7 percent (Ricklefs 2008:326, 344).

The growth under the New Order regime continued in the 1990s, averaging eight per cent annual GDP growth until 1996. But the Asian Financial Crisis starting in 1997 caused a depreciation of the Indonesian Rupiah and led to severe recession and inflation.[3] The Crisis triggered the fall of the New Order regime. Consequently, Indonesia went through major reforms of its monetary, exchange rate, and fiscal policies and structural adjustments to the banking sector and industries under the IMF Recovery Program until 2003 (Lane et al. 1999:4-5; Michida 2005:58-61). Under the Yudhoyono administration which began in 2004, the economic confusion was finally resolved, and growth rates recovered to around five to six percent per annum from 2005 to 2014 (Hondai and Nakamura 2017:26).

Reflecting the trait of Indonesia being an archipelago stretching over 5,000 kilometers in area, the diversity of cultures, ethnicities, and religions brings a certain amount of difficulty to the distribution of resources, balancing of ethnic representation, and ensuring equality across regions. In particular, relations between Java, an island which accounts for fifty-nine percent of the population, and other outer islands continued to be a potential source of tension (Shiraishi 2010:9-11). According to the World Bank national accounts data, Indonesia's GDP per capita (constant 2010 USD) in 2016 is USD 3,974, up from USD 2,084 in 1998, which makes it a middle-income country according to the World Bank classification.[4] By the national standards, the poverty rates are 9.9 per cent in urban areas and 16.6 percent in 2010, both lower than 21.9 percent and 25.7 percent in 1998. Still, the poverty rates differ between provinces, where the rural poverty rate reaches over twenty-five percent in Papua and West Papua, and around fifteen percent in Ache, Maluku, and East Nusa Tenggara in 2009, which are all from "outer island" areas (Hondai and Nakamura 2017:107-115).[5]

5.1.3 Civil Society and Social Movements

Pre-modern societies in Indonesia had self-help and mutual support groups and associations, such as burial associations (*kelompok kematian*), funeral insurance groups (*beras perelek*), saving and credit groups (*arisan*), and mutual-help (*gotong royong*) groups. In the early 20th century, modern associations like Budi Oetomo (1908), Muhammadiyah (1912) or Nahdlatul Ulama (1926) were formed to support education, and other religious and social issues in colonial societies, and some of them became involved in political and independent movements (Hadiwanata 2003;

Nakamura et al. 2001:13).

The 1950s after Indonesia's independence saw a short period of associational freedom, but under the New Order corporatism, social organizations remained weak and fragmented. But after the 1970s, some NGOs such as Bina Desa or Lembaga Bantuan Hukum were established by the growing middle-class groups and slowly grew. The number of NGOs grew from a few hundred in 1970s to 3,000 in the 1980s, and to 6,000 by the mid-1990s (Beittinger-Lee 2009:70). This was made possible because the government also needed the contribution from these "development NGOs" to implement governmental development programs, for which the government itself did not have sufficient capacity. NGOs also received support from international donor agencies. In the 1980s and 1990s, advocacy NGOs (WALHI, ELSAM) and NGO forums (INGI, INFID) were established and raised "democratization" (*demokratisasi*) as their agenda. Abdurrahman Wahid (1999-2001) became the first president who was also a civil society leader (as the leader of Islamic organization Nahdlatul Ulama). Some authors observe that civil society organizations and social movements are impacting the policy-making processes at a central level in post-Suharto Indonesia with examples such as anti-corruption, the 2011 Social Security Law, and the 2014 Village Law (Nyman 2009: 252; Okamoto 2015a:169-171). However, NGOs' presence and mobilization power in local communities are rather weak due to their limitations including their dependency on foreign donors, lack of capacity and wide support from the public, and their own corruption (Beittinger-Lee 2009:123; Honna 2013:153).

It is worth mentioning the importance of Muslim civil society or organizations, which are growing in post-Suharto Indonesia as the providers of education and community services (Nyman 2009: 259). Beittinger-Lee (2009:26-27) points out that even the concept of civil society is becoming divided into a more Western-oriented way that stresses independence from the state (*Masyarakat sipil / warga*) and a more Islam-oriented way (*Masyarakat madani*), which sees the ideal form of social and political frameworks in the seventh century city-state of Medina (Azra 2006:39-40; Miichi 2004:123).

5.2 Case Analysis: Governmental Decentralization
5.2.1 Background

B. J. Habibie, who took over as President after Suharto's resignation, undertook major political reforms. These included the release of political prisoners, securing the freedom of the press, political parties, trade unions, and other associations, free election, and considering the autonomy or independence of military-occupied East Timor. In the absence of military/authoritarian rule, the pressure from long-continuing regional separatist movements were becoming strong, especially in Papua, East Timor, and Aceh. There were also inter-group conflicts between ethnic or religious groups (Ricklefs 2008:382-390). Such risk of national disintegration was the major cause of decentralization. Also, some politicians and bureaucrats in the central government supported the idea of transferring power to local governments, with backing from some international financial institutions and bilateral donors (IMF, the World Bank, the Asian Development Bank, and German DFZ) after the economic crisis, to improve the quality of public services and to increase accountability by bringing the services closer to the people (Buehler 2010:269; Hadiz 2010:10; Schulze and

Sjahrir 2014:186-187).

5.2.2 Processes
1999 Decentralization Reform

It was also Habibie's concerns about separatism which led to the radical decentralization process. And being from South Sulawesi, one of the outer islands, Habibie publicly blamed the Java-centrist state system (Buehler 2010:268). In the special session of the People's Consultative Assembly (MPR) in 1998, an ambitious Decentralization Plan was approved, and in May 1999, two laws to fundamentally change the relationships between the central and local governments were passed (Lewis 2014:136).

The first was Law No. 22/1999 on Regional Government, which granted autonomy to local governments. It transferred most governmental functions - apart from national defense, foreign affairs, finance, justice, religion, and few others saved for the central government - to the local governments, which were district and city level governments.[6] It also outlined the governance mechanisms of local governments and councils and released the district level government from the supervision of provincial level government (Holtzappel 2009:6-7, 11).

The second was Law No. 25/1999 on Intergovernmental Fiscal Balance. It stated that the central government was to pass a minimum of twenty-five percent of its revenue to local levels, of which ten percent goes to provincial and ninety percent to district-level governments (Buehler 2010:267-268). So far, nearly forty percent of central government expenditure has been transferred to local governments, and the revenue of local governments grew from IDR fifty-seven trillion (USD seven billion) in 2001 to IDR 120 trillion (USD fourteen billion) in 2009 in constant 2000 prices (Lewis 2014:137-138).[7] And in the 2016 Governmental Budget Plan, the expenditure of local governments was IDR 782 trillion (USD fifty-two billion), for the first time ever higher than the central ministries' expenditure of IDR 780 trillion (ARC 2017:64-65).

These two laws took effect in January 2001. The reform was done as a "big bang," without providing much time for preparation (Nasution 2016:1). Together they increased the political and financial autonomy of the local governments, mainly at the district (*kabupaten*) and city (*kota*) level. Also, national governmental offices at local levels (apart from courts and religious offices) were abolished and approximately two million people, or two-thirds of central governmental staff, were transferred to the local levels. And for the first time, the creation of new provinces, districts, and sub-districts was allowed.[8]

After 2005, district heads (*bupati*) were directly elected instead of being elected by the local council, and by 2010 all heads were replaced with directly elected ones (Schulze and Sjahrir 2014:193). Democratization through election was expected to improve vertical accountability to the local constituency.

Furthermore, in 2014 the government issued a new Law No. 6 / 2014 on Villages to increase the responsiveness of local governments to community needs. Around 74,000 villages are now granted autonomy from upper-level local governments and given access to a village fund (IDR 1 billion, which is approx. USD 75,000) per year directly from the national budget (Antlov et al. 2016; Reality Check Approach 2016). This was made possible by the long-lasting campaigns of village head groups requesting more funding for villages and village officials, and other activists demanding rights and cultural autonomy for indigenous communities as well as land rights (Shimagami 2012:99; Vel et al 2017).

Attempt at Re-centralization

The drastic decentralization process caused a certain amount of confusion and unintended issues. Some of the major ones were: i) the arbitrary policies and decisions made by the newly-elected local government heads without paying much attention to legal frameworks, or without coordination or consultation with the neighboring local governments and upper levels, ii) corruption and misappropriation of government resources by governors, mayors and local council representatives who could choose or dismiss the local government heads, iii) the creation of new provinces and districts or cities in order to obtain the resources allocated to it, which often showed poor performance in their administration, and iv) the creation of new departments and positions at the local government and the increase of personnel and administrative expenses (Ikawa 2015:35-36; Okamoto 2012:46-47).

Therefore, in 2004, Law No. 32/2004 on Regional Government and Law No. 33/2004 on Intergovernmental Fiscal Balance revised the two 1999 Laws. The former, while establishing that local government heads were to be elected through direct election, also placed some limits on the autonomy of district / city governments and set some policy areas that they are obliged to implement together with provincial and central levels. It also prescribed the supervisory power of provincial and central governments over lower level governments. The latter provision gave the upper level governments the authority to approve local governments' budgets and local taxes and fees (Ikawa 2015:30). It was a response from the central government (mainly the Ministry of Internal Affairs) to re-balance and fine-tune intergovernmental power relationships, and to secure the quality of services provided by the local governments (Mahi 2014:63).⁹

Also in 2014, after Jokowi was elected as the new President, 2014 Law 23/2014 was passed by Parliament, establishing that local government heads were to be elected by local parliaments, not by direct elections. This caused a huge amount of discontent and opposition in both online and off-line public debates, and Yudhoyono and Jokowi issued Presidential Orders / Laws to maintain the direct election of local government heads. This case showed a conflict of interest between the major political parties who sought to control local government heads through their majority in local parliaments, and the general public who had shown their preference for the direct-election system since 2005 (Ostwald et al. 2016:143).

Results: Accomplishments

There were some significant achievements as a result of the decentralization process. First, Indonesia avoided the feared disintegration of the nation and "balkanization" and the country stayed united with a limited amount of violence, other than ex-Portuguese East Timor's independence in 2002 (Kimura 2013:1). Shiraishi (2010:19) points out that this stability has been brought about partly by the birth of new provinces and districts / cities, in which a single ethnicity can more easily have a majority and control resources, thus reducing the chances of inter-ethnic / religious conflicts.

Second, decentralization made it possible to maintain cultural and regional identities for the first time in decades. The creation of new provinces and districts helped, at least for the new ethnic majorities that were created by the reshuffling (for example, the Banten people who had remained a minority compared to the Sunda people in West Java province before the creation of Banten province), to reclaim cultural and ethnic identity after the long years of oppression during the New Order period (Schulze and Sjahir 2014:191).

Third, it opened up an opportunity for public participation and local-level democracy (Suharyo 2009:96). Mahi also points out that elections in Indonesia have been conducted successfully, with a minimal level of hostility and violence (Mahi 2014:59-60).

And fourth, although arguably, it has improved the delivery of public services by bringing it down closer to the people (Ostwald et al. 2016:140). Schulze and Sjahir (2014:196-198, 201-203) conclude, based on the extent of district-level infrastructure (middle schools, community health centers (*buskesmas*), and percentage of village with paved roads) and service delivery (net enrollment rate of secondary school children, percentage of births attended by professional staff, and percentage of households with access to clean water), that decentralization has increased local governments' responsiveness to the local population in all three of these areas. Mahi (2014) also highlights the improvement of local welfare and the efficiency of public goods provision brought by decentralization, which is measured by i) regional economic growth, ii) the changes in the local Human Development Index, iii) significant increase in education and health spending from local government budgets, and iv) the availability of local public facilities and infrastructure such as the number of local hospitals, roads, and schools especially in the outer island areas. Shimagami (2012:88) witnesses improved performance in village-level local administrative services, though seeing differences between regions.[10]

As a result of the direct election of local government heads, a number of "reformist" heads who implement innovative policies have emerged at different levels. Miharti et al. (2016) argue that the decentralization processes created more autonomy and space for decision-making for local governments and community health centers, and some of them managed to develop their own innovative policies like universal health coverage in Jembrana district, or introducing computer ultrasonography at Jagir, Surabaya city with the cooperation of both internal and external stakeholders such as politicians (mayors) and private hospitals and clinics. Among many others like Mulyadi Jayabaya in Lebak district, President Joko Widodo was also first known as the reformist mayor of Solo city for his innovative policies such as administrative reforms and free medical services and holding open dialogue with local people (Honna 2013:62-63; Okamoto 2012:58-59).

Results: Limitations and Controversies

However, there are some limitations in the results as well as unintended side effects and controversial paradoxes as the result of decentralization. Research works on the subject tend to agree that the capacity of local governments remains largely weak especially when they are newly established, and reform initiatives are dependent on individual leaders (Buehler 2010:281; Lewis 2014:143). During the long years of the New Order regime, local governments were not asked to develop their own plans, policies, or projects, or to handle complicated financial arrangements with the central government or negotiations with foreign companies. Thus, many are not able to fully utilize the opportunities opened up by decentralization, even after a variety of support projects from the central government and international donor agencies. A report issued by USAID in 2009, among other authors, says that the quality of public service delivery has not improved significantly, or not as much as they expected it to (Pratikno 2011; Schulze and Sjahrir 2014:203; USAID 2009:90). Some authors point out that local governments spend too much (26.7 percent of the revenue in 2009) on general administration, which is higher compared to international best practice – or that it is sometimes misused for expensive buildings and cars, and overstaffing, and sees this being caused by a lack of downward accountability of local governments towards their consistencies (Lewis 2014:145, 150; Schulze and Sjahrir 2014:199).

Still, the majority of local citizens seem to be satisfied with the quality of services provided, which may be partly reflecting their attachment to local identities as well as low expectations for public service delivery (USAID 2009:164). According to a 2007 AsiaBarometer Survey, they also show greater trust in local governments (29.3 percent)[11] than the central government (23.2 percent) (Pratikno 2011:279). According to Lewis (2014:150), a large-scale survey found that seventy-eight, ninety, and eighty-five percent of respondents answered that they are at least somewhat satisfied with the quality of local administrative, health, and educational services respectively. As seen above in the case of the 2014 Local Government Law, they are even responding to some recent efforts made by the central government or political parties to re-centralize power, showing their contentment with the current electoral and administrative systems.

Moreover, the new institutional settings and systems at the local level have been dominated by a "new alliance" of New Order elites who were either bureaucrats, appointed governors / mayors, or military officer during the Suharto era, together with local businesspeople[12] who have connections with local governments, and local aristocrats and nobilities (Hadiz 2010:92-94; Schulze and Sjahrir 2014:191).[13] They have reinvented themselves as party politicians to fit into new election systems (Mahi 2014:62; Mietzner 2013:111-113). Often local gangsters (*preman*) and/ or militia – what Beittinger-Lee calls 'uncivil society' (non-governmental groups who have a negative influence on society, such as those involved in drug dealing, human trafficking, or terrorism) - are used as their muscle, and some of them like Syamsul Arifin who was a *preman*, even became elected politicians (a *bupati* and later the Governor of North Sumatra) themselves (Beittinger-Lee 2009:20, 77; Ford and Pepinsky 2014).

Okamoto provides a detailed observation on how the late Chasan Sochib controlled the politics of the newly established Banten province. He was the leader of *jawara*, a local martial arts group and the owner of a construction business with strong connection with Golkar and the Army. His family ultimately held the positions of provincial governor and four district/city-level governors or vice-governors in the province. They used the identity and culture of the Banten people, violence and threats, and bribes and benefits through governmental projects to mobilize political support and control political parties, politicians, and bureaucrats. They even established their own NGOs and foundations to improve their reputation, while oppressing civil society groups and media who were against them (Okamoto 2015b).

These local elites and gangsters managed to transform themselves into democratic politicians or put their agents in the post-*reformasi* local governmental systems to capture the resources allocated to local governments. As money politics in regions grew, corruption such as kickbacks to politicians are becoming a normal practice, and corruption is "decentralized," but no less intense (Morishita 2015:29-30; Schulze and Sjahir 2014:189). Those who cannot play this game of money politics, such as farmers or workers, are excluded from these systems (Hadiz 2010:95).

And as the use of "identity politics" is increasing, it is becoming easier to condemn political opponents based on their ethnic or religious background – something which was carefully avoided in the history of the Republic of Indonesia. The most prominent case is Basuki Tjahaja Purnama (known as "Ahok") who became the governor of Jakarta after Jokowi left to take his position as President. A Christian of Chinese descent, he was known as a "reformist" governor but was charged with blasphemy for mentioning a verse from the Quran during his campaign, causing mass uproar from Islamic groups (*The Diplomat* 2017). If this kind of logic of playing identity politics to divide groups between "indigenous" and others, for instance to provide jobs first to "local" Betawi people in Jakarta as Honna (2013:184) reports, takes a greater hold in the future, it may ultimately damage the unity of the nation.

5.2.3 Analysis

As observed above, governmental decentralization started as a "top-down" process, coming as an emergency operation from the central government to keep the country from disintegrating and international organizations expecting administrative efficiency and improved transparency (Morishita 2015:27).

After 18 years since its implementation, the decentralized government and democratic election systems seem to have already taken deep root in the country – partly as a result of the strong alliances between

Chapter 5: Indonesia *179*

local elites and other groups (businesses and "uncivil society" groups) to win the seats of elected local government heads and a majority of local councils and to control the resources allocated to local administrations (Table 5.1). Although this system excludes powerless civil society and ordinary people, as Honna states, a "paradox of democratization," democratization and decentralization in Indonesia are stable because the groups who hold a vested interest and power in local communities are basically happy about the situation and not willing to overthrow the system.[14] As Honna points out, "it would have been more unstable if it was cleaner, more egalitarian and transparent" (Honna 2013:200). Therefore, we may say that this is an example of a top-down approach finding strong response at the bottom and thus consolidating the initiative, no matter how vicious it may be.

Table 5.1 Scaling Patterns and Paths for Governmental Decentralization, Indonesia

	Stage 1: Ideation	Stage 2: Incubation	Stage 3: Acceleration	Stage 4: Institutionalization
Government	※ (Centralized system during the Suharto regime)		○ (central gov.) (1999 Laws)	○ (local govs.)
Business		Risk of regional separation after the crisis	Top-down policy with resource redistribution gets locally embedded	○ (local businesses)
Civil Society	○ (requesting as a reform agenda)			○ (support from local people and "uncivil society")

○ minor / ◯ : major involvement from each sector
※ : conflict with the initiative / ▢ : multi-sectoral alliance
💭 : new ideation / ▢ : legislation (central / local levels)

However, decentralization has not yet significantly changed the quality of public service provision as expected due to various reasons, such as the limited capacity of local governments, lack of vertical accountability to the local communities, and the weak pressure to perform from local citizens and civil society. Thus, we have to say that this was a success in term of its stability / embeddedness, but not fully achieving the expected results.

A part of the reason why the elections are not holding local government officials accountable as expected is the marginalized role NGOs or other civil society organizations (CSOs) play in local politics. Indonesian NGOs played a significant role during the *reformasi* and *demokrasi* period to challenge the legitimacy of the New Order regime and to fill in the gaps after the collapse of authoritarian rule, and they tend to influence national level policies as we saw in the 2014 Village Law process (Beittinger-Lee 2009:69-71, 123). Still they are largely based on the urban middle-class and do not have many links to influence the local population, or local politics.[15] Without a wide basis of support, they depended heavily first on Suharto's developmental programs and later on foreign donors' funding to implement their agendas (Beittinger-Lee 2009:129-130; Okamoto 2015b:150).

For the decentralization process to bring the desired results, first it needs more eyes and pressure from the public, with the support of civil society to set policy agenda, as well as to improve the capability and accountability of local governments. Okamoto (2015b) finds hope in the way local activists in Banteng province worked with an anti-corruption NGO in Jakarta, finally leading to the national Corruption Eradication Commission's arrest of Chasan Sochib's children for bribery. Then there may be more chances for regional governments to rightly utilize the political, administrative and financial authority given to them, and to produce local-level service innovations as they already do in some areas.

With all the limitations, when we examine the process of governmental decentralization as a social innovation process, we can see some significant changes compared to the pre-*reformasi* era such as i) the change of the central-local relationships and resources allocation, ii) the level of service provision, and iii) the people's attachment to the new system. First, local people now have the power to replace local government heads through election. Second, they have various grounds to request a certain amount of services and accountability from local governments, ranging from commitments made by the candidate during election campaigns, a national service standard which has a legally binding force, and a national agency for anti-corruption. Third, there is the potential for local government heads who were elected by local people to implement reforms which are rather independent from the local power elites.

These may be potential effects rather than the reality at the moment, but when we see how the public responded to the legislated termination of direct election of local government heads in 2014 and how it pushed back the decision, we can say that these changes have already gained a certain amount of legitimacy in the society and people's mindsets. In addition to sustained changes and improved welfare, we shall conclude that the most prominent change brought by decentralization is the people's side winning such legitimacy. And we should also be aware of civil society's contributions to lead these changes by proposing the value of decentralization, democratization, and anti-corruption, even when they do not have much influence at the local politics level.

5.4 Summary

The drastic shift of governmental decentralization happened as a top-down measure to avoid possible regional revolts and independence after the end of the New Order rule led by Java-centric Suharto and his regime. As a result of the major shift of financial, human, and administrative resources from central to local governments, locally elected officials are at least in some regions starting to provide public services in better quality, and moreover the new systems of decentralization and local democracy seems to be already embedded as a value in people and society. However, the local level "alliance" comprises from local elites including politicians, military officers, and leaders in Suharto-era as well as newly established businesses and oligarchy, and "*premans,*" gangsters who benefit from administrative systems and local democracy. Without a check from the upper governmental / political institutions or civil society, they can enjoy the resources newly made available by decentralization. It seems that as far as the power balance works, the "alliance" can make an SI initiative quite stable – no matter whether it is virtuous or vicious in nature.

---

1 Later the local government systems were made uniform by Suharto with Law No.5/1974 on Standard Regional Governance and Law No. 5/1979 on Standard Village Administration (Holtzappel 2009:8).

2 The members of the Presidential Economic Advisory Team set up in 1966 were called the "Berkeley Mafia" and later appointed to different ministerial positions under the Suharto regime (Hondai and Nakamura 2017:22).

3 The GDP fell 13.1 percent in 1998 and it took until 2003 to return to the pre-crisis level (Michida 2005:60).

4 "GDP per capita (constant 2010 US$) All Countries and Economies" page, The World Bank website: https://data.worldbank.org/indicator/NY.GDP.PCAP.KD?end=2016

&start=1960&view=chart&year=1998 (Retrieved 2nd Nov. 2018)

5   Please note that these rates are based on a new governmental definition on poverty which began in 1996, based on different consumption baskets data. According to World Bank data, the poverty headcount ratio, defined as less than USD 1.9 a day (2011 PPP), was 6.8 percent in 2016. "Poverty & Equity Data Portal: Indonesia" page, The World Bank website: http://povertydata.worldbank.org/poverty/country/IDN (Retrieved 2nd Nov. 2018)

6   The reform gave district / city level the most power, budget, and human resources. Provinces were largely bypassed since they were seen as a potential threat to national integrity by becoming a unit that could seek independence (Buehler 2010:268).

7   "IDR/USD calculated by 2000 rate", Trading Economics website: https://trading-economics.com/indonesia/currency (Retrieved 2nd Nov. 2018)

8   As a result, the numbers of provinces and districts/cities have increased from twenty-seven and 292 respectively in 1999 to thirty-four and 477 in 2010 (Schulze and Sjahrir 2014:191).

9   Later the central government created the "Minimum Service Standard" (*Standar Pelayanan Minimal*) in 2008 to set minimum requirements for services provided by local governments (Okamoto 2012b:54).

10 However, we have no way to identify whether performance improved *because of* the decentralization process, or it improved *even with the (negative) impact of* decentralization. In other words, it may be true that performance may have been even better if Indonesia had kept its centralized system. But here we shall follow the scholarship noting the decentralization of Indonesia as a "successful case" of improving government service standards, compared to other countries.

11 Comparing the AsiaBarometer 2004 and 2007 surveys, respondents' trust in local governments rose from 26.6 percent to 29.3 percent during the period. Trust in the central government dropped from 29.0 percent to 23.2 percent. Trust in local governments in Indonesia is also relatively higher than the regional average of 18.5 percent. It is interesting that the respondents also stated that the governments' performance in responding to issues is getting worse (economy, corruption, and crime) or not changing (human rights, quality of administrative service, and environmental protection) during the same time period (Pratikno 2011:278-280).

12 President Joko Widodo (Jokowi) himself is well-known example of a local

businessperson who climbed up the ladder as a politician, but Lane criticizes that his "hollow" campaign shows that he does not have a new and progressive agenda (Lane 2014: vii-ix). Okamoto (2012:59) reports that the local merchants who were removed by then-Mayor Jokowi from the center of Solo city to a market area on the outskirts had to close their businesses and questions the usefulness of his populistic approach.

13   Beard and Phakphian (2012) have also reported a similar elite capture of community resources and the lack of transparency through community-based planning initiatives in a local community in Northern Thailand.

14   Hasegawa (2014) argues that local elites are starting to cover the request from non-elites to win fierce competition, and providing free education / health services and improving government efficiency as a policy. Perhaps these policies are helping satisfy local people about the result of decentralization.

15   According to a 2007 AsiaBarometer survey, Indonesians show much stronger trust in religious organizations (48.5 percent) than NGOs (21.2 percent) (Pratikno 2011:280).

Chapter 6 : Conclusion

This chapter responds to the research questions set in the Introduction and presents findings from the case studies, including the two-axes model of SI scaling. Then it discusses what may be some contributions this study can make to the research of social innovation theory, and some possible policy implications. Finally it proposes future research topics based on the findings that this study managed to obtain.

6.1 Findings
Factors and Causal Mechanisms for SI Initiative Scaling

First, this section responds to the main research question of: "What are the factors and causal mechanisms that affect the scaling of (or the failure of) social innovation initiatives in selected Asian countries?", summarized as eight findings. Then it shows a model to describe the SI scaling by two axes of top-down or bottom-up initiatives, and the degree to which multi-sectoral "alliances" proliferate.

Finding 1: Opportunities Created by Crises

The first finding is that in many cases, opportunities are born out of crises. In the case studies, we can see that many of the significant SI initiatives arise as a consequence of a major social crisis which may damage the unity or stability of the entire society. The Great Hanshin Earthquake opened an opportunity to create legislation for private nonprofit organizations. Environmental pollution in Japan was a serious health hazard to thousands of people. Increasing inequality in post-reform China and post-financial crisis South Korea both urged stakeholders including policymakers to take drastic measures. Indonesian decentralization was also a response to the confusion and increasing risk of regional revolt and disintegration following the Asian Financial Crisis and the political turmoil after the fall of the Suharto regime.

Even after the remarkable economic growth in East Asian countries, severe inequality, unemployment (or lack of decent work) and poverty remain in the society, together with aging populations and weakening

Figure 6.1 Resilience and Adaptability Cycle

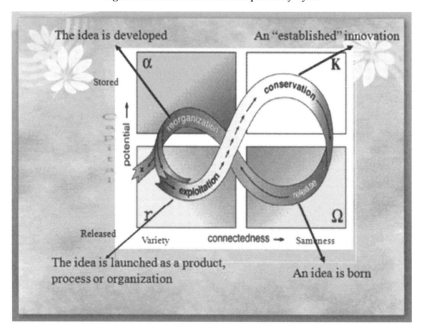

Source: Social Innovation Generation website[1]

traditional social safety nets. The governments, not only in Japan but also in China, South Korea, and Indonesia, are all gradually shifting to more universal systems of social welfare and social services, but they are hesitant to move to a full-service welfare state considering the financial sustainability and capacity limitation. "Social innovation" – no matter what it means to the people who mention it - is expected to be a solution in many such societies, especially when governments are failing to cope with the situation caused by a crisis. As Westley et al. (2007) notes, the crisis may be a "release" of existing resources and spaces from the public sector, which are then opened up as opportunities for different SI initiatives (Figure 6.1).

Finding 2: Strong but Weak States

Another finding is that while Asian states are powerful, they are not powerful enough to force all others to follow their decisions. Most of the target countries once had (or still have) a history of authoritarian rule and state-corporatism. This includes Party-state China, South Korea during military rule, the Suharto regime in Indonesia, and is also somewhat true for postwar Japan, which continued to have a strong connection between the mainstream political-bureaucratic-industrial sectors. Such experiences have left behind significant traits in the state of civil societies and in the relationships between government, business, and civil society, such as mainstream governmental bodies and businesses' deep-rooted suspicion of civil society.

Still, we should not think of Asian governments as having unlimited power to do whatever they desire. As we see in the case of community-based integrated care in Japan and the social enterprise scheme led by the South Korean Ministry of Employment and Labor, top-down policies without the engagement of different players tend to end up in failure, or an inactive scheme relying solely on governmental support. Successful cases of top-down initiatives have corresponding partners on local levels, like NPOs and local governments who needed the former's operational capacity in Japan, social organizations in China or local elites in Indonesia fully utilizing the spaces opened for them (though not necessarily in an ideal or expected way).

Finding 3: Social Enterprise is NOT the Cure

A third finding is that social enterprise is not the cure for all problems, at least for now. While disappointment in governments' ability to tackle social issues grows, society's expectations for SI are on the rise. In particular, there are high hopes for social entrepreneurs or social enterprises to both solve social issues and be financially self-sustainable. From the civil society side as well, there is the hope that transforming themselves into a form of social enterprise may make them more financially sustainable, and release them from the stigma placed on "civil society" in some countries (The Hope Institute 2017:271). However, we should be fully aware that no civil society or social enterprise / social entrepreneur is able to solve systemic social problems by themselves (Ganz et al. 2018). Even in our case studies of social economy organizations in South Korea, social organizations in China, and NPOs in Japan – although all of them are growing considerably and firmly established as a sector, their scale and presence within their respective societies is still limited, if not marginal. Their presence is also biased towards urban areas and certain social issues. In other words, we should not expect social entrepreneurs / social enterprises themselves to be the solution for all the diverse and enormous social issues, or to replace the full function of the welfare state, at least at the moment or in any near future.

Finding 4: The Power of Local-level "Alliances"

Fourth is the power of local-level multi-sectoral "alliances." In the case analyses, the existence of and proliferation of multi-sectoral "alliances," especially on the local level, was the key determining factor in the successful scaling and fixation of SI initiatives in the society. Local governments in "progressive" local governments' areas in Japan working together with local residents and businesses created solutions for environmental pollution prior to the nation. Local governments like Shanghai, Beijing or Guangdong became experimental sites for social organizations in China. And Mayor Park Won-soon's Seoul city, with its partnerships with social businesses and civil society organizations, is becoming the "social economy city" of East Asia. Indonesian decentralization found strong unions on the local level to support (or utilize) the resources released for them. On the contrary, when community-based integrated care in Japan failed to establish a multi-stakeholder collaboration in most local areas, it could not take a firm hold in the society. The establishment and proliferation of such local-level "alliances" can be a crucial step toward the SI initiatives becoming rooted in the society and bringing it up to a macro-level change.

But this does not happen automatically, and even in our limited number of case studies, we can observe that there are some different paths to formulate such local-level alliances. First, it can be resource-driven partnership to utilize the available resources, like in the case of Indonesian governmental decentralization. Second, it can be initiated by the leadership of local government, mostly by elected heads but in some cases by active bureaucrats to facilitate different stakeholders, such as the cases of the "progressive" local governments in Japan or Mayor Park in Seoul. Third, it can be created as a result of social movement or grass-roots activities, like what happened in the case of 1963/1964 anti-pollution movement in Shizuoka prefecture, Japan. Of course it can be a mixture of any of these, as typical in the case of social organizations in China which may be a mixture of all three, depending on the region and time.

Also, the formation of "alliances" is affected by other factors such as the seriousness of the issue and the existence of a social consensus to tackle the issue, in other words the amount of pressure being exerted upon the stakeholders. Such force from the society urges politicians to take actions and businesses to follow new standards, as well as seeking out new business opportunities.[2] The resources allocated for forming such "alliances" definitely helps – what may have happened, if community-based integrated care in Japan had been given enough monetary incentives,[3] or if Indonesian local governments had not been given enough resources after decentralization? Perhaps the results would be quite different.

Finding 5: The Danger of Power Capture
A fifth point taken from this study is the danger of power capture. While we appreciate the value of an "alliance" of stakeholders, especially at the local level, we must be fully aware of the reality that this does not always create the expected, or "desirable" output and in some case, and even the "alliance" can be a "vicious" one. As in the case of Indonesian decentralization, an alliance of powerful elites can monopolize the benefits created by new political systems and exclude those who do not

have power or access to resources. Or as in the cases of NPOs in Japan, Social Enterprise Promotion Law in South Korea or social organizations in China, governmental agencies can manipulate the system to suit their own agendas. Having alternative options and spaces (such as cooperatives in South Korea, or Private-Run Non-Enterprise Units / corporates in China) may help to avoid this kind of capture, though it is not always available. Having more resources available, such as governmental funding, may also increase the risks of misuse and rent-seeking.

Finding 6: Processes Going Back and Forth

The sixth finding is that the SI processes are not straightforward. We should be aware that SI processes do not always happen as a linear process starting from small initiatives and scaling to macro-level as some SI theories or models suggest. In the case studies, environmental pollution in Japan was the only initiative in which the scaling from grassroots to local, then to the central government level happened as the conventional model suggests. Others may go back and forth like the cases of social organizations in China and decentralization in Indonesia. Or some even start as a top-down central government policy, and after the failure of the initial attempt, grow again at different levels, as we see in the cases of community-based integrated care in Japan, social organizations in China, and social economy organizations in South Korea. These processes are a result of negotiation and compromise, and reframing of acceptable concepts between the changing actors.

Finding 7: The Power of Ideals and Values

Seventh is the power of ideals and values. What makes a significant difference between everyday political negotiations and SI is the existence of a novel idea or value behind an SI. It is not only a nice phrase or slogan, but if the idea can convince people that it can work to resolve a major issue, it may serve to push the negotiation process forward. The newly invented values of "environmental protection" and "environment rights" became a force to stop businesses from continuing to openly pollute and to force them to cooperate with governmental regulations. In South Korea, the concept of "social economy" introduced from Europe and the U.S. led the bipartisan politics to an agreement to move the initiatives forward. In China, ambiguous words like "charity," "philanthropy," or "public benefit" and their various translations are used to support social organizations. Even in the Indonesian decentralization process, people now have the vocabulary and the logic for requesting government services that are closer to the people or to meet their needs.

And in the case studies we can find two different sources of such ideas. First is learning from other countries, as we saw in the cases of civil society leaders in Japan designing schemes for NPOs by studying the U.S. and the U.K. nonprofit and voluntary sectors, the concept of social economy being brought in from Europe in South Korea, the Charity Law and other initiatives to support social organizations in China, and the decentralization agenda introduced by international donors to Indonesia. Second is ideas that are derived from existing local problems and initiatives. Intellectuals including Dr. Tsuru in Japan who led the environmental pollution studies, Dr. Hwang in South Korea, or the group of scholars that developed the concepts of Chinese civil society were closely in touch with the reality of local communities (for instance, Dr. Tsuru visited all major pollution sites and Dr. Hwang worked together with civil society practitioners) and indigenous values, and were able to derive important values and concepts from them. They then shape these elements into a positive value which is more easily accepted by other stakeholders and society. In other words, they can act as an interpreter between social reality and foreign concepts.

However, it is important to note that these ideas are also a result of negotiation and conflict between different stakeholders, and it can be easily changed or "hijacked" by someone with more manipulative power or influence. In the case of South Korea, the Ministry of Employment and Labor took the idea of social enterprise from civil society leaders and researchers and utilized it for their own agenda. Even in the case of environmental pollution, the idea of "public harm (*Kogai*)" was shifted (or sanitized) to environmental value and rights as it became mainstreamed in society.

Finding 8: Information and Governance

The eighth and final finding is the use of information technology to change information availability, resource mobilization, and governance mechanisms. As seen in some of the case studies, although the cases are limited, such as the utilization of big data for community-based integrated care in Japan or online platforms for social organizations in China, the development of ICT is changing the information sharing, governance mechanisms, resource allocation and power balance in societies. It may work either to strengthen the coercive power of the state, or to release more information and data to the public and allow more resource mobilization and participatory governance, as we see in the case of Chinese social organizations. Table 6.1 gives a summary of all eight findings and the case studies applicable.

Table 6.1 Summary of the Findings of Causal Relationships and Patterns Found from Case Studies

Findings	Case Study Country* (and Cases for Japan**)
Finding 1: Opportunities Created by Crises	JP (NPO, EP), SK, IN
Finding 2: Strong but Weak States	JP (CBIC), CH, SK, IN
Finding 3: Social Enterprise is NOT the Cure	JP (NPO), CH, SK
Finding 4: The Power of Local-level "Alliances"	JP (NPO, EP, CBIC), CH, SK, IN
Finding 5: The Danger of Power Capture	JP (NPO), CH, SK, IN
Finding 6: Processes Going Back and Forth	JP (NPO, CBIC), CH, SK, IN
Finding 7: The Power of Ideals and Values	JP (NPO, EP), CH, SK, IN
Finding 8: Information and Governance	JP (CBIC), CH

* JP: Japan, CH: China (Social Organization), SK: South Korea (Social Economy), IN: Indonesia (Decentralization)
** NPO: Non-Profit Organization, EP: Environmental Pollution, CBIC: Community-Based Integrated Care

Source: Developed by the author

Four Types of Social Innovation Scaling

Next is the four types of social innovation scaling, based on the two axes we set in Figure 1.12 to analyze different case studies and scaling patterns: i) different flows of initiatives – top-down or bottom-up, and ii) whether the case had the establishment and proliferation of local "alliances" to support the initiative or not. Figure 6.2 divides the SI initiatives into four types according to these two categories, the flow of the initiatives and the scale of local-level support:

Figure 6.2 Four Types of Social Innovation Scaling

	Proliferation of local-level alliances	Lacked local-level alliances
Top-down	**i. Caught on Locally** Wide range of local-level alliances to support and sustain the policy / initiative coming from central government (e.g. NPO sector in Japan / Decentralization in Indonesia)	**iii. Hollow Policy** Lack of local-level alliances to support the central policy / initiative (e.g. Gov-led Social Enterprise scheme in South Korea / Community-based integrated care in Japan)
Bottom-up	**ii. Successful Scaling** Diffusion of local level-alliances allows the momentum to scale up and make a change on the macro level (e.g. Environmental pollution in Japan / Social Organizations in China (partly))	**iv. Failed to Scale** An SI initiative that does not find stakeholders to support or expand it (e.g. none from the case studies - but numerous SI initiatives fail to scale and stay small)[4]

Source: Developed by the author

i. Caught on Locally

Type i. is "Caught on Locally." This is a pattern for top-down policies which find a number of local-level alliances to support or sustain the policy. When there is a wide range of such alliances, SI initiatives can continue and become embedded in society. It is like a ball caught by and then passed between people waiting at the local level, so we shall name this the "caught on locally" pattern. Examples of this pattern include the NPO sector in Japan, or governmental decentralization in Indonesia.

ii. Successful Scaling

Type ii. is "Successful scaling." This pattern starts from the grassroots or a local community, then after proliferation or dissemination to other areas, with local level "alliances" formed in each area, reaches societal change on a macro level, including central governmental policies. This may be the most typical way of scaling, though it happens. Examples of this pattern are environmental pollution in Japan, social economy organizations in South Korea, or social organizations in China, though the last two are a mixture with top-down policies.

iii. Hollow Policy

Type iii. is "Hollow Policy." This is a pattern which is seen when a top-down initiative could not find any (or not so many) local-level "alliances" to support the initiative. Therefore, the policy cannot be sustained or take root in society, but disappears after the funding disappears or the leadership changes. Therefore, we should call this a "Hollow Policy" pattern, and the examples of this process (at least at the moment) are community-based integrated care in Japan, or the Social Enterprise scheme in South Korea created by the Ministry of Employment and Labor.

iv. Failed to Scale

Type iv. is "Failed to Scale." Although this pattern is not found in the case studies, this is actually how most SI initiatives or projects end up – started on a local level, often by a single organization. and unable to find a sufficient number of local partners, or "alliances" to adopt the initiative, or to create a certain macro-level impact. Indeed, this is the reason why the scaling of SI initiatives remains a major issue to be resolved.

By looking at these four patterns, we can see that the proliferation of local level "alliances" is the crucial key for the SI initiative to scale, or to have a significant impact on a society, no matter if it is a top-down or a bottom-up process. Thus if we want an SI initiative to have a significant impact on society, building a number of local level, inter-sectoral "alliances" may be a shortcut, or perhaps another way might be preparing a policy incentive to create these types of multi-stakeholder networks.

6.2 Arguments
What the Two-Axes Model Means for SI Theory and Policies

This section discusses what the two-axes model and other findings as well as the methodology of this study may contribute to the study of SI theory and policy. The model sees the primary significance of the establishment and proliferation of local-level "alliances" formed by different sectors, as it functions as the driver to create macro-level social changes by an SI initiative and for them to take root. The role of such multi-sectoral "alliances" were previously overlooked as a consequence of a few established academic patterns and methodologies taken in SI study. First, there was a dichotomy in SI research of focusing either on i) micro-level analysis of a "social innovator" or single project/organization, or on ii) macro-level concepts or models. Second, since there was a strong tendency to see SI from the perspectives of individual organizations or social movements, multi-sectoral governance or negotiation processes were mostly ignored, partly because of the unavailability of data and framework to analyze such processes, and scaling was considered to be the linear expansion of a homogeneous movement or an initiative without substantive change to its original principle or characteristics.

Of course this book is not the first to focus on the interaction of multi-sectoral actors (Pel and Bauler 2014; Westley et al. 2017). What is new about this research is first the application of the methodology of historical process-tracing of the interactions between various stakeholders, instead of analyzing one organization or movement. Also different from the historical process-tracing conducted by Westley and her group, it uses a tri-sectoral relationship framework as a unit of analysis instead of individuals and organizations. Second, by applying that methodology and multi-faceted perspective, this study enables us to see how an SI initiative proliferates and takes root (or does not) in the society as a result of inter-sectoral collaboration, negotiation, and conflict, as well as how the ideas and concepts - not only practices – of the SI initiative can be modified or diverted, based on the interaction of actors.

To explain further about the latter point, Figure 6.3 presents another model which looks a little bit like a game of billiards. An SI initiative may start at the individual (i) level by a civil society organization (Ic), drawn as a double-line arrow. When it comes into a local ecosystem level (ii), there may be other actors such as local government (Lg), businesses (Lb), or other local civil society organizations or local communities (Lc)[5] that affect the initiative (single-line arrow from each showing their influence), and the arrow may change direction slightly or drastically as a result. Meanwhile, the initiative may be "diffused" to another local ecosystem, with another set of local stakeholders, so the direction of the arrow may or may not be same as the original one. When they scale to the national or macro level (iii), there is more involvement from national stakeholders (Ng, Nb, Nc) and as a result, more alteration of the initiative may happen.[6]

Figure 6.3 Model of Inter-Sectoral Relations in a Social Innovation Initiative

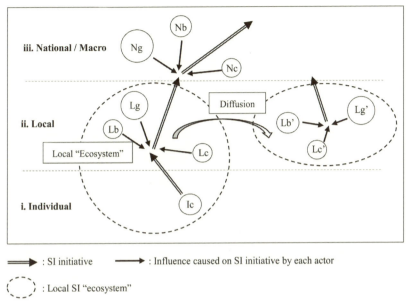

Source: Developed by the author

These models and the methodology can provide strong empirical evidence to establish a theoretical linkage between the micro and macro levels of SI processes and may contribute to the field as a long-wished for "middle-range" theory. Applying these models together with SI ecosystem study opens a new field for SI research to analyze i) a dynamic process of how an "alliance" is formed in a local or national ecosystem, and what the possibly different interests and aims that stakeholders have in it are, and ii) how the "alliance" is expanded or scaled to other areas or countries, and how they are changed from the "original", based on other local contexts and actors. From such analyses, there will be more nuanced empirical evidence to solve the mystery of SI scaling, and SI theoretical models can be further refined.

The model also provides a suggestion as to why the policies to support SI development that focus primarily on incubation of social entrepreneurs or supporting individual projects, or on reforming laws and/or tax incentives have mostly failed to scale or to have a significant social impact. For an SI initiative to have a certain degree of impact, or even possibly to replace the welfare state model and establish a welfare society, there is a need to harness multi-sectoral collaboration in local communities rather than supporting one single sector. This needs to go beyond empty slogans or directions asking for "collaboration," or providing a negligible amount of subsidy from the government alone. What is needed is the creation of a framework for local governance between different stakeholders that allows them to take substantial actions, and this needs to be done by contribution from all sectors, including civil society organizations and local communities.

The Roles of Governments, Businesses, and Civil Society

Then what are the roles of central and local governments, businesses, and civil society / social sectors (including the nonprofit/charity, voluntary, and social business sectors) in creating such collaborations? Here are some of the roles each sector plays in the processes, based on the findings from the case studies.

Governments

First is the government. What only governments can do is to create space for innovative actors, and to recognize the legitimacy of such attempts (Clarence 2014:55). Without such acknowledgement, it will be difficult for innovative actors to raise resources and win society's trust. The significant contribution of the NPO Law in Japan or the Charity Law in China was to give such recognition and legitimacy to nonprofit / social organizations, albeit selectively. The Social Enterprise Promotion Act and Basic Law on Cooperatives in South Korea, among other schemes also provided space for different actors.

Providing funding and other resources is often considered the most important role of the government. It may be a useful tool for short-term achievement, but scholars tend to agree that it also brings about some side effects, such as creating dependency and impairing the creativity of social actors as we saw in the case of certified social enterprises in South Korea (Defourny and Nyssens 2008; Hwang et al. 2016), and to some extent in NPOs in Japan. Indonesian decentralization is another example of local elites enjoying rent-seeking of newly provided resources to local governments and councils.

Probably another role – which is often overlooked – is the coordination of various stakeholders for effective and fruitful cooperation, which in some cases leads to forming successful "alliances" as well as setting some standards for good governance and quality operation, which may or may not happen without such intervention. Again, the Seoul Metropolitan Government focused on this to create supportive partnerships for social economy development. And in the 1960s, local governments in Japan played a significant role in coordinating businesses and other sectors to reduce pollution in their areas ahead of the central government.

Businesses

Second is businesses. By definition, the goal of business is to maximize profit and not to maximize public benefit or to solve social issues.

Therefore, it is not particularly helpful to expect businesses to be "drivers" of SI. However, businesses have the best capacity to scale up any new initiatives once they are given the right incentive, as in the case of corporate sectors joining the environmental protection movement once society became hostile to polluting businesses and there was a new opportunity for pro-environmental business. In some ways, they are the ones who have the "casting vote" in the SI process. In a society with limited resources (as most of our societies are), a change in social values which results in the consumers' choices and pressure posed from them may be the best incentives for businesses to adapt their operations accordingly, rather than generous subsidies from the government.

Civil Society

Thirdly, the civil society sector including academics and independent intellectuals is most suitable to find and develop new values and ideas, either from their own experiences or by referring to what others are doing. The value comes from the real circumstances of the society they work with, as the practitioners in South Korea accumulated experience in diverse forms of cooperatives and other alternative businesses with disadvantaged groups or how social organizations in China developed new fields of social services (conversely, civil society in Indonesia is blamed for focusing too much on central politics and foreign donors rather than the needs of society at the grassroots level). It can also come from foreign practices or concepts. Also, they have more freedom for innovation than governments, for example being free from the boundaries that restrict governments (for example, legal justification or geographical jurisdiction). Therefore, if they have the capacity to collaborate with others (which is not always the case) and to find resources, they are in the best position to start new initiatives on the ground together with other stakeholders. Finally, they can create an atmosphere or a pressure to change the attitude of other sectors, like the pressure from civil society and mass demonstrations changing social welfare policies in China, South Korea, and Indonesia, or the environmental policies and nonprofit laws and regulations of local and central governments in Japan.

The East and The West – How Different are They?

Now is there any major difference or heterogeneousness in the pattern and processes of SI scaling between the existing SI literature which is largely based on the experience of Western countries, and this study based on an analysis of Northeast and Southeast Asian countries? The findings in this study show a strong commonality between the findings of Western SI literature, especially of Westley et al. (2017), which puts emphasis on i) the importance of meaning and initial vision, ii) development from a niche, iii) negotiation and compromise between stakeholders, sometimes over a long time-span, and iv) the failure of regime-led innovations, or Haxeltine et al. (2017) which sees the process of SI as a replacement of existing institutions by creating new social relations. The structure and mechanisms of the multi-stakeholder processes of SI scaling seems to have no essential difference between Asian and Western societies.

Although the state influence on civil society seems to be strong in most of our case studies in Asian countries, they are not almighty. Also the government-led approach towards SI is becoming increasingly normal in Western contexts as well, as Defourny and Nyssens (2008) point out that social enterprise in Europe is also dependent on governmental support. Haxeltine et al. (2015:35-36) also state that SI initiatives are implemented by state policies, and people are motivated either by incentives or enforcement to do it as an "imposed change pathway" of SI, showing examples of young people obliged to do community work, or the "Big Society" policy taken under the U.K. Conservative-Liberal Democratic coalition government. Westley et al. (2017) presents some cases of an SI initiative (such as intelligence testing) utilizing the interests of the state during wartime that was quickly adopted and spread throughout society. Martinelli (2013) stresses contextual differences and the use of bottom-up approach for space, funding, and the ownership of locality, which seems to correspond to the findings of this study.

Still, we should not overlook the power of values and meanings in different political, social, and cultural contexts. These differences may affect the goals and processes of SI initiatives - as we saw how the word "civil society" may have very different meanings in Communist China or Muslim Indonesia. Differences in values may also affect the relationships between actors (Pel et al. 2017:13).

Furthermore, we notice from the case studies (NPOs in Japan, social organizations and "civil society" concepts in China, social economic organizations in South Korea, and decentralization in Indonesia), that even the ideas and principles behind an SI initiative may not stay coherent, as Westley (2017:242-243) suggested, but may be amended, distorted, or hijacked depending on local contexts and the interactions and power relations between different actors.[7] For instance, NPOs in Japan became largely a tool for governmental service outsourcing, rather than a vibrant sector for grassroots mobilization or civil society partitipation. The concept of social economy was altered by the South Korean Ministry of Employment and Labor to increase employment opportunities for marginalized groups by giving subsidies, while the Chinese translation of "civil society" has changed (and is still changing) quickly to obtain the approval of the Party-state system, and the ideal of decentralization in Indonesia to bring services closer to people has been manipulated by local elites, though they may be still using the same language.

Nevertheless, we should not see this as a divide between the East and the West, but something which urges us to be more conscious of such contexts in any given setting or local "ecosystem," including what values each region and actor may give priority to, compared to others. Even in one country, any particular community or region may have very different local contexts from the stereo typical "national" images, depending on the history, social settings, and actors it has.

6.3 Policy Implications and Way Forward

Finally, based on the results of analyses, this study attempts to provide some policy implications, both to generate and also to scale up SI initiatives. Based on the findings above, here are some of the infrastructures and policy recommendations that may be useful to establish and scale up successful SI processes.

Creating Inclusive Spaces and Resources at Local Levels

First is to create inclusive spaces and resources at local levels, for the local stakeholders to form an "alliance" to resolve their own issues. From some of the successful SI cases we have observed, such as some local governments in Japan during the 1960s-1970s stopping environmental pollution, or the Seoul Metropolitan Government under Mayor Park creating an environment to enhance social economy and social services, we can see that local community stakeholders are in a better position than policy makers in the central government to identify diverse local issues and priorities, and to form local-level alliances to tackle those issues together with other stakeholders. Therefore, creating more spaces, authority, and resources for stakeholders in local communities can help to utilize a limited amount of resources more effectively by forming an "alliance" of local stakeholders. However, to avoid any elite capture in which specific groups exclusively access and manipulate power and resources, rules and governance mechanisms should be put in place to form inclusive partnerships between different stakeholders in the community.

Securing a Minimum Level of Social Safety Nets and Safeguarding from Harmful Results

Second is to secure a minimum level of social safety nets and safeguarding from harmful results. One of the findings throughout this study is that none of the cases, including NPOs or community-based integrated care in Japan, social organizations in China, social economy organizations in South Korea, and decentralization in Indonesia, are able, at least not at the moment, to provide all or most of the services that are needed in an entire society by themselves. Even for the best practices, they are either i) dependent on capable / charismatic leaders, or ii) unable to collaborate with other sectors (governments and businesses), or iii) limited in their coverage areas, geographically or issue-wise.

And perhaps we cannot realistically expect that local communities will be able to deal with all issues, especially for minorities and marginalized groups. With the limited amount of resources and power dynamics in a community, the services provided may miss a number of critical issues for those groups. Therefore, while having more resources, decision-making power, and time in the locality may improve the situation, it is also necessary for the national government to set a minimum level of social safety nets and service standards, which can be universally applied for all citizens regardless of their position in society. Furthermore, governments and civil society together need to monitor the results, to avoid any "innovation" that causes unexpected damage to others and to ensure quality control for any possible violation.

Creating "Playgrounds" or "Regulative Sandboxes" for Social Innovation Experiments

Third is to create "playgrounds" or "regulatory sandboxes" for SI experiments. Despite civil society organizations including social enterprise perhaps not being able to "solve" any social issue by themselves without working with other sectors, it is also true that they are in the best position to develop and try new ideas to tackle any issues within local communities. And while new technologies enable different options which did not exist before, they are often in conflict with existing rules and regulations. Thus, such trials for innovative practices can be encouraged by easing regulatory frameworks during the "experimental" stage. Nevertheless, it needs to be monitored and recorded closely first so that it will not cause critical harm to anyone, and second to extract useful knowledge for scaling and disseminating to others.

Building an Infrastructure to Share Success and Failure of Different Initiatives

Fourth is to build an infrastructure to share success and failure of different initiatives. Both to maximize the impact and avoid any possible damage, the openness of information and data should be pursued for all attempts and policies. The use of the latest information technology can definitely aid these efforts. This is not only to present the results, but also to create an opportunity for people to be engaged and provide their inputs. Also, the exchange of people and information between different areas needs to be expanded, so that people can learn from others' successes and failures. This is not only for people in the same countries. The case studies show how social innovators are inspired by the best practices of other countries, and it will be helpful to provide such experiences for more of them.

Scaling Up Successful Initiatives

Fifth is to support scaling up successful initiatives, in a sustainable way. When a useful SI initiative is consolidated in one place, and if it is not too context-specific or dependent on external funding, it may be scaled up. But for the initiative to be sustainable, it is preferable if the scaling does not depend on policy funding, coercive regulations, or a "special" leader, but is disseminated instead through knowledge sharing, or as a sustainable business activity, in so far as it is relevant.

Final Thoughts on Power Relationships and Ideas, and Possibile Future Research

Now as the final thought of this research, I shall note some points what I find to be its limitations and the possible way forward. This book focused mostly on inter-sectoral relationships, or how those relationships influence the scaling processes of a SI initiative. It managed to present the crucial role of local-level "alliances" between different stakeholders for SI initiatives to scale, and how the initiative may be altered as the result of interactions between various players. Still from its focus, scope, methodologies, and cases selected, it has certain limitations and left unanswered questions. One of the major ones is how different ideas and values affect the power dynamics. Does the new idea always precede the initiative, or is it that the new idea can be embedded within society (and replace the old ideas and values) only after the practice becomes a new "normal" in the society? Both seem to be true in our case studies, but this is something we could not cover enough in this study. Another limitation is the lack of in-depth study of SI processes in a specific local "ecosystem," which naturally happened due to this research's scope in which the whole process of scaling in one country was covered. Sector or issue-based (such as health care, education, among others) cases are another thing discarded from this study that can benefit from the findings of this research.

Based on the findings and unanswered questions, there are some new research questions, including i) how ideas and values embedded in societies affect the SI processes, including the formation and fixation of new ideas and values, ii) how a succesful "alliance" can be formed in a local ecosystem, and how the sense of crisis / urgency or a new resource provided for an initiative affect it, and iii) how technology can help to form successful SI and its diffusion and scaling, among others.

Some of the next possible steps to take are first to conduct more detailed case studies and comparisons of SI formulation and scaling processes within specific "SI ecosystem" contexts to see how different social values, traditions, available resources, stakeholders, and societal relationships within an ecosystem affect the development of SI initiatives, formation of "alliances," and creation of a "welfare community" at local levels. A second step would be to investigate how different technologies (big data, artificial intelligence, and mobile devices, remote cares, among others) can help (or not help) create more inclusive and effective SI processes, and a third to exchange empirical findings and theoretical models among other scholars working globally on SI theories and empirical studies.

---

1   "Social Innovation" page, SiG website: http://www.sigeneration.ca/social-innovation/ (Retrieved 5th May 2018)
2   We can recall how Japanese corporates developed pollution control / prevention as a new industrial area, or how South Korean *chaebols* participated in a newly established social enterprise sector, as well as finding them to be "clean" areas to operate in to avoid criticism from the general public.
3   Although this is unlikely, since one of the main reasons to introduce community-based integrated care was to reduce the cost of elderly care, and the lion's share of the long-term care insurance funding was already being used for various service providers.
4   Deiglmeier (2018); Howaldt et al. (2014a)
5   There may be more than one of any or all stakeholders (Lg, Lb, Lc / Ng, Nb, Nc), but the figure is simplified.
6   And perhaps at this national / macro stage, the initial organization (Ic) may not have significant influence over the whole initiative, or there may be many more who are involved. This is one of the reasons why one-organizational analysis is limited in its ability to analyze the whole scaling process of an SI initiative.
7   Westley also acknowledges the effect of complex dynamics and "we do not expect consistency… across time" especially for practice, still seeing a "surprising degree of coherence… which in this case seemed to be guided by the thread of the original idea or principles that undergirded it" (Westley 2017:242), so it may be whether you argue that the cup is half empty, or half full.

References

Abe, H. (2016). Shakai Gabanansu no Shiten. in Tsujinaka, Y., Choi, S., and Abe, H. (eds.) *Gendai Nihon no Rokaru Gabanansu Netowaku: Jichitai, juminjichisoshiki, oyobi hieirisoshiki no kousatsu*. CAJS/ICR Monograph Series No.8. Tsukuba: ICR, University of Tsukuba, 1-24.

Akiba, T. (2012). Kankoku no Shakaitekikigyo to Gensetsu no Tayosei. in Akiba, T., Kawase, S., Kikuchi, K., Kikkawa, J., Hiroishi, T., and Moon, K. (eds.) *Kiki no Jidai no Shimin Katsudo: Nikkan syakaitekikigyo saizensen*. Osaka: Toho Shuppan, 165-178.

Ako, T. (2012). Chugoku no Kouminshakai to Minshuka no Yukue: Kyokusetu suru sosharumedia to seiji seido kaikaku no kankei. *Kokusai Seiji*, (169), 45-59.

Ako, T. (2014). *Hinja wo Kurau Kuni: Chugoku kakusa shyakai kara no keikoku*. Tokyo: Shincho Sha.

Amako, S. (2013). *Chuka Jinmin Kyowakoku Shi*. Tokyo: Iwanami Shoten.

Amako, S. (2015). *Chugoku Kyosanto Ron: Shukinpei no yabo to minshuka no shinario*. Tokyo: NHK Shuppan.

Antadze, N. (2017). National Parks in the United States. In Westley, F., McGowan, K., and Tjornbo, O. (eds.) *The Evolution of Social Innovation: Building resilience through transitions*. Cheltenham and Northampton, MA: Edwar Elgar Publishing, 18-39.

Antlov, H., Wetterberg, A. and Dharmawan, L. (2016). Village Governance, Community Life, and the 2014 Village Law in Indonesia. *Bulletin of Indonesian Economic Studies*, 52(2), 161-183.

Aoo, K. (2017). Aging Society in Japan: A process of social innovation and the roles of civil society. *Korean NPO Review*. 16(2), 67-85.

Aoo, K. (2018). Sosyaru Inobeshon Riron no Tenkai to Kadai: Nihon, oushu, hokubei no hikaku bunseki wo chushin ni. *Kokusai Nihon Kenkyu*, (10), 103-119.

Aoo, K. (2019a, forthcoming). *A Summary of and the Outlook for Research on Five Countries: Research on Social Innovation Eco-System in East Asia*. A deliverable of "Research on the Social Innovation Eco-System in Asia" project funded by the Toyota Foundation.

Aoo, K. (2019b, forthcoming). *Social Innovation Eco-system Study in East Asia: Japan*. A deliverable of "Research on the Social Innovation Eco-System in Asia" project funded by the Toyota Foundation.

ARC (2017). *ARC Repoto: Indonesia 2017/18*. Tokyo: ARC.

Asakawa, S. (2017). Kaigohoken no Shinsogojigyo Kaishi de Ittai Nani ga Kawaru noka? *Diamond Online*. https://diamond.jp/articles/-/129131 (Retrieved 17th Dec. 2017).

Asakura, M. (2010). Chiki Kea Sisutemu Zukuri he no Chosen. in Asakura, M. and Ota, S. (eds.) *Chiki Kea Sisutemu to sono Henkaku Shutai*. Tokyo: Kosei Kan, 1-10.

Asian Venture Philanthropy Network (2017). *Social Investment Country Report: South Korea*. Singapore: AVPN.

Azra, A. (2006). *Indonesia, Islam, and Democracy: Dynamics in a global context*. Singapore: Equinox Publishing.

Barnes, M. (2010). Stepping up to Support the Social Innovation Fund and Other Community Solutions. *The White House (President Barack Obama) website*: https://obamawhitehouse.archives.gov/blog/2010/05/27/stepping-support-social-innovation-fund-and-other-community-solutions (Retrieved 12th Sep. 2017)

Beard, V. A. and Phakphian, S. (2012). Community-based Planning in Thailand: Social capital, collective action and elite capture. In Daniere, A. and Luong, H. V. (eds.) *The Dynamics of Social Capital and Civil Engagement in Asia*. London: Routledge, 141-159.

Beittinger-Lee, V. (2009). *(Un) Civil Society and Political Change in Indonesia: A contested arena*. Abingdon: Routledge.

Bell, D. A., Translated by Seko, T., and Hasumi, J. (2006) *Ajiateki Kachi to Riberaru Demokurashi: Toyo to Seiyo no Taiwa*. Tokyo: Fukosha.

Bennett, A. (2010). Process Tracing and Causal Inference. In Brady, H. E. and Collier, D. (eds.). *Rethinking Social Inquiry: Diverse tools, shared standards.* (2nd edition). Lanham: Rowman & Littlefield, 207-219.

BEPA (Bureau of European Policy Advisers, European Commission) (2011). *Empowering People, Driving Change: Social innovation in the European Union*. Luxemburg: European Union.

Bidet, E. and Eum, H. (2011). Social Enterprise in South Korea: History and diversity. *Social Enterprise Journal,* 7(1), 69-85.

Borzaga, C. and Defourny, J. (eds.) (2001). *The Emergence of Social Enterprise*. London and New York: Routledge.

Bradach, J. and Grindle, A. (2014). Emerging Pathways to Transformative Scale. *Stanford*

Social Innovation Review, Spring 2014 (Special Supplement), 7-11.

Brady, H., Collier, D., and Seawright, J. (2010). Refocusing the Discussion of Methodology. In Brady, H. E. and Collier, D. (eds.). *Rethinking Social Inquiry: Diverse tools, shared standards.* 2nd edition, Lanham: Rowman & Littlefield, 15-31.

Brennan, M. (2017). Why is WeChat Pushing So Hard for Charity? *China Channel online* (30th Aug. 2017). https://chinachannel.co/wechat-pushing-hard-charity/ (Retrieved 4th May 2018)

Buehler, M. (2010). Decentralisation and Local Democracy in Indonesia: The marginalization of the public sphere. In Aspinall, E. and Mietzner, M. (eds.). *Problems of Democratisation in Indonesia: Elections, institutions and society.* Singapore: ISEAS.

Bunte, M. and Ufen, A. (2009). The New Order and Its Legacy: Reflections on democratization in Indonesia. In Bunte, M. and Ufen, A. (eds.). *Democratization in Post-Suharto Indonesia.* Abingdon: Routledge, 3-29.

Byrne, D. and Callaghan, G. (2014). *Complexity Theory and the Social Sciences: The state of the art.* Abingdon and New York: Routledge.

C. (2018, forthcoming). *Social Innovation Eco-system Study in East Asia: South Korea.* A deliverable of "Research on the Social Innovation Eco-System in Asia" project funded by the Toyota Foundation.

Cabinet Office (2011). *Heisei 23 Nendo Tokuteihieirikatudohojin no Jittai oyobi Ninteitokuteikatudohojin Seido no Riyojyoko ni kansuru Chosa (Gaiyo).* Tokyo: Cabinet Office.

Cabinet Office (2016a). *Heisei 28 Nendo Shimin no Shakaikoken ni kansuru Jittaichosa.* Tokyo: Cabinet Office.

Cabinet Office (2016b). *Heisei 28 Nendo Koreishakai Hakusho.* Tokyo: Cabinet Office.

Cabinet Office (2018). *Heisei 29 Nendo Tokuteihieirihojin ni Kansuru Jittaichosa.* Tokyo: Cabinet Office.

Cajaiba-Santana, G. (2014). Social Innovation: Moving the field forward. A conceptual framework. *Technological Forecasting & Social Change,* 82 (2014), 42-51.

Campbell, J. (2000). Changing Meanings of Frail Old People and the Japanese Welfare State. In Long, S. O. (ed.). *Caring for the Elderly in Japan and the U.S.: Practices and policies.* London: Routledge, 82-97.

Campbell, J. Ikegami, N., Gori, C., Barbella F., Chomik R., d'Amico, F., Holder, H., Ishibashi T., Johansson, L., Komisar, H., Ring, M., and Theobald, H. (2016). How Different

Countries Allocate Long-Term Care Resources to Older Users: A comparative snapshot. In Gori, C., Fernandez, J.-L., and Wittenberg, R. (eds.). *Long-Term Care Reforms in OECD Countries*. Bristol: Policy Press, 47-76.

Charlton, S. E. M. (2010). *Comparing Asian Politics: India, China, and Japan*. (Third edition) Boulder: Westview Press.

Chen, W. (2009). Choken, Yukirei ni Miru Kindaishakai Kouekisiso no Tenkai. Tao, T., Jiang, K., Kenjo, T., and Kirihara, K. (eds.) *Higashi Ajia ni okeru Koueki Shiso no Henyo: Kinsei kara kindai he.* Tokyo: Nihon Keizai Hyoronsha, 31-51.

Cheng, L., Lin, S., and Shao, S. (2011). Higashi Ajia ni okeru Fukushi Seisaku no Saikento. in Sonoda, S. (ed.) *Risuku no Naka no Higasi Ajia*. Tokyo: Keiso Shobo, 115-137.

Cheon, H. (2018). Kankoku Gensyu ni okeru Kyodokumiaiundo ni tuite no Ichikosatu: Genshu kyodo syakaikeizai netowaku no torikumi wo chushin ni. *Bukkyo Daigaku Daigakuin Kiyo*, (46), 67-80.

Chiappero-Martinetti, E. and Jacobi, N. V. (2015). *How can Sen's "Capabilities Approach" Contribute to Understanding the Role for Social Innovations for the Marginalized?* CRESSI Working Papers, Oxford: Said Business School.

China Association of Fundraising Professionals (2015). *Online Fundraising in China: A research report on third party platforms in 2014*. Beijing: CAFP.

Cho, C., Translated by Hando, H. and Hando, C. (2007). *Gendai Kankoku no Chiho Jichi.* Tokyo: Hosei Daigaku Syuppankai.

Choi, S., Translated by Isozaki, N. et al. (2012). *Minshuka Igo no Kankoku Minsyusyugi: Kigen to kiki.* Tokyo: Iwanami Shoten.

Christensen, C. M. (1997). *The Innovator's Dilemma: When new technologies cause great firms to fail*. Boston, Mass.: Harvard Business School Press.

Chu, Y.-H., Diamond, L., Nathan, A. J., and Shin, D. C. (2008). Introduction: Comparative perspectives on democratic legitimacy in East Asia. In Chu, Y.-H., Diamond, L., Nathan, A. J., Shin, D. C. (eds.) *How East Asians View Democracy*. New York: Colombia University Press, 1-38.

Clarence, E. (2014). Good Governance for Scaling Social Innovations. In Sgaragli, F. (ed.) *Enabling Social Innovation Ecosystems for Community-Led Territorial Development.* Rome: Fondazione Giacomo Brodolini, 47-59.

Collier, D., Brady, H., and Seawright, J. (2010). Causal Inference: Old dilemmas, new tools. In Brady, H. E. and Collier, D. (eds.). *Rethinking Social Inquiry: Diverse tools, shared standards*. 2nd edition, Lanham: Rowman & Littlefield, 201-204.

Colombo, F., Llena-Nozal, A., Mercier, J., and Tjadens, F. (2011). *Help Wanted?: Providing and paying for long-term care*. OECD Publishing.

Dees, K. G. (1998). Enterprising Nonprofits. *Harvard Business Review*, 76(1), 55-68.

Deiglemeier, K. (2018). Scaling Social Innovations: Gaps and opportunities. In SI-DRIVE (ed.) *Atlas of Social Innovation: New practices for a better future*. Dusseldorf: SI-DRIVE, 198-201.

Defourny, J. and Develtere, P. (1999). The Social Economy: The worldwide making of a third sector. In Defourny, J., Develtere, P., and Fonteneau, B. (eds.). *Social Economy: North and South*. Centre d'Economie Sociale, 3-35.

Defourny, J. and Kim, S. (2011). Emerging Models of Social Enterprise in Eastern Asia: A cross-country analysis. *Social Enterprise Journal*, 7(1), 86-111.

Defourny, J. and Nyssens, M. (eds.) (2008). Social Enterprise in Europe: Recent trends and developments. *Working Paper Series*, No. 08/01, Liege: EMES European Research Network.

Defourny, J. and Nyssens, M. (2013). Social Innovation, Social Economy and Social Enterprise: What can the European debate tell us? In Moulaert, F. MacCallum, D., Mehmood, A. and Hamdouch, A. (eds.). *The International Handbook on Social Innovation: Collective action, social learning and transdisciplinary research*. Cheltenham and Northampton: Edward Elgar Publishing, 13-24.

Deng, Z. (ed.) (2011). *State and Civil Society: The Chinese perspective*. Singapore: World Scientific Publishing.

Diplomat, The. (2017). The Fall of Ahok and Indonesia's Future. April 21, 2017. https://thediplomat.com/2017/04/the-fall-of-ahok-and-indonesias-future/ (Retrieved 27th Mar. 2018)

Dixon, J. (1981). *The Chinese Welfare System 1949-1979*. New York: Praeger.

Domanski, D. (2018). Developing the Social Innovation Ecosystem of the Vienna Region. *ZSI Discussion Paper, Nr. 37*. Wien: Zentrum for Soziale Innovation.

Domanski, D. and Kaletka, C. (eds.) (2017). *Exploring the Research Landscape of Social Innovation*. A deliverable of the project Social Innovation Community (SIC), Dortmund: Sozialforschungstelle.

Drucker, P. F. (1986). *Innovation and Entrepreneurship: Practice and principles*. New York: Harper & Row.

Eastman, L. E., (Translated by Ueda, S. and Fukao, Y.) (1994). *Chugoku no Shakai*. Tokyo: Heibon Sha.

Economic Planning Agency (2000). *Tokuteihieirihoujin no Katudo, Un-ei no Jittai ni Kansuru Chosa Hokokuho*. Tokyo: EPA.

Economist, The. (2010). Let's Hear Those Ideas. 12th August 2010. http://www.economist.com/node/16789766 (Retrieved 28th Aug. 2017)

Elderly Care Study Group (2003). *2015 Nen no Koureisha Kaigo: Koureisha no songen wo sasaeru kea no kakuritu ni mukete*. Tokyo: MoHLW.

Esping-Andersen, G. (1990). *The Three Worlds of Welfare Capitalism*. Cambridge: Polity Press.

Esping-Andersen, G. (1996). After the Golden Age? Welfare State Dilemmas in a Global Economy. In Esping-Andersen, G. (ed.). *Welfare States in Transition: National adaptations in global economics*. London: SAGE Publications, 1-31.

Esping-Andersen, G. (1999). *Social Foundations of Postindustrial Economics*. Oxford and New York: Oxford University Press.

Estevez-Abe, A. (2003). State-Society Partnerships in the Japanese Welfare State. In Schwartz, F. J. and Pharr, S. (eds.) *The State of Civil Society in Japan*. New York: Cambridge University Press, 154-172.

Estevez-Abe, M. (2008). *Welfare and Capitalism in Postwar Japan*. New York: Harvard University Press.

European Commission (2010). *Europe 2020: A strategy for smart, sustainable and inclusive growth*. Brussels: European Commission.

European Commission (2013). *Guide to Social Innovation*. Luxemburg: European Union.

European Commission (2017). *Projects Funded by the European Union Programme for Employment and Social Innovation (EaSI) Report VI*. Brussels: European Commission Directorate-General for Employment, Social Affairs and Inclusion.

Evers, A. (1995). Part of the Welfare Mix: The third sector as an intermediate area between market economy, state and community. *Voluntas*, 6(2), 159-182.

Ford, M. and Pepinsky, T. B. (eds.) (2014). *Beyond Oligarchy: Wealth, power and contemporary Indonesian politics*. Ithaca: Cornell University Press.

Franz, H.-W., Hochgerner, J., and Howaldt, J. (2012). Challenge Social Innovation: An introduction. In Franz, H.-W., Hochgerner, J., and Howaldt, J. (eds.) *Challenge Social Innovation: Potentials for business, social entrepreneurship, welfare and civil society*.

Heidelberg: Springer.

Fujii, A., Harada, K., and Ootaka, K. (2013). *Tatakau Shakaitekikigyo: Komuniti enpawamento no ninaite.* Tokyo: Keiso Shobo.

Fujikawa, K. (2017). Kaiketu to Hochi wo Meguru Shakaikatei. in Fujikawa, K., Watanabe, S., and Horibata, M. (eds.) *Kogai, Kankyomondai no Hochi Kozo to Kaiketsu Katei.* Tokyo: Toshindo, 17-42.

Fujisawa, Y., Ishida, Y., Nagatomi, and Iwasaki, K. (2017). Social Innovation and Some Japanese Cases. *Asia Pacific Tech Monitor* (33), 38-44.

Fukunaga, F. (2014). *Nihon Senryoshi 1945-1952: Tokyo, Washinton, Okinawa.* Tokyo: Chuo Koron Shinsya.

Fukuoka City (2017). *ICT wo Katuyo Shita Chiki Hokatu Kea Sisutemu no Kochiku: Hokengai sabisu no katuyo to sosyutu ni mukete.* Nihon Soken Website: http://www.jri.co.jp/MediaLibrary/file/column/opinion/detail/20170330_4.pdf (Retrieved 20th Apr. 2018)

Fuma, S. (2009). Chugoku Shakaifukushi Shijo ni okeru Kindai no Hajimari: Tokuni kyoyokenshi no atarashisa ni tuite. in Tao, T., Jiang, K., Kenjo, T., and Kirihara, K. (eds.) *ibid*, 195-228.

Funatsu, T. and Nagai, F. (2012). *Kawariyuku Tonan Ajia no Chihojichi.* Chiba: IDE.

Gabriel, M. (2014). *Making It Big: Strategies for scaling social innovations.* London: Nesta.

Ganz, M., Kay, T., and Spicer, J. (2018). Social Enterprise is not Social Change. *Stanford Social Innovation Review*, Spring 2018 https://ssir.org/articles/entry/social_enterprise_is_not_social_change (Retrieved 8th Apr. 2018).

George, A. L. and Bennett, A. (2005). *Case Studies and Theory Development in the Social Sciences.* Cambridge, Mass.: The MIT Press.

Giddens, A. (1998). *The Third Way.* Cambridge: Polity Press.

Giddens, A. (2010). The Rise and Fall of New Labour. *New Statesman*, 17th May 2010 http://www.newstatesman.com/uk-politics/2010/05/labour-policy-policies-blair (last accessed 28th Aug. 2017),

Global Social Economy Forum (2016). *Status of Social Economy Development in Seoul: A case study of Seoul.* Seoul: GSEF.

Goldsmith, S., Georges, G., and Burke, T. G. (2010). *The Power of Social Innovation.* San Francisco: Jossey-Bass.

Goodman, R. and Peng, I. (1996). The East Asian Welfare States: Peripatetic learning, adaptive change, and nation-building. In Esping-Andersen, G. (ed.) *Welfare States in Transition: National adaptations in global economics.* London: SAGE Publications, 192-224.

Guida, F. and Maiolini, R. Introduction: Social innovation, actors, contexts and trends. Opening the black box. In Sgaragli, F. (ed.) *Enabling Social Innovation Ecosystems for Community-Led Territorial Development.* Rome: Fondazione Giacomo Brodolini, 13-19.

Guo, L. (2017). *Nichu no Syoshikoreika to Fukushi Rejimu: Ikuji shien to koreisha fuyo, kaigo.* Sapporo: Hokkaido Daigaku Shuppankai.

Guo, C. and Lai, W. (2017). Community Foundations in China: In search of identity? *Voluntas* (2017), 1-17.

Guo, D. and Min, S. (2011). Chugoku: Chugoku ni okeru fukushikan to shakaiteki chowa. in Inoguchi, T. (ed.) *Ajia Barometa: Higashi ajia to Tonan ajia no kachikan.* Tokyo: Jigakusya Shuppan, 39-59.

Habermas, J., Translated by Hosoya, S. (1994). *Kokyosei no Kozo Tenkan: Shiminshakai no ichi kategori ni tuite no tankyu.* Tokyo: Mirai Sya.

Hadiwanata, B. S. (2003). *The Politics of NGOs in Indonesia: Developing democracy and managing a movement.* London: Routledge.

Hadiz, V. (2010). *Localising Power in Post Authoritarian Indonesia: A Southeast Asia perspective.* Stanford: Stanford University Press.

Haggard, S. and Kaufman, R. R. (2008). *Development, Democracy and Welfare States: Latin America, East Asia, and Eastern Europe.* Princeton and Oxford: Princeton University Press.

Hamada, E. and Kim, S. (2018). Shakaiteki Toshi Senryaku no Sogohyoka. in Miura, M. (ed.) *Shakai heno Toshi: Kojin wo sasaeru tsunagari wo kizuku.* Tokyo: Iwanami Shoten, 3-30.

Hamalainen, T. and Heiskala, R. (eds.) (2007). *Social Innovations, Institutional Change and Economic Performance: Making sense of structural adjustment processes in industrial sectors, regions, and societies.* Cheltenham: Edward Elgar.

Hansalim Cooperative (2016). *Hito to Hito Hito to Shizen Mata Isshoni Motto Atarashiku.* Hansalim Cooperative Website: http://www.hansalim.or.kr/wp-content/uploads/2016/06/2016-0622.pdf (Retrieved 7th Apr. 2018)

Happiness Foundation, The (2018). *2017 Annual Report.* Seoul: The Happiness Foundation.

Harada, K. (2013). Sado Sekuta to Seifu Sekuta no Kyodo: Nichiei no Seisaku Doko to Akauntabiriti. in Fujii, A., Harada, K., and Otaka, K. (eds.) *ibid*. 144-175.

Harada, S. (2015). NPO Hou Kaisei, Shinkifuzeisei no Seisaku Katei: Shodo rengo to seisakushikouteki gakusyu no hensen ni chakumoku site. *Nonprofit Review,* 15(1), 1-12.

Harada, S. (2017). NPO Hou Seitei Katei ni okeru Rippou Undou no Soshikikan Renkei: Bunyanai, bunyakan no renkei ni chakumoku site. *Nonprofit Review,* 17(2), 77-87.

Hasegawa, T. (2014). *Local Government Responsiveness in Indonesia after Decentralization: Examining elite initiatives and citizen participation.* A PhD Dissertation submitted to the University of Tsukuba. (Abstract only) https://tsukuba.repo.nii.ac.jp/?action=pages_view_main&active_action=repository_view_main_item_detail&item_id=32357&item_no=1&page_id=13&block_id=83

Hashimoto, Y. (2010). Hieiri, Kyodo to Chiki Kea Sisutemu. in Asakura, M. and Ota, T. (eds.) *Chiki Kea Sisutemu to sono Henkaku Shutai.* Tokyo: Kouseikan, 175-190.

Hashimoto, S. (2017). Kankoku ni okeru Shakaiteki Keizaisoshiki no Saikin no Douko: Shakaiteki kyodokumiai to shakaitekikigyo no jirei wo chushin ni. *Kansai Daigaku Shakaibakubu Kiyo,* 49(1), 33-61.

Hashiya, H. (2000). Keizai Kensetu to Kokusaika no Shinten. in Takeda, Y. (ed.) *Chosenshi.* Tokyo: Yamakawa Shuppansya, 363-436.

Hattori, T. (2005). 1980 Nendai Kankoku no Shakaikeizaiteki Henka: Kankoku ni totte 80 nendai to iunowa donoyona jidai data noka? in Hattori, T. and Kim, M. (eds.) *Kankoku shakai to Nihon Shakai no Henyo: Shimin, shiminundo, kankyo.* Tokyo: Keio Gijuku Daigaku Syuppankai, 1-33.

Hattori A., Muto, K., and Shibusawa, K (2010). *Sosharu Inobeshon: Eiri to hieiri wo koete.* Tokyo: Nihon Keizai Hyoronsha.

Haxeltine A., Kemp, R., Dumitru, A., Avelino, F., Pel, B., and Wittmayer, J. (2015). *TRANSIT WP3 Deliverable D3.2 – "A first prototype of TSI theory".* TRANSIT.

Haxeltine, A., Kemp, R., Cozan, S., Ruijsink, S., Backhaus, J., Avelino, F. and Dumitru, A. (2017). *How Social Innovation Leads to Transformative Change: Towards a theory of transformative social innovation.* TRANSIT Brief No.3, TRANSIT.

Hayase, N. and Matsubara, A. (2004). *NPO ga Wakaru Q&A.* Iwanami Booklet No. 618, Tokyo: Iwanami Shoten.

Hayashi, Y. and Imata, T. (eds.) (1999). *Firansoropi no Shiso: NPO to borantia.* Tokyo:

Nihon Keizai Hyouronsha.

Heals, C. and Green, H. (2016). *Social Innovation in Health and Social Care: Case study results*. A deliverable of the project: Social Innovation: Driving Force of Social Change (SI-DRIVE). Dortmund: Sozialforschungsstelle.

Heiskala, R. (2007). Social Innovations: Structural and power perspectives. In Hamalainen, T. and Heiskala, R. (eds.). *Social Innovations, Institutional Change and Economic Performance: Making sense of structural adjustment processes in industrial sectors, regions, and societies*. Cheltenham: Edward Elgar, 52-79.

Hirose, T. (2014). *Kaigo, Kango Sabisu Tokei Detashu 2015*. Tokyo: Santo Sha.

Hishida, M. (ed.) (2010). Chugoku Kisou karano Gabanansu. Tokyo: Hosei Daigaku Syupankyoku.

Holtzappel, C. J. G. (2009). Introduction: The regional governance reform in Indonesia. In Holtzappel, C. and Ramstedt, M. (eds.) *Decentralization and Regional Autonomy in Indonesia: Implementation and challenges*. Singapore: ISEAS, 1-56.

Hondai, S. and Nakamura, K. (2017). *Indonesia no Keizaihatten to Shotoku Kakusa: Nihon no keiken to hikaku bunseki*. Tokyo: Nihon Hyoronsha.

Honna, J. (2013). *Minshuka no Paradokusu: Indonesia ni miru ajia seiji no shinso*. Tokyo: Iwanami Shoten.

Hope Institute, The (2017). Social Innovation in Asia: Trends and characteristics in China, Korea, India, Japan and Thailand. In Morris-Suzuki, T. and Soh, E. J. (eds.) *New Worlds from Below: Informal life politics and grassroots action in Twenty-first-century Northeast Asia*. Acton: ANU Press. 249-274.

Howaldt, J., Butzin, A., Domanski, D., and Kaletka, C. (2014a). *Theoretical Approaches to Social Innovation – A critical literature review*. A deliverable of the project: Social Innovation: Driving Force of Social Change (SI-DRIVE). Dortmund: Sozialforschungsstelle.

Howaldt, J., Scroder, A., Kaletla, C., Refheld, D., and Terstriep, J. (2014b). *Mapping the World of Social Innovation: A global comparative analysis across sectors and world regions*. A deliverable of the project: Social Innovation: Driving Force of Social Change (SI-DRIVE). Dortmund: Sozialforschungsstelle.

Howaldt, J., Domanski, D., and Kaletka, C. (2016). Social Innovation: Towards a new innovation paradigm. *Mackenzie Management Review*, 17(6), 20-44.

Hu, M. and Guo, C. (2016). Fundraising Policy Reform and its Impact on Nonprofits in

China: A view from the trenches. *Nonprofit Policy Forum*, 7(2), 213-236.

Huang, M. (2014a). Seido. in Tsujinaka, Y. Lee, K., and Kojima, N. (eds.) *Gendai Chugoku no Shiminshakai, Riekidantai: Hikaku no naka no Chugoku*. Tokyo: Bokutakusha, 85-109.

Huang, M. (2014b). Minbenhikigyotani. in Tsujinaka, Y. Lee, K., and Kojima, N. (eds.) *ibid*, 199-216.

Huntington, S. P., Translated by Tsubouchi, M., Nakamichi, J., Yabuno, Y. (1995). *Daisan no Nami: 20 seiki kohan no minshuka*. Tokyo: Sanrei Shobo.

Hyun, D. (2011). Kankoku: Bunkateki henyo wo togetutu aru jukyoshakai. in Inoguchi, T. (ed.) *Ajia Barometa: Higashi ajia to tounan ajia no kachikan*. Tokyo: Jigakusha, 111-136.

Hwang, D. S., Jang, W., Park, J. S. and Kim, S. (2016). Social Enterprise in South Korea. *ICSEM Working Papers*, No. 35, Liege: The International Comparative Social Enterprise Models (ICSEM) Project.

Iijima, N. (2000). *Kankyomondai no Shakaishi*. Tokyo: Yuhikaku.

Ikawa, H. (2015). Indonesia ni okeru Chihojichi to Chihobunkenkaikaku. Ikawa, H. (ed.) *Ajia shokoku ni okeru chihobunken to chihojichi* (Vol.1). Tokyo: GRIPS, 11-46.

Imai, T. (2016). Igirisu ni Okeru Seikenkotai to Fukushi Gabanansu no Henyo. in Osawa, M. and Sato, I. (eds.) *Gabanansu wo toinaosu II: Shijo, shakai no henyo to kaikakuseiji*. Tokyo: Tokyo Daigaku Shuppankai, 173-198.

Inoue, K. (2006). *Nihon Kankyoshi Gaisetsu*. Okayama: Daigaku Kyoiku Shuppan.

Inoue, H. (2010). Sekai ni okeru Shakai Inobeta no Katuyaku. in Kaneko, I., Kokuryo, J., and Gen M. (eds.) *Shakai Inobeta heno Shotai: Henka wo tsukuru hito ni naru*. Tokyo: Keio Gijuku Daigaku Shuppan, 29-49.

Inoguchi, T. (2014). *Deta kara Yomu Ajia no Kofukudo: Seikatu no shitu no kokusaihikaku*. Tokyo: Iwanami Shoten.

Inoguchi, T. and Carlson, M. (2006). Introduction. In Inoguchi, T. and Carlson, M. (eds.) *Governance and Democracy in Asia*. Melbourne: Trans Pacific Press.

Inogchi, T. and Fujii, S. (2011). Nihon: Seikatu no shitu, shakaikankei shihon, gabanansu ni tsuiteno shimin no ninshiki. in Inoguchi, T. (ed.) *Ajia Barometa: Higashi ajia to Tounan ajia no kachikan*. Tokyo: Jigakusha, 137-161.

Ishii, T., Ogata, Y., Suzuki, K. (eds.) (2014). *Gendai Chugoku to Shiminshakai: Fuhenteki kindai no kanosei*. Tokyo: Bensei Shuppan.

Isobe, Y. (2008). *Gendai Chugoku no Chuo Chiho Kankei: Kantonsho in okeru chihobunken to sho shidosha*. Tokyo: Keio Gijuku Daigaku Shuppankai.

Isozaki, N. (2004). Taiseihendo to Shiminshakai no Netowaku. Tsujinaka, Y. and Yeom J. (eds.) *Gendai Kankoku no Shiminshakai, Riekidantai: Nikkan hikaku ni yoru taiseiiko no kenkyu*. Tokyo: Bokutaku Sha, 51-83.

Ito, S. and Kondo, Y. (2010). Gabanansuron no Tenkai to Chihoseifu, Shiminshakai: Rironteki kento to jisho ni muketa sosaka. Tsujinaka, Y. and Ito, S. (eds.) Rokaru gabanansu: Chihoseifu to shiminshakai. Tokyo: Bokutaku Sha, 19-38.

Ito, T. (2013). Nichio Nenkinkaikaku ni okeru Fukushikaikaku to Fukushiseiji: Hikakujireibunseki kara no sekkin. Japan Association for Comparative Politics (ed.) *Jireihikaku kara miru fukushiseiji*. Kyoto: Minerva Shobo, 1-31.

Ito, Y. (2016). *Kankyo Seisaku to Inobeshon: Kodoseichoki nihon no iosankabutsu taisaku no jireikenkyu*. Tokyo: Chuokeizaisha.

Iwabuchi, Y. (2018). Kankyo Machizukuri wo Toinaosu (Jyo) Mizushima Zaidan no Tanjo kara. *Sanyo Shimbun Digital*, 15th May 2018. http://www.sanyonews.jp/article/715441/1/?rct=machitan (Retrieved 24th Sep. 2018)

Jang, J. (2017). The Development of Social Economy in South Korea: Focusing on the role of the state and civil society. *Voluntas* 28(6), 2592-2613.

Japan Association of Charitable Organizations, The (2013). *Charitable and Non-profit Organizations in Japan*. Tokyo: JACO.

Japan Institute for Labour Policy and Training (JILPT) (2004). *NPO Houjin ni Okeru Noryoku Kaihatuto Koyo Sosyutu ni Kansuru Chosa*. Tokyo: JILPT.

Japan Institute for Labour Policy and Training (JILPT) (2015). *NPO Houjin no Katsudo to Hatarakikata ni Kansuru Chosa*. Tokyo: JILPT.

Japan Institute for Labour Policy and Training (JILPT) (2016). *NPO no Shuro ni Kansuru Kenkyu: Kojyoteki seicho to shinsai wo ki to shita henka wo toraeru*. Tokyo: JILPT.

Japan NPO Research Association (2017). *Higashinihon Daishinsaigo no NPO ni okeru Katudojittai to Kongo no Tenbo Chosahokokusho*. Japan NPO Research Association.

Jessop, B., Moulaert, F., Hulgard, L., and Hamdouch, A. (2013). Social Innovation Research: A new stage in innovation analysis? In Moulaert, F., MacCallum, D., Mehmood, A., and Hamdouch, A. (eds.) *The International Handbook on Social Innovation: Collective action, social learning and transdisciplinary research*. Cheltenham and Northampton: Edward Elgar Publishing, 110-130.

Jervis, R. (1997). *System Effects: Complexity in political and social life*. Princeton, N.J.: Princeton University Press.

Jia, X. (2017). China's Implementation of the Overseas NGO Management Law. *China Development Brief*. http://www.chinadevelopmentbrief.cn/articles/chinas-implementation-of-the-overseas-ngo-management-law/ (Retrieved 21st Mar. 2018)

JICA (Japan International Cooperation Agency) (2004). *Nihon no Sangyo Kogai Taisaku Keiken: Kaihatutojokoku to kakaku, shijo, kurinapurodakushon no kanten kara*. JICA.

Jolin, M. (2008). Innovating the White House: How the next president of the United States can spur social entrepreneurship. *Stanford Social Innovation Review*, 6(2), 23-24.

Jung, I. (2009). Explaining the Development and Adoption of Social Policy in Korea: The case of the National Basic Livelihood Security Act. *Health and Social Welfare Review*, 29(1), 52-79.

Jung, K., Jang, H., and Seo, I. (2015). Government-driven Social Enterprises in South Korea: Lessons from the social enterprise promotion program in the Seoul Metropolitan Government. *International Review of Administrative Sciences*, 82(3), 1-19.

Kabumoto, C. (2006). Kankoku no Jikatsukigyo: Koteki fujo ni yoru shuroshien no kanosei. In Noguchi, S. (ed.) *Fukushikokka no keisei, saihen to shakaifukushi seisaku*. Tokyo: Chuohoki Shuppan, 125-140.

Kanagawa, K. (2008). *Kyodogata Gabanansu to NPO: Igirisu no patonasipu seisaku wo jirei to site*. Kyoto: Koyo Shobo.

Kaneko, Y. (2014). Shakaihosho Kenkyu no Makuroteki Kokusai Hikaku: Hikaku fukushikokkaron no tenkai. in Nishimura, S., Kyogoku, T., and Kaneko, Y. (eds.) *Shakaihosho no Kokusai Hikaku Kenkyu: Seidosaiko ni muketa gakusaiteki, seisakukagakuteki apurochi*. Kyoto: Minerva Shobo, 19-40.

Kaneko, I., Kokuryo, J., and Gen M. (eds.) (2010). *Shakai Inobeta heno Shotai: Henka wo tukuru hito ni naru*. Tokyo: Keio Daigaku Shuppankai.

Kang, M. (2014). Korean Decentralization: Achievements and Future Challenges. In GRIPS *Achievements and Future Challenges of Decentralization in Asian Countries*. Tokyo: GRIPS, 133-150.

Kang X. and Han, H. (2007). Administrative Absorption of Society: A further probe into the state-society relationship in Chinese Mainland. *Social Sciences in China*, Special Issue: NGOs and Social Transition in China, 116-128.

Kang, X. and Han, H. (2008). Graduated Controls: The state-society relationship in

Contemporary China. *Modern China*, 34(1), 36-55.

Kashiwagi, H. (2004). *NPO Hojin Unei, Zeimu Kanzen Manyuaru: Darenidemo wakaru NPO no jitumu*. Tokyo: J Risachi Shuppan.

Kashiwagi, H. (2008). *NPO to Seiji: Adobokasi to shakaihenkaku no aratana ninaite no tameni*. Tokyo: Akashi Shuppan.

Kawamura, K. (2015). *Shinko Minsyusyugi Taikoku Indonesia: Yudoyono seiken no jyunen to jokowi daitoryo no tanjo*. Chiba: IDE.

Kawamura, M. (2014). *Kaigohoken Saitenken: Seido jishi jyunen no hyoka to 2050 nen no gurando dezain*. Kyoto: Minerva Shobo.

Kawato, Y., Pekkanen, R. J., and Yamamoto, H. (2011). State and Civil Society in Japan, In Gaunder, A. (ed.) *Routledge Handbook of Japanese Politics*. Abingdon: Routledge, 117-129.

Kelly, M., Yutthaphonphinit, P., Seubsman, S.-A., and Sleigh, A. C. (2012). Development Policy in Thailand: From top-down to grass roots. *Asian Social Science*, 8(13), 29-39.

Kikkawa, J. (2012). Kankoku no Komuniti Dukuri no Jisen: Sonmisan mauru no aratana chosen. in Akiba, T. et al. (eds.) *ibid*, 203-217.

Kim, S. (2000). *The Politics of Democratization in Korea: The role of civil society*. Pittsburgh: University of Pittsburgh Press.

Kim, S. (2008). *Kouhatsu Fukushikokkaron: Hikaku no nakano kankoku to higasi ajia*. Tokyo: Tokyo Daigaku Shyuppankai.

Kim, K. (2013). Chaebols and Their Effect on Economic Growth in South Korea, *Korean Social Sciences Review*, 3(2), 1-28.

Kim, S. (2014). Nihon: Sengo ni okeru shakaihosyo seido no seiritu to sono tokucho. in Tada, H. (ed.) *Sekai ha Naze Shakaihosho Seido wo Tsukuta noka: Shuyo kyukakoku no hikaku kenkyu*. Kyoto: Minerva Shobo, 231-263.

Kim, K. (2015). Kankoku ni okeru Shakaitekikigyo no Tenkai. in Ikemoto, Y. and Matsui, H. (eds.) *Rentai Keizai to Sosharu Bizinesu: Hinkonsakugen, tomi no saibunpai no tameno keipabiriti apurochi*. Tokyo: Akashi Shoten, 185-207.

Kim, S. (2016). *Fukushikoka no Nikkan Hikaku: Kouhatsukoku ni okeru koyohosho, shakai-hosyo*. Tokyo: Akashi Shoten.

Kim, I. and Hwang, C. (2002). *Defining the Nonprofit Sector: South Korea*. Working Papers of the Johns Hopkins Comparative Nonprofit Sector Project, No. 41. Baltimore: The

Johns Hopkins Center for Civil Society Studies.

Kimura, E. (2013). *Political Change and Territoriality in Indonesia: Provincial proliferation.* Abingdon and New York: Routledge.

Kishimoto, M. (1998). Chugoku toha Nanika. Ogata, I. and Kishimoto, M. (eds.) *Chugoku Shi.* Tokyo: Yamakawa Shuppansha, 3-23.

Kishimoto, M. (2012). *Chikishakairon Saiko: Minshinshi ronsyu 2.* Tokyo: Kenbun Syuppan.

Koga, S. (2010). *Chugoku Toshishakai to Kusanone NGO.* Tokyo: Ochanomizu Shobo.

Kojima, H. (2003). *Seisaku Keisei to NPO Hou: Mondai, seisaku, sosite seiji.* Tokyo: Yuhikaku.

Kojima, N. and Kobashi, Y. (2014). Kikinkai. in Tsujinaka, Y. Li, K., and Kojima, N. (eds.) *ibid*, 217-233.

Kooiman, J. (2003). *Governing as Governance.* London: SAGE Publications.

Kramer, M. R. (2017). Systems Change in a Polarized Country. *Stanford Social Innovation Review.* Online edition, April 11, 2017 https://ssir.org/articles/entry/systems_change_in_a_polarized_country (Retrieved 10th Jul. 2017).

Kwon, H. (1999). *The Welfare State in Korea: The politics of legitimation.* Basingstoke: Palgrave Macmillan.

Lake, R. W. (2016). The Subordination of Urban Policy in the Time of Financialization. In DeFilippis, J. (ed.). *Urban Policy in the Time of Obama.* Minneapolis: University of Minnesota Press, 49-64.

Lane, M. (2014). *Decentralization & Its Discontents: An essay on class, political agency and national perspective in Indonesian politics.* Singapore: ISEAS.

Lane, T., Ghosh, A., Hamann, J., Phillips, S., Schulze-Ghattas, M., and Tsikata, T. (1999). *IMF-Supported Programs in Indonesia, Korea, and Thailand: A preliminary assessment.* Occasional Paper 178, Washington D.C.: IMF.

Laratta, R., Nakagawa, S., and Sakurai, M. (2011). Japanese Social Enterprises: Major contemporary issues and key challenges. *Social Enterprise Journal*, 7(1), 50-68.

Lee, E. (2012). Kankoku no Shakaitekikigyo no Genkyo to Shiminshakai no Inisiatibu. in Akiba, T. et al. (eds.) *ibid*, 121-164.

Lee, W. (2017). Innovating Local Government. *Social Innovation and Social Transition in East Asia*, a supplement of the *Stanford Social Innovation Review*, 18-19.

Leung, J. C. B. and Xu, Y. B. (2010). The Emergence of Social Assistance in China. In Midgley, J. and Tang, K.-L. (eds.) *Social Policy and Poverty in East Asia: The role of social security.* Abingdon: Routledge, 47-65.

Lewis, B. D. (2014). Twelve Years of Fiscal Decentralization: A balance sheet. In Hill, H. (ed.) *Regional Dynamics in a Decentralized Indonesia*. Singapore: ISEAS, 135-155.

Li, Y. (2008). Chishiki Bunshi no Yakuwari. in Li, Y. (ed.) *ibid*, 63-80.

Li, X. (2018a). *Gendai Chugoku no Shosatu: Hyakusei shakai no shiten kara*. Tokyo: Kokusai Shoin.

Li, Y. (2018b). *Shita kara Kouchiku Sareru Chugoku: Chugokuteki shiminshakai no riariti*. Tokyo: Akashi Shoten.

Lim, S. H. and Endo, C. (2016). The Development of the Social Economy in the Welfare Mix: Political dynamics between the state and the third sector. *Social Science Journal*, 53(4), 486-494.

Lin, C. Y.-Y., and Chen, J. (2016). *The Impact of Societal and Social Innovation: A case-based approach*. Singapore: Springer.

Liu, P. (2008). Chugoku ni Okeru Kusanone NGO Taito no Shakaiteki Haikei. in Li, Y. (ed.) *ibid*, 21-33.

Lowe, R. (1993). *The Welfare State in Britain since 1945*. Basingstoke: Macmillan Press.

Lupton, R., Hills, J., Stewart, K., and Vizard, P. (2013). *Labour's Social Policy Record: Policy, spending and outcomes 1997-2010*. Social Policy in a Cold Climate Research Report 1. London: Centre for Analysis of Social Exclusion, LSE.

Lyon, F. (2012). Social Innovation, Co-operation, and Competition: Inter-organizational relations for social enterprises in the delivery of public services. In Nicholls, A. and Murdock, A. (eds.) *Social Innovation: Blurring boundaries to reconfigure markets*. Basingstoke: Palgrave Macmillan. 139-161.

Ma, C. (2014). Chugoku Shiminshakairon Kenkyu no Genjo to Kadai, Tenbo: Shiminshakai to hochikokkakan no kankei kenkyu ni motozuku kousatu. in Ishii, T., Ogata, Y., and Suzuki, K. (eds.) *ibid*, 77-101.

Maezawa, M. (2011). Byoin Kinou Bunka to Chiki Houkatu Kea. in Ota, T. and Morimoto, Y. (eds.) *Chiki Houkatu Kea Sisutemu: Sono kangaekata to kadai*. Tokyo: Koseikan.

Mahi, B. R. (2014). Indonesian Decentralization: Achievements and the Future Prospect. In GRIPS *Achievements and Future Challenges of Decentralization in Asian Countries*. Tokyo: GRIPS, 51-81.

Martinelli, F. (2013). Learning from Case Studies of Social Innovation in the Field of Social Services: Creatively balancing top-down universalism with bottom-up democracy. In Moulaert, F. MacCallum, D., Mehmood, A. and Hamdouch, A. (eds.) *The International*

Handbook on Social Innovation: Collective action, social learning and transdisciplinary research. Cheltenham and Northampton: Edward Elgar Publishing, 346-360.

Marukawa, T. (2013). *Gendai Chugoku Keizai.* Tokyo: Yuhikaku.

Masuda, M. (2013). Ajia no Shakaihosho. in Masuda, M. and Kim J. (eds.) *Ajia no Shakaihosho.* Tokyo: Horitu Bunkasha, 1-23.

Masuda, H. (ed.) (2014). *Chiho Shometu: Tokyo ikkyoku shuchu ga maneku jinko kyugen.* Tokyo: Chuo Koron Shinsha.

Masumi, J. (2005). Sengoshi no Kigen to Isou. in Nakamura M., Tankawa, A., Yun, K., and Igarashi, T. (eds.) *Senryo to Kaikaku.* Tokyo: Iwanami Shoten, 1-30.

Matsue, A. (2014). Kankoku: IMF Keizailiki to Shakaihosho Seido no Sosetu. in Tada, H. (ed.) *ibid*, 265-296.

Matsushita, K. (2002). *Atarashi Kokyo to Jichitai: Jichitai ha naze NPO to patonashipu wo kumanakereba ikenai noka.* Tokyo: Shinzansha.

McGowan, K., Westley, F., and Tjornbo, O. (2017). The History of Social Innovation. in Westley, F., McGowan, K., and Tjornbo, O. (eds.) *The Evolution of Social Innovation.* Cheltenham and Northampton: Edward Elgar Publishing, 1-17.

Meckstroth, T. W. (1975). "Most Different Systems" and "Most Similar Systems": A study in the logic of comparative inquiry. *Comparative Political Studies*, 8(2), 132-157.

Mendell, M., Spear, R., Noya, A., and Clarence, E. (2010). *Improving Social Inclusion at the Local Level Through the Social Economy: Report for Korea.* OECD Local Economic and Employment Development Working Papers 2010/15. Paris: OECD.

Michida, E. (2005). Makuro Keizai no Doko to Kadai: Toshi no kaifuku ni mukete. in Ishida, M. (ed.) *Indonesia Saisei heno Chosen.* Chiba: IDE, 58-74.

Mietzner, M. (2013). *Money, Power and Ideology: Political parties in post-authoritarian Indonesia.* Honolulu: University of Hawai'i Press.

Miharti, S., Holzhacker, R. L. and Wittek, R. (2016). Decentralization and Primary Health Care Innovations in Indonesia. In Holzhacker, R. L., Wittek, R. and Woltjer, J. (eds.) *Decentralization and Governance in Indonesia.* New York and London: Springer, 53-78.

Miichi, K. (2004). *Indonesia Isuramu Shugi no Yukue.* Tokyo: Heibonsha.

Ministry of Health, Labour and Welfare (2016). *Heisei 28 Nen Kaigo Sabisu Shisetu, Jigyosyo Chousa no Gaikyo.* MoHLW Website: https://www.mhlw.go.jp/toukei/saikin/hw/kaigo/service16/index.html (Retrieved 11th Sep. 2018)

Ministry of Health, Labour and Welfare (2017). *Chiki Kyosei Shakai no Jitugen ni Mukete (Toumen no Kaikaku Koutei).* Tokyo: MoHLW.

Mitsubishi UFJ Research & Consulting (2010). *Chiki Houkatu Kea Kenkyukai Hokokusyo.* Tokyo: Mitsubishi UFJ Research & Consulting.

Miyamoto, T. (2006). Fukushikokka no Saihen to Gensetsu Seiji: Atarashi bunseki wakugumi. in Miyamoto, T. (ed.) *Hikaku Fukushi Seiji: Seidotenkan no akuta to senryaku.* Tokyo: Waseda Daigaku Shupanbu, 68-88.

Miyamoto, K. (2014a). *Sengo Nihon Kogai Shiron.* Tokyo: Iwanami Shoten.

Miyamoto, K. (2014b). Nihon no Kougai no Rekishiteki Kyokun. in Miyamoto, K. and Awaji, T. (eds.) *Kogai, Kankyo Kenkyu no Paioniatachi.* Tokyo: Iwanami Shoten, 3-40.

Miyamoto, T. (2014c). Chiki Shakai wo Ikani Sasaeru noka: Seikatsu hosho no saihen to chiki hokatu kea. in Miyamoto, T. (ed.) *Chiki Hokatu Kea to Seikatu Hosho no Saihen: Atarashi sasaeai sisutemu wo tukuru.* Tokyo: Akashi Shoten, 15-44.

Miyazaki, I. (1963). *Kakyo: Chugoku no juken jigoku.* Tokyo: Chuo Koron Shinsya.

Miyogawa, K. (2002). Minamatabyo to Kagaku. iin Kato, T. and Watanabe, M. (eds.) *Hitotsubashi Daigaku Kokusai Sinpozium 20 Seiki no Yume to Genjitu: Senso, Bunmei, Fukushi.*Tokyo: Sairyusha, 271-285.

Mohan, A., Harsh, S., Ganesh, D., Jha, P., Raote, R., Detorre, R., and Sharma, V. (2017a). *Social Investment Landscape in Asia: Insights from North and South Asia.* Singapore: AVPN.

Mohan, A., Harsh, S., Modi, A. (2017b). *Social Investment Landscape in Asia: Insights from Southeast Asia.* Singapore: AVPN.

Moore, M.-L., Westley, F. R., Tjornbo, O., and Holroyd, C. (2012). The Loop, the Lens, and the Lesson: Using Resilience Theory to examine public policy and social innovation. In Nicholls, A., and Murdock, A. *Social Innovation: Blurring boundaries to reconfigure markets.* Baskingstoke: Palgrave Macmillan, 89-113.

Morgan, K. J. and Campbell, A. L. (2011). *The Delegated Welfare State: Medicare, Markets, and the Governance of Social Policy.* Oxford: Oxford University Press.

Morgenthau, H. J. (1968). *Politics among Nations: The struggle for power and peace.* Fourth Edition. New York: Alfred A. Knopf.

Morishita, A. (2015). *Tennen Shigen wo Meguru Seiji to Boryoku: Gendai Indonesia no chiho seiji.* Kyoto: Kyoto Daigaku Shuppankai.

Morris-Suzuki, T. (2017). Introduction: Informal Life Politics in Northeast Asia. In

References *229*

Morris-Suzuki, T., and Soh, E.-J. (eds.) *New Worlds from Below: Informal life politics and grassroots action in twenty-first-century Northeast Asia*. Acton: Australian National University, 1-14.

Moulaert, F., MacCallum D., and Hiller J. (2013). Social Innovation: Intuition, precept, concept, theory and practice. In Moulaert, F. MacCallum, D., Mehmood, A. and Hamdouch, A. (eds.) *The International Handbook on Social Innovation: Collective action, social learning and transdisciplinary research*. Cheltenham and Northampton: Edward Elgar Publishing, 13-24.

Mukai, K. (2015). *Posuto Fukushikokka no Sado Sekutaron: Shiminteki kokyoken no ninaite to shitenokanosei*. Kyoto: Minerva Shobo.

Mulgan, G. (2012). The Theoretical Foundations of Social Innovation. In Nicholls, A., and Murdock, A. (2012). *Social Innovation: Blurring boundaries to reconfigure markets*. Baskingstoke: Palgrave Macmillan, 33-65.

Mulgan, G., Tucker, S., Ali, R., and Sanders, B. (2007). *Social Innovation: What it is, why it matters and how it can be accelerated*. Skoll Centre for Social Entrepreneurship Working Paper, Oxford: Said Business School.

Mun, G. *Shin Kankoku Gendaishi*. Tokyo: Iwanami Shoten.

Muramatsu, Y. (1994). *Nihon no Gyosei: Katudogata kanryosei no henbo*. Tokyo: Chuo Koron Shinsha.

Muramatsu, Y., Ito, M., and Tsujinaka, Y. (2001). *Nihon no Seiji* (Second Edition). Tokyo: Yuhikaku.

Murray, J. H. (2012). Choose Your Own Master: Social enterprise, certifications, and benefit corporation statutes. *American University Business Law Review*, 2(1), 1-53.

Murray, R., Caulier-Grice, J., and Mulgan, G. (2010). *The Open Book of Social Innovation*. Social Innovator Series, London: The Young Foundation and NESTA.

Nagashima, Y. (2016). Toritsu Tama Shakai Kyoiku Kaikan Shiminkatudo Sabisu Kona Siryo to sono Akaibuka ni kansuru Kosatu. *The Bulletin of the National Institute of Japanese Literature*. (12), 75-95.

Najita, T. (2009). *Ordinary Economies in Japan: A historical perspective 1750-1950*. Berkeley: University of California Press.

Nakamura, Y. (2000). Shiminkatudo no Tojo to Tenkai. in Nakamura, Y. and Japan NPO Center (eds.) *Nihon no NPO/2000*. Tokyo: Nihon Hyoronsha, 31-39.

Nakamura, M., Siddique, S., and Bajunid, O. F. (eds.) (2001). *Islam and Civil Society in*

Southeast Asia. Singapore: ISEAS.

Nasution, A. (2016). *Government Decentralization Program in Indonesia*. ADBI Working Paper 601. Tokyo: Asian Development Bank Institute.

National Institute of Population and Social Security Research (2017). *The Financial Statistics of Social Security in Japan*. Fiscal Year 2015, Tokyo: NIPSSR.

Nicholls, A. and Murdock, A. (2012). The Nature of Social Innovation. In Nicholls, A. and Murdock, A. (eds.) *Social Innovation: Blurring boundaries to reconfigure markets*. Basingstoke: Palgrave Macmillan, 1-30.

Nicholls, A., Simon, J., and Gabriel, M. (2015). Introduction: Dimensions of Social Innovation. In Nicholls, A., Simon, J., and Gabriel, M. (eds.) *New Frontiers in Social Innovation Research*. Basingstoke: Palgrave Macmillan, 1-26.

Nie, J.-B. (2016). Erosion of Eldercare in China: A socio-ethical inquiry in aging, elderly suicide and the government's responsibilities in the context of the one-child policy. *Ageing International*, 41(4), 350-365.

Nihei, N. (2011). *Borantia no Tanjo to Syuen: Zoyo no paradokusu no chishiki shakaigaku*. Nagoya: Nagoya Daigaku Syuppankai.

Nippon Institute for Research Advancement (NIRA) (1994). *Shimin Koeki Katsudo Kiban Seibi ni kansuru Chosakenkyu*. Tokyo: NIRA.

Nishimura, H. (ed.) (2014). *Sosharu Inobeshon ga Hiraku Mirai*. Kyoto: Horitsu Bunka Sha.

Noguchi, Y. (2015). *Sengo Keizaishi: Watashi tachi ha dokode machigaetanoka*. Tokyo: Toyo Keizai.

Nonaka, I., Hirano, F., and Hirata, T. (2014). *Jissen Sosyaru Inobeshon: Chi wo kachi ni kaeta komyuniti, kigyo, NPO*. Tokyo: Chikura Shobo.

Numao, N. (2014). Chiki Hokatu Kea ni okeru Jichitai Gyozaisei Un-ei no Kadai. in Miyamoto, T. (ed.) *Chiki Hokatu Kea to Seikatuhosho no Saihen: Atarashi sasaeai sisutemu wo tukuru*. Tokyo: Akashi Shoten, 119-150.

Nyman, M. (2009). Civil Society and the Challenges of the Post-Suharto Era. In Bunte, M. and Ufen, A. (eds.) *Democratization in Post-Suharto Indonesia*. Abingdon: Routledge, 251-275.

O'Byrne, L., Miller, M., Douse, C., Vankatesh, R., Kapucu, N. (2014). Social Innovation in the Public Sector: The case of Seoul Metropolitan Government. Journal of Economic and Social Studies, 4(1), 51-68.

Ochiai, E. (2009). Care Diamonds and Welfare Regimes in East and South-East Asian Societies: Bridging family and welfare sociology. *International Journal of Japanese Sociology*, 18(1), 60-78.

Ochiai E. (2013). Higashi Asia no Teishuseiritu to Kazokushugi: Hanashuku kindai to shiteno nihon. in Ochiai, E. (ed.) *Shinmituken to Kokyoken no Saihensei: Ajia kindai karano toi.* Kyoto: Kyoto Daigaku Shuppankai, 67-97.

Ochiai, E., Abe, A., Uzuhashi, T., Tamiya, Y., and Shikata, M. (2010). Nihon ni okeru Kea Daiamondo no Saihensei: Kaigohoken ha kazokushugi wo kaetaka. *Kaigai Shakai Hosho Kenkyu.* (170), 4-19.

OECD (2010). *OECD Environmental Performance Reviews JAPAN.* Paris: OECD.

OECD (2011). *Fostering Innovation to Address Social Challenges.* LEED Forum on Social Innovations.

OECD (2016). *Social Expenditure Update 2016.* http://www.oecd.org/els/soc/OECD2016-Social-Expenditure-Update.pdf (Figure from http://www.oecd.org/social/expenditure.htm) (Retrieved 11th Apr. 2017).

Ohmura, K. (2013). Igirisu. in Shizume M. and Kondo M. (eds.) *Hikaku Fukushikokka: Riron, keiryo, kakkokujirei.* Kyoto: Minerva Shobo, 244-266.

Ohmuro, N. (2009). Sosyaru Inobeshon Riron no Keifu. *Kyoto Management Review* (15), 13-40.

Okada, I. (2016). *Kakushin Jichitai: Nekkyo to zasetsu ni nani wo manabu ka.* Tokyo: Chuo Kouron Shinsha.

Okamoto, M. (2012). Gyakukosu wo Ayumu Indonesia no Chihojichi: Chuoseifu ni yoru gabamento kyokaheno kokoromi. in Funatsu T. and Nagai, F. (eds.) *Kawariyuku tounanajia no chihojichi.* Chiba: IDE, 27-66.

Okamoto, M. (2015a). Yudoyono Seiken no Jyunenkan: Seijiteki antei, teitai to shiminshakai no taido. In Kawamura, K. (ed.) *Shinko Minshushugi Taikoku Indonesia: Yudoyono seiken no jyunenkan to jokowi daitoryo no tanjo.* Chiba: IDE, 159-184.

Okamoto, M. (2015b). *Boryoku to Tekio no Seijigaku: Indonesia minshuka to chihoseiji no antei.* Kyoto: Kyoto Daigaku Shuppankai.

Okamura, S. (2017). Chugoku no Jizenho to Jizenjigyo no Hatten. *Gaikoku no Rippo,* (271), 250-274.

Onishi, Y. (2014). *Senshinkoku Kankoku no Yuutsu: Shosikoreika, keizaikakusa, gurobaruka.* Tokyo: Chuo Koron Shinsha.

Ooi, C. (2010). Takayamashi Shakaifukushikyogikai no Juminsoshikika Katsudo. in Asakura, M. and Ota,T. (eds.) *Chiki Kea Sisutemu to Sono Henkaku Shutai*. Tokyo: Koseikan, 107-122.

Ostwald, K., Tajima, Y. and Samphantharak, K. (2016). Indonesia's Decentralization Experiment: Motivations, successes, and unintended consequences. *Journal of Southeast Asian Economics* 33(2), 139-156.

Ozaki, T. (2001). Kaigohoken to NPO. in Yamaoka, Y., Hayase, N., and Ishikawa, R. (eds.) *NPO Hieiri Sekuta no Jidai: Tayo na kyodo no kanosei wo saguru*. Kyoto: Minerva Shobo, 221-237.

Park, W. (2012). Nikkan no Shiminshakai, Shakaitekikigyo wo Kataru. in Akiba, T. et al. (eds.) *ibid*, 12-38.

Park, H. (2016). Sanka to Kyodo ni Hisomu Katto: Chiiki ni okeru fukushi gabanansu. in Osawa, M., and Sato, I. (eds.) *Gabanansu wo Toinaosu I: Ekkyo suru riron no yukue*. Tokyo: Tokyo Daigaku Shuppankai, 135-157.

Pekkanen, R. (2006). *Japan's Dual Civil Society: Members without advocates*. Stanford: Stanford University Press.

Pel, B. and Bauler, T. (2014). *The Institutionalization of Social Innovation: Between transformation and capture*. TRANSIT working paper no. 2, TRANSIT.

Pel, B., Bauler, T., Avelino, F., Backhaus, J., Ruijsink, S., Rach, S.et al. (2017). *The Critical Turning Points Database: Concept, methodology and dataset of an international transformative social innovation comparison*. TRANSIT Working Paper No. 10, TRANSIT.

Peng, I. (2009). *The Political and Social Economy of Care: Republic of Korea Research Report 3*. Geneva: UNRISD.

Pestoff, V., Translated by Fujita, A. et al. (2000). *Fukushishakai to Shiminminshushugi: Kyodokumiai to shakaitekikigyo no yakuwari*. Tokyo: Nihon Keizai Hyoronsha.

Phills, J. A., Deiglmeier, K., and Miller, D. T. (2008). Rediscovering Social Innovation. *Stanford Social Innovation Review*, Fall 2008, 34-43.

Pierre, J. (2000). Introduction: Understanding governance. In Pierre, J. (ed.) *Debating Governance: Authority, steering, and democracy*. Oxford: Oxford University Press, 1-12.

Pierson, P. (1996). The New Politics of the Welfare State. *World Politics*, 48(2), 143-179.

Pierson, C. (2002). 21 Seiki he to Mukau Fukushikokka. in Kato, T. and Watanabe, M. (eds.) *ibid*, 63-74.

Potts, M. (2017). Social Innovation Comes to Pennsylvania Avenue. *Stanford Social Innovation Review*, Spring 2017, 20-27.

Pratikno (2011). Indonesia: Seiji kaikaku kara 8 nen, fumanzoku na kekka. in Inoguchi, T. (ed.) *ibid*, 271-282.

Prewitt, K. (2006). Foundations. In Powell, W. and Steinberg, R. (eds.) *The Non-profit Sector: A research handbook*. 2nd edition, New Haven & London: Yale University Press, 355-377.

Przeworski, A. and Teune, H. (1970). *The Logic of Comparative Social Inquiry*. New York: Wiley-Interscience.

Ra, I. (2015). *Sosharu Bijinesu no Seisaku to Jissen*. Kyoto: Horitu Bunkasha.

Ragin, C. C., Translated by Shikamata, N. (1993). *Shakaikagaku ni Okeru Hikaku Kenkyu: Shituteki bunseki to keiryoteki bunseki no togo ni mukete*. Kyoto: Minerva Shobo.

Ramage, D. E. (1997). *Politics in Indonesia: Democracy, Islam and the ideology of tolerance*. Paperback version, London and New York: Routledge.

Rana, P. B. and Hamid, N. (eds.) (1996). *From Centrally Planned to Market Economics: The Asian approach Volume 2 People's Republic of China and Mongolia*. Oxford: Oxford University Press.

Reality Check Approach (2016). *Local perspectives and experiences of the Village Law in Indonesia*. Jakarta: KOMPAK.

Rhodes, R. A. W. (1997). *Understanding Governance: Policy Networks, Governance, Reflexivity and Accountability*. Maidenhead: Open University Press.

Ricklefs, M. C. (2008). *A History of Modern Indonesia since c. 1200*. 4th edition, Basingstoke and New York: Palgrave Macmillan.

Robinson, D. T. and Stuart, T. E. (2007). Network Effects in the Governance of Strategic Alliances. *Journal of Law, Economics and Organization*, 23(1), 242-273.

Rogers, E. M. (1983). *Diffusion of Innovations*. 3rd edition, New York: Free Press.

Rosenbluth, F. M. and Thies, M. F. (2010). *Japan Transformed: Political change and economic restructuring*. Princeton: Princeton University Press.

Saito, J. (2010). *Jiminto Chokiseiken no Seijikeizaigaku: Riekiyudo seiji no jikomujun*. Tokyo: Keiso Shobo.

Sakamoto, F. (2004). *NPO no Keiei: Sikin chotatu kara unei made*. Tokyo: Nikkei.

Sakamoto, H. and Tsujinaka, Y. (2012). NPO Seiji no Bunseki Sikaku. in Tsujinaka, Y., Sakamoro, H., and Yamamoto, H. (eds.) *Gendai Nihon no NPO Seiji: Shiminshakai no shinkyokumen.* Tokyo: Bokutakusha, 23-48.

Salamon, L. M. (1995). *Partners in Public Service.* Baltimore: John Hopkins University Press.

Salamon, L. M., Translated by Egami, A., and Ono, A. (2007). *NPO to Kokyo Sabisu: Seifu to minkan no patonashipu.* Kyoto: Minerva Shobo.

Salamon, L. M. and Anheier, H. K. (1998) Social Origins of Civil Society: Explaining the nonprofit sector cross-nationally. *Voluntas*, 9(3), 213-248.

Sato, S. (2003). *Kaigohoken Un-ei ni okeru Jichitai no Kadai.* Kyoto: Houritu Bunkasha.

Sawada, Y. (2014). Revisions to the Long-Term Care Insurance System. In Sumii, H. and Sawada, Y. (eds.) *Achievements and Future Directions of the Long-Term Care Insurance System in Japan: Toward social "kaigo" security in the global longevity society.* Okayama: University Education Press, 192-205.

Sawada, Y. and Sumii, H. (2014). Introduction to and Background of Long-Term Care Insurance in Japan: Creating and maintaining "kaigo" security". In Sumii, H. and Sawada, Y. (eds.) *ibid.* 3-16.

Sawai, M. and Tanimoto, M. (2016). *Nihonkeizaishi: Kinsei kara gendai made.* Tokyo: Yuhikaku.

Schulze, G. G. and Sjahrir, B. S. (2014). Decentralization, Governance and Public Service Delivery. In Hill, H. (ed.) *Regional Dynamics in a Decentralized Indonesia.* Singapore: ISEAS, 186-207.

Schumpeter, J. A., Translated by Nakayama, I. and Tohata, S. (1937). *Keizai Hatten no Riron: Kigyosha rijun, shihon, shinyo, rishi oyobi keiki no kaiten ni kansuru ichikenkyu.* Tokyo: Iwanami Shoten.

Schumpeter, J. A. (1994). *Capitalism, Socialism and Democracy.* Paperback reprinted version of first published in 1943, London: Routledge.

Seol, D. and Haruki, I. (2011). Kankoku Shakai ga Chokumen suru Mittu no Kadai. in Haruki, I. and Seol, D. (eds.) *Kankoku no Shosikoreika to Kakusashakai: Nikkan hikaku no siza kara.* Tokyo: Keio Gijuku Daigaku Shuppankai, 1-18.

Seoul Innovation Center (2017). *Seoul Innovation Research Lab at Seoul Innovation Center 2016 Annual Report.* Seoul: Seoul Innovation Center.

Seoul Metropolitan Government. (2015). *Seoul Innovation Report.* Seoul: Seoul

Metropolitan Government.

Sgaragli, F. and Giacomo Brodolini Foundation (2014). Preface. In Sgaragli, F. (ed.) *Enabling Social Innovation Ecosystems for Community-Led Territorial Development*. Rome: Fondazione Giacomo Brogolini, 7-11.

Shen, J. (2014). *Chugoku no Shakaifukusi Kaikaku ha Nani wo Mezasou to Shiteirunoka: Shakaishugi, shihonshugi no chowa*. Kyoto: Minerva Shobo.

Shen, J. (2016). Posuto Kaikakuki no Chugoku Shakaihosho. in Shen, J. and Sawada, Y. *Posuto Kaikakuki no Chugoku Shakaihosho ha Dou naru noka: Senbetushigi kara fuhenshigi heno tankan no naka de*. Kyoto: Minerva Shobo, 1-19.

Shen, D. and Li, F. (2017). East Asia's Role in Global Social Innovation. *Stanford Social Innovation Review,* Spring 2017 Supplement, 3-4.

Shim, J. (2011). Kankoku Shakaifukushi Sabisu no Henka to Chikifukushi. in Goto, S., Komatsu, R., and Noguchi, S. (eds.) *Kazoku: Komuniti no henbo to fukushishakai no kaihatu*. Tokyo: Chuohoki Shuppan, 151-165.

Shimagami, M. (2012). Indonesia Bunkenka Jidai no Sonraku Kaikaku: Sonraku jichi wo meguru rinen to genjitu. in Funatsu T. and Nagai, F. (eds.) *Kawariyuku tounanajia no chihojichi*. Chiba: IDE, 67-104.

Shinoda, T. (2011). Prime Ministerial Leadership. In Gaunder, A. (ed.) *The Routledge Handbook of Japanese Politics*. Abingdon: Routledge, 48-59.

Shiraishi, T. (1997). *Sukaruno to Suharuto: Idai naru Indonesia wo mezasite*. Tokyo: Iwanami Shoten.

Shiraishi, T. (2006). *Shinpan Indonesia*. Tokyo: NTT Shuppan.

Shiraishi, T. (2010). Indonesia ni oite Keizai Seicho no Seiji ha ikanishite Fukkatu shitaka. in Otsuka, K.and Shiraishi, T. (eds.) *Kokka to Keizaihatten: Nozomashi kokka no sugata wo motomete*. Tokyo: Toyo Keizai Shinposha, 9-29.

Shirasawa, M. (2011). *Kaigohoken Seido no Arubeki Sugata: Riyosha shutai no kea manejimento wo motoni*. Tokyo: Tsutsui Shobo.

SI-DRIVE (2018). *Atlas of Social Innovation: New practices for a better future*. A deliverable of the project: Social Innovation: Driving Force of Social Change (SI-DRIVE). Dortmund: Sozialforschungsstelle.

Simon, K. W. (2013). *Civil society in China: The legal framework from ancient times to the "New Reform Era"*. Oxford and New York: Oxford University Press.

Sorensen, E. and Torfing, J. (2006). Introduction: Governance Network Research: Towards a second generation. In Sorensen, E. and Torging, J. (eds.) *Theories of Democratic Network Governance*. London: Palgrave Macmillan, 1-21.

SSIR Editor's Note (2003). Helping Those Who Do the Important Work of Improving Society Do It Even Better. *Stanford Social Innovation Review*, Spring 2003, 4-5.

SSIR (2017). *Spring 2017 Supplement: Social Innovation and Social Transition in East Asia*. Digital Edition. http://stanford.ebookhost.net/ssir/digital/45/index.php?e=45&open=1 (Retrieved 7th Mar. 2018).

Sugaya, H. (2013). *ASEAN Shokoku no Shakaihosho*. Tokyo: Nippon Hyoron Sha.

Suharyo, W. J. (2009). Indonesia's Transition to Decentralized Governance: Evolution at the local level. In Holtzappel, C. J. G. and Ramstedt, M. (eds.) *Decentralization and Regional Autonomy in Indonesia: Implementation and challenges*. Singapore: ISEAS, 75-98.

Suzuki, K. (2014). Kenryoku ni Jujun na Chugokuteki Shiminshakai no Houtekikouzo. in Ishii, T., Ogata, Y., and Suzuki, K. (eds.) *ibid*. Tokyo: Bensei Syuppan, 536-565.

Tada, H. (2014). Jyoron: Shakaihosho toha Nanika. in Tada, H. (ed.) *ibid*, 1-19.

Takahara, A. and Maeda, H. (2014). *Kaihatushugi no Jidai he: 1972-2014*. Tokyo: Iwanami Shoten.

Takahashi, H. (2012). *Chikihoukatu Kea Sisutemu*. Tokyo: Ohm Sha.

Takahashi, M, Kimura, T., and Ishiguro, T. (2018). *Sosharu Inobeshon wo Rironka suru: Kirihirakareru shakaikigyoka no aratana jisen*. Tokyo: Bunshindo.

Takayasu, T. (2014). *Kankoku no Shakai Hosho: Teifukushi, teifutan shakaihosho no bunseki*. Okayama: Gakubunsha.

Tao, M. (2004). *Jissen NPO Manejimento: Keieikanri no tameno rinen to giho*. Kyoto: Minerva Shobo.

Tamamura, M. (2014). *Shakai Inobeshon no Kagaku: Seisaku maketingu, SROI, tourongata yoronchosa*. Tokyo: Keiso Shobo.

Tanaka, Y. (2008). *NPO Shinjidai: Shiminsei shouzou no tameni*. Tokyo: Akashi Shoten.

Tanaka, Y. (2011). *Shiminshakai Seisakuron: 3.11 Go no seifu, NPO, borantia wo kangaeru tameni*. Tokyo: Akashi Shoten.

Tang, L. (2012). *Gendai Chugoku no Seiji: Kaihatu dokusai to sono yukue*. Tokyo: Iwanami Shoten.

Tang, J. (2017). *Chugoku no Taisei Iko to Keizai Hatten*. Okayama: Okayama Daigaku Keizaigakubu.

Tanimoto, K., Ohmoro, N., Ohira, S., Doi, M., and Komura, K. (2013). *Sosharu Inobeshon no Sosyutu to Fukyu*. Tokyo: NTT Shyuppan.

Tao, D. (2009). Higasi Ajia no Kyusai Shisetu to shiteno Shaso: Nakai chikuzan shaso shigi kou. in Tao,D., Jiang, K., Kenjo, T., and Kirihara, K. (eds.) *ibid*, 31-51.

Taylor-Gooby, P. (2004). New Risks and Social Change. In Taylor-Gooby, P. (ed.) New Risks, New Welfare: The Transformation of the European Welfare State. Oxford: Oxford University Press, 1-28.

Teets, J. C. (2011). Reforming Service Delivery in China: The emergence of a social innovation model. *Journal of Chinese Political Science*, Vol.17, 15-32.

TEPSIE (2014). *Social Innovation Theory and Research: A summary of the findings from TEPSIE*. A deliverable of the project: The theoretical, empirical and policy foundations for building social innovation in Europe (TEPSIE), Brussels: European Commission, DG Research.

Tjemkes, B., Vos, P., and Burgers, K. (2012). *Strategic Alliance Management*. London and New York: Routledge.

Tomizawa, K. (1999). Hieiri, Kyodo Sekuta toha Nanika. in Kawaguchi, K. and Tomizawa, K. (eds.) *Fukushishakai to Hieiri Kyodo Sekuta: Yoropa no chosen to nihon no kadai*. Tokyo: Nihon Keizai Hyoronsha, 17-28.

Tomozawa, Y. (2014). *Toi to shiteno Kougai: Kankyo Shakaigakusha Iijima Nobuko no Shisaku*. Tokyo: Keiso Shobo.

Toyota Foundation, The (2007). *30 Years of History 1974-2004*. Tokyo: The Toyota Foundation.

Tsai, L. L. (2007). *Accountability without Democracy: Solidarity groups and public goods provision in rural China*. Cambridge: Cambridge University Press.

Tsujimoto, K., Hayase, N., and Matsubara, A. (2000). *NPO Hayawakari Q&A*. Iwanami Booklet No. 511, Tokyo: Iwanami Shoten.

Tsujinaka, Y. (2003). From Developmentalism to Maturity: Japan's civil society organizations in comparative perspective. In Schwartz, F. and Pharr, S. J. (eds.) *The State of Civil Society in Japan*. New York: Cambridge University Press, 83-115.

Tsujinaka, Y. (2010). Jyosho. in Tsujinaka, Y. and Ito, S. (eds.) *Rokaru Gabanansu: Chihoseifu to Shiminshakai*. Tokyo: Bokutakusha, 9-17.

Tsujinaka, Y. (2012a). Maegaki. in Tsujinaka, Y., Sakamoto, H., and Yamamoto, H. (eds.) *Gendai Nihon no NPO Seiji: Shiminshakai no Shinkyokumen*. Tokyo: Bokutaku Sha.

Tsujinaka, Y. (2012b). *Seijigaku Nyumon: Koutekikettei no kouzo, akuta, jyokyo.* Tokyo: Hoso Daigaku Kyoiku Shinkokai.

Tsujinaka, Y. (2014). Ketsuron. in Tsujinaka, Y., Li, K., Kojima, N. (eds.) *ibid*, 373-388.

Tsujinaka, Y. and Choi, S. (2004). Dantai Keisei to Seiji Taisei no Henka: Kokka koporatizumu kara rodoseiji wo hete futu no tagenshugi he. in Tsujinaka, Y. and Yeoh, T. (eds.) *ibid*, 101-139.

Tsujinaka, Y. and Kojima, N. (2014). Jyosho. in Tsujinaka, Y., Li, K., Kojima, N. (eds.) *ibid*, 15-32.

Tsujinaka, Y., Li, K., and Yuan, R. (2014). Houhou. in Tsujinaka, Y., Li, K., Kojima, N. (eds.) *ibid*, 35-50.

Tsujinaka, Y., Yamamoto, H., and Kubo, Y. (2010). Nihon ni okeru Dantai no Keisei to Sonritu. in Tsujinaka,Y. and Mori, H. (eds.) *Gendai Shakaishudan no Seijikenno: Riekidantai to shiminshakai.* Tokyo: Bokutakusha, 33-64.

Tsukamoto, I. and Kaneko, I. (2017). *Sosharu Inpakuto Bondo toha Nanika: Fainansu ni yoru shakai inobeshon no kanosei.* Kyoto: Minerva Shobo.

Tsukamoto, I., Yanagisawa, T., and Yamagishi, H. (2007). *Igirisu Hieiri Sekuta no Chosen: NPO, seifu no senryakuteki patonasipu.* Kyoto: Minerva Shobo.

Tsuru, S. (1999). *The Political Economy of the Environment: The case of Japan.* London: The Athlone Press.

Tsuru, S. (2001). *Tsuru Shigeto Jiten: Ikutu mono kiro wo kaiko shite.* Tokyo: Iwanami Shoten.

Uchiyama, Y. (2010). Nihon Seiji no Akuta to Seisaku Kettei Patan. *Kikan Seisaku Keiei Kenkyu*, Vol.3, 1-18.

Ueno, C. (2011). *Kea no Shakaigaku.* Tokyo: Ota Shuppan.

Ueyama, S. (2002). *Seisaku Renkei no Jidai: Chiki, jichitai, NPO no patonashipu.* Tokyo: Nippon Hyoron Sha.

Ui, J. (2014). *Ui Jun Selection Vol.2: Kogai ni daisansha ha inai.* Tokyo: Shinsensha.

United Nations, The (2015). *The Millennium Development Goals Report 2015.* New York: United Nations.

USAID (2009). *Decentralization 2009: Stock taking on Indonesia's recent decentralization reforms Summary Report.* Washington DC: USAID.

Ushiro, F. (2009). *NPO ha Kokyo Sabisu wo Ninaeruka: Tsugi no jyunen heno kadai to senryaku.* Kyoto: Horitsu Bunka Sha.

Van Dyke, N., McCammon, H. J. (eds.) (2010). *Strategic Alliances: Coalition building and social movements*. Minneapolis: University of Minnesota Press.

Vatikiotis, M. R. J. (1996). *Political Change in Southeast Asia: Trimming the banyan tree.* London and New York: Routledge.

Vatikiotis, M. R. J. (1998). *Indonesian Politics Under Suharto: The rise and fall of the new order.* 3rd edition, London and New York: Routledge.

Vel, J., Zakaria, R. Y., and Bedner, A. (2017). Creating Indonesia's Village Law. *Inside Indonesia*, May 9, 2017. http://www.insideindonesia.org/creating-indonesia-s-village-law (Retrieved 13th Dec. 2017)

Wang, M. (2011). The Development of Civil Organizations and the Road to Civil Society in China. In Wang, M. (ed.) *Emerging Civil Society in China, 1978-2008*. London / Boston: Brill, 1-57.

Wang, M. and Liu, G. (2017). Incremental Co-governance: Investigation of Hangzhou Experience of Driving Reform Through Innovation. In Wang, M. (ed.) *A Discussion on Chinese Road of NGOs: Reform and co-governance by society*. Singapore: Springer.

Watanabe, T. and Tsuyuki, M. (2009). *Shakaiteki Kigyoka to Shakai Inobeshon: Giron no kokusaiteki keifuto nihon no kadai*. ESRI Discussion Paper Series No. 215, Tokyo: Economic and Social Research Institute.

Westley, F. (2017). Conclusion: Recognizing transformative potential. In Westley, F., McGowan, K., and Tjornbo, O. (eds.) *The Evolution of Social Innovation*, Cheltenham and Northampton: Edward Elgar Publishing, 239-255.

Westley, F. and Antadze, N. (2010). Making a Difference: Strategies for scaling social innovation. *The Innovation Journal*, 15(1), 2-9.

Westley, F., Zimmerman, B., and Patton, M. (2007). *Getting to Maybe: How the world is changed* (Paperback edition). Toronto: Vintage Canada.

Williams, M. S. (2016). Reasons to Obey: "Multiple Modernities" and constructions of political legitimacy. In Chan, J., Shin, D. C., and Williams, M. S. (eds.) *East Asian Perspectives on Political Legitimacy: Bridging the Empirical-Normative Divide*. New York: Cambridge University Press, 25-54.

Wittmayer, J., Avelino, F., Dorland, J., Pel B., and Jorgensen, M. S. (2015). *Methodological Guidelines Batch 2*. TRANSIT.

World Bank (1993). *The East Asian Miracle: Economic growth and public policy*. New York: Oxford University Press.

World Bank (2003). *Decentralizing Indonesia: A regional public expenditure review overview report.* Washington DC: World Bank.

Xu, Y. and Li, Y. (2008). Chugoku ni okeru Kusanone NGO no Genjo. in Li, Y. (ed.) *Taito suru Chugoku no Kusanone NGO: Shiminshakai heno michi wo saguru.* Tokyo: Koseisha, 3-19.

Xu, Y. and Zhang, X. (2010). Rural Protection in China: Reform, performance and problems. In Midgley, J. and Tang, K.-L. (eds.) *ibid.* 116-127.

Yamaoka, Y. (1999). *Jidai ga Ugoku Toki: Shakai no henkaku to NPO no kanosei.* Tokyo: Gyosei.

Yamaoka, Y. (2001). 21 Seiki Seido Kaikaku: Sekengata shakai kara shimingata shakai he. Sonotoki NPO no yakuwari wa. in Yamaoka, Y., Hayase, N., and Ishikawa, R. (eds.) *NPO Hieiri Sekuta no Jidai: Tayo na kyodo no kanosei wo saguru.* Kyoto: Minerva Shobo, 7-47.

Yamaoka, Y. (2007). Tokuteihieirikatudosokushin-ho to Koekihojinseido Kaikaku Kanren 3 Ho no Rippkatei: Tokuni rippo eno shimin sanka no shiten kara. in Kojima, T. (ed.) *Nihon Hosei no Kaikaku: Rippo to Jitumu no Saizensen.* Tokyo: Chuo Daigaku Shuppanbu, 549-608.

Yamauchi, N. (1997). *Nonpurofito Ekonomi: NPO to firansoropi no keizaigaku.* Tokyo: Nihon Hyoronsha.

Yamauchi, N. (2002). *NPO no Jidai.* Osaka: Osaka Daigaku Shuppankai.

Yang, Y., Wilkinson, M. and Zhang, X. (2016). Beyond the Abolition of Dual Administration: The challenges to NGO governance in 21st Century China. *Voluntas*, 27(5), 2292-2310.

Yashiro, N. (2017). *Nihonkeizairon Nyumon* (New Edition). Tokyo: Yuhikaku.

Yeon, S. (2012). *Kankoku ni Okeru Chihobunken Kaikaku no Bunseki.* Tokyo: Koujin no Tomosha.

Yokohama, Y. (2012). Chugoku Toshibu ni Okeru Kusanone NGO no Chiiki Fukushi Katudo ni Kansuru Kenkyu. *Kochi Gakuen Tanki Daigaku Kiyo*, (42), 75-85.

Yonezawa, H. (2017). *Shakaitekikigyo heno Atarashi Mikata: Shakaiseisaku no nakano Sado Sekuta.* Kyoto: Minerva Shobo.

Yu, K. (2014). Chugoku Kominshakai no Seidoteki Kankyo. in Ishii, T., Ogata, Y., and Suzuki, K. (eds.) *ibid.* 102-154.

Yu, Z. (2016). Chugoku ni Okeru NPO Sekuta no Genjo to Kadai. *Doshisha Seisaku Kagaku*

Kenkyu, 17(2), 53-67.

Yu, Z. (2017). *Gendai Chugoku no NPO Sekuta no Tenkai: Kokyosei no henyo no siten kara*. Kyoto: Yamaguchi Shoten.

Yui, D. (2016). *Mikan no Senryokaikaku: Amerika chisikijin to suterareta nihon minshukakousou* (New Edition). Tokyo: Tokyo Daigaku Shuppankai.

Yuuki, Y. (2011). *Nihon no Kaigo Sisutemu: Seisaku kettei katei to genba nizu no bunseki*. Tokyo: Iwanami Syoten.

Zhang, J. (2012). Higashi Ajia Fukushi Moderu to Shakai Shihon: Tansu, soretomo fukusu? in Sonoga, S. (ed.) *Bokko suru Higashi Ajia no Chusankaikyu*. Tokyo: Keiso Shobo, 207-232.

Zhang, X. and Sun, J. (2016). *Meta-Analysis of Evaluations across the Social Innovation Fund Program: Final Report*. Prepared for the Corporation for National and Community Service, Office of Research and Evaluation, Fairfax: ICF International.

Zhao, W. (2015). Chugoku ni okeru Shakai Kigyoka no Zouka to Sosharu Inobeshon no Doukou ni Kansuru Kousatu. in *Kenkyu Inobeshon Gakkai Dai 30 Kai Nenji Gakujutu Taikai Kouen Youshishu*.

Zhao, X. (2001). An Analysis of Unofficial Social Organizations in China: Their emergence and growth. *The Nonprofit Review*, 1(2), 133-142.

Zhao, X. (2010). Toshibu Kisou Seifu to NGO no Renkei: Shaku ni okeru dekasegi roudousha NGO chosa kara. Hishida, M. (ed.) *Chugoku: Kisou karano gabanansu*. Tokyo: Hosei Daigaku Syuppankai, 211-234.

Zhu, M. (2014). Chugoku: Tani hosho kara shakaihosho seido he. in Tada, H. (ed.) *ibid*, Kyoto: Minerva Shobo, 297-331.

Zhu, M. (2017). Zenmenteki Shokoshakai no Jitugen ni Muketeno Hinkon Taisaku: Seijyunfuhin wo chusin ni. in Taniguchi, H. (ed.) *Chugoku Seijikeizai no Kozotekitenkan*. Tokyo: Chuo Daigaku Shuppanbu, 89-106.

Zimmeck, M. (2010). The Compact 10 Years On: Government's approach to partnership with the voluntary and community sector in England. *Voluntary Sector Review*, 1(1), 125-133.

■著者紹介

青尾　謙（あおお・けん）

岡山大学大学院ヘルスシステム統合科学研究科　講師、立教大学社会デザイン研究所　研究員、（公財）助成財団センター　参与。
東京大学：学士（教養・国際関係論）、英国サセックス大学：修士（開発学）、筑波大学：博士（社会科学）。
住友銀行、国際協力NGO（国際開発救援財団）、国際組織（UNDP）、助成財団（トヨタ財団、日本財団）を経て現職。
専門はソーシャル・イノベーション理論と事例、地域コミュニティ研究、SDGsとウェルビーイング、国際開発学、アジア研究等。

Social Innovation Scaling Process in East Asia: Bridging the gaps between stakeholders

2019年5月10日　初版第1刷発行

■著　者──青尾　謙
■発　行　者──佐藤　守
■発　行　所──株式会社 大学教育出版
　　　　　　　〒700-0953　岡山市南区西市 855-4
　　　　　　　電話(086)244-1268㈹　FAX(086)246-0294
■印刷製本──モリモト印刷㈱
■Ｄ Ｔ Ｐ──林　雅子

© Ken Aoo 2019, Printed in Japan
検印省略　　落丁・乱丁本はお取り替えいたします。
本書のコピー・スキャン・デジタル化等の無断複製は著作権法上での例外を除き禁じられています。本書を代行業者等の第三者に依頼してスキャンやデジタル化することは、たとえ個人や家庭内での利用でも著作権法違反です。

ISBN978-4-86692-025-2